W9-BBR-187

MYTH, SACRED HISTORY, AND PHILOSOPHY

Cornelius Loew
WESTERN MICHIGAN UNIVERSITY

MYTH, SACRED HISTORY, AND PHILOSOPHY

The Pre-Christian Religious Heritage of the West

HARCOURT, BRACE & WORLD, INC.
New York | Chicago | San Francisco | Atlanta

Library of Congress Catalog Card Number: 67-16822

Printed in the United States of America

Acknowledgments

The author wishes to thank the following publishers for permission to reprint portions of the works listed below:

BASIL BLACKWELL & MOTT, LTD. For *Ancilla to the Pre-Socratic Philosophers* by Kathleen Freeman; for *Discovery of the Mind* by Bruno Snell.

THE BOLLINGEN FOUNDATION For *Cosmos and History* by Mircea Eliade, originally published as *The Myth of the Eternal Return*.

WILLIAM COLLINS SONS & CO., LTD. For *Before the Bible* by Cyrus H. Gordon.

Acknowledgments continue on page 283.

Preface

Ten years ago when I was invited to introduce courses in religion at Western Michigan University I decided to construct a new kind of introductory course. *Myth, Sacred History, and Philosophy* is the text that has evolved.

Since contemporary scholarly research has extended our knowledge of the Western religious heritage back as far as primitive cultures, I believed it necessary that a survey of that heritage include the religious traditions of ancient Mesopotamia and Egypt. The key to understanding these traditions is the exploration of their fundamental convictions by means of an analysis of the linguistic forms through which these convictions were expressed. Three different forms of expression were used by the pre-Christian creators of our religious heritage: myth, sacred history, and philosophy. The Mesopotamians and Egyptians created a rich and comprehensive image of society and expressed this image in sacred stories or *myths*. The Hebrews replaced this concept with their own distinctive image of a covenant people under Yahweh and developed a special story form to express it, *sacred history*. The Greeks drew on the mythic tradition and focused this tradition on their principle of life-orientation, the image of the city-state. Their distinctive form of expression was *philosophy*, by which they critically analyzed the traditional myths.

In developing this method of introducing students to the religious heritage of the West I have provided introductory and illustrative material and then have had the students spend most of their time exploring the tremendous wealth of original source materials, and the interpretations of those texts, now available in paperback editions. For the convenience of the reader, I have included at the end of each chapter a short list of recommended paperbacks for supplementary reading and at the end of the book bibliographies of both hardbound and paperback editions.

I should like to acknowledge a special debt to Professor Eric Voegelin. My discovery, several years ago, of the first three volumes of his *Order and History* was an exciting and rewarding experience. The similarity of many, but not all, of our views has reinforced my belief in my approach and has been of great profit to my teaching.

Many sections of the following chapters, developed originally for the course "Introduction to the Religious Heritage of the West," have been presented to adult groups. The response encourages me to hope that my attempt to present in compact and simplified form some of the work of many great contemporary scholars will be useful not only to college and university students but to a wider audience as well.

CORNELIUS LOEW

Kalamazoo, Michigan

Contents

MYTH, SACRED HISTORY, AND PHILOSOPHY

Introduction

The great human community of the Western world is at least five thousand years old, yet the earliest beginnings of high civilization in the Near East have been rediscovered only within the past century. The archeologists and scholars who began excavating sandswept, barren mounds in the northern Mesopotamian valley during the 1840's were looking for remains of the Assyrian and Babylonian civilizations, about which they had considerable information from classical and Biblical sources. It soon became obvious that the Assyrians had been culturally dependent on the Babylonians, much as the Romans were dependent on the Greeks. But the archeologists themselves were astounded when evidence piled up to demonstrate that the Babylonian culture had been inherited from a civilization older than itself—even older than the Egyptian civilization, which had been believed the earliest of all high civilizations. At first, the evidence was a matter of references in Babylonian inscriptions, one of which noted that the earliest-known ruler of the southern region of Mesopotamia had called himself "king of Sumer and Akkad." This led one French enthusiast, Jules Oppert, to predict that sooner or later the Sumerians would become recognized as the creators of the first civilization. Finally, in 1877, excavations were begun that brought to light the actual cities, temples, artifacts, and writings of the Sumerians, dating back to about 4000 B.C. After vanishing completely from human history for over twenty-five hundred years, the Sumerians have now become one of the best-known peoples of the ancient Near East.[1]

---

[1] The story of modern archeology is fascinating, especially as told by C. W. Ceram in *Gods, Graves, and Scholars* (New York, 1952). Except for a final section on the early empires of Central and South America, the entire book deals with Near Eastern cultures related to the present study. A more detailed survey of the remarkable rediscovery of Sumer is S. N. Kramer's *History Begins at Sumer* (New York, 1959). See also Henri Frankfort's *The Birth of Civilization in the Near East* (Garden City, N.Y., 1956).

A word of explanation should be given regarding "Akkad," which ap-

The flood of material that has been pouring into the hands of scholars ever since the rediscovery of Sumer has given us nothing less than a "new" cultural heritage. We can no longer be content with studies of the pre-Christian roots of Western culture that make a few preliminary remarks about Mesopotamia and Egypt and then hurry on to the Biblical Israelites and the classical Greeks. In fact, evidence of extensive cross-cultural contacts between the early civilizations is changing our understanding of the Israelites and the Greeks themselves.

Consider, for instance, what is now known about the literary career of the Gilgamesh Epic, one of the greatest literary works produced in the Mesopotamian valley cultures. Committed to cuneiform writing around 2000 B.C., it spread westward and northward until by 1500 B.C. it was probably the most widely known and most influential literary work in the world. The epic reached Palestine at least three centuries before the Israelites emerged as a people and claimed Palestine for their homeland. In Anatolia, the text was known not only in the Babylonian language but in Hurrian and Hittite translations as well. No one who is familiar with the Biblical Book of Genesis or with Homer's *Iliad* and *Odyssey* can read the Gilgamesh Epic without experiencing again and again a shock of recognition. Parallels of various kinds are so numerous that it is hard to believe they are purely coincidental.

Literary parallels are only one of several types of evidence that make the traditional view that Israel and Hellas developed completely independently of each other no longer convincing. These civilizations were parallel structures erected on the same Eastern Mediterranean cultural foundation. Thus, our pre-Christian cultural heritage is "new" in two important ways: it has been expanded by the addition of new knowledge about the earlier cultures, and it has been deepened by new insights into the relationships of the Hebrews and the Greeks to these cultures.

The implications of the expansion and reinterpretation of Near Eastern history for study of the Western pre-Christian

---

peared with Sumer in the Babylonian inscription mentioned above. The Akkadians were a Semitic-speaking folk who lived north of the Sumerians and gradually became dominant in central Mesopotamia. By about 2400 B.C., some eight hundred years after Sumerian civilization began to flourish, the Akkadians had taken over Sumer, to the south, and had gained control over considerable territory to the north.

religious heritage are numerous and far-reaching. Particularly significant is that certain forms of experience and expression, which have persisted throughout the past five thousand years, are still contributing to the meaningfulness as well as to the complexity and confusion of our contemporary religious situation. This may seem unlikely to persons who simply assume that Christianity superseded all earlier religious orientations and rendered them obsolete. Such an assumption does not do justice either to the contributions the Hebrew and the Greek traditions have continued to make to religious experience and expression in Western culture or to the persistence in the modern West of convictions that are strikingly similar to convictions that were the lifeblood of the earliest Near Eastern cultures.

The key term is *convictions.* Convictions that shape men's orientation to life are religious phenomena. But what actually are convictions? They are all persuasions about good and bad; about gods and devils; about representations of the ideal man, the ideal state, and the ideal society; about the meaning of history, nature, and the All. The Latin root of the phrase "to be convinced" means "to be overcome thoroughly." A conviction points to someone or something that does the overcoming, which is experienced as an exterior force by those who hold the conviction. This experience from outside, or objective referent, has been called the gods, the highest good, the truth, the Holy Spirit, the law of nature, the nation. The decisive quality in the experience of being convinced we will call the quality of *ultimacy,* the quality that causes men to acknowledge that the objective referent has final authority over them and, therefore, that the convictions with which they deal with the "facts of life" are valid and binding, permanent and sacred. In this study, conviction refers specifically to those persuasions about the meaning, purpose, and proper ordering of life that are so fundamental and so widely shared that they function as comprehensive orienting and integrating factors in a culture or in communities of faith within a culture.

How can basic convictions be identified and studied? One familiar feature of the Christian tradition makes identification seem deceptively easy. The early Christians expressed their faith in such summaries as the Apostles' and the Nicene Creeds. Over the centuries more detailed confessions of faith and impressive systems of doctrine were—and continue to be—formulated. This conscious and sustained effort over many centuries to define the essential Christian convictions and to draw out the logical implications of the definitions has often created the impression that basic convictions are normally expressed in the form of a series of propositional statements. A study of Mesopotamian and Egyptian materials with the expectation of finding definitions of essential beliefs would be frustrating. Nor would such definitional forms of expression be found in Israel or in classical Greece. The first known step toward definition of convictions was taken by Hellenistic philosophical schools—such as the Epicureans and the Stoics—who raised the teachings of their founders to a position of final and unalterable truth and made correct belief (orthodoxy) a requirement for membership in their communities of faith.

The Mesopotamians, Egyptians, Hebrews, and Greeks all developed distinctive linguistic forms through which they expressed their fundamental convictions. One of the forms was Greek philosophy, which paved the way for the type of reflective, systematic, definitional statements taken over by the Christians from the Hellenistic schools. The other verbal forms were presentational rather than definitional and portrayed basic convictions in story form. The Mesopotamians and the Egyptians told myths; the Hebrews recounted sacred history. And in their dramas of tragedy, the Greeks created a distinctive form of storytelling closely related both to myth and to philosophy. One has only to remember that the stories of Christmas and Easter lie at the heart of Christian tradition to sense the possibility of a continuity of sacred-story telling that stretches back from the present far beyond the Hebrews and the Greeks into the mythical traditions of primitive cultures. The first answer, then, to the question of how we can identify basic convictions in the pre-Christian cultures is that we must take seriously the sacred stories these peoples accepted as authoritative.

A second answer grows out of the fact that the most important sacred stories of a culture, or of a religious community within a culture, often are acted out in liturgy and ritual. Thus, we must also take seriously the dramatic forms that combine language with action, especially ritual activities associated with annual festivals, and that include the reciting and acting of sacred stories or the representation of major themes of sacred stories. Again, if we remember that the most sacred act of worship in the Christian tradition, the Holy Communion, involves the joining of sacred history and dramatic ritual to present anew the story of Jesus' death and resurrection, we can sense the possibility of a continuity of sacred acting preceding even the Hebrews and the Greeks. Since linguistic and action forms are so closely intertwined, descriptions of certain religious festivals will be included in our study where they help to illuminate the character, meaning, and function of basic convictions.

The Mesopotamian and Egyptian cultures were permeated by a cosmological conviction—that is, by the conviction that the meaning of life is rooted in an encompassing cosmic order in which man, society, and the gods all participate. Both the Mesopotamians and the Egyptians realized that society is greater and more enduring than any man and that the cosmos is greater and more enduring than any society. They were convinced that the gods *are* the cosmos and that the order of their society was a small-scale copy of the gods' vast cosmic society. Therefore, they experienced the quality of ultimacy most directly in and through the compact unity of their society. For example, the temple of Anu and Ishtar in the ancient Sumerian city of Uruk was the political, economic, military, and social center of the total life of the city-state. It was the community's capitol, board of trade, bank, supreme court, and military citadel as well as its official center of worship. The gods that were worshiped there were the models and guarantors of every standard pattern of attitude and activity. Loyalty to the gods meant obedience to the customs and mores of the society. The church stood beside the state as part of the same institution. Organized communities of faith, living within the general community but differentiated from it, were unknown in Mesopotamia or in Egypt at any time. The myths (sacred stories) that expressed the cosmological conviction in these cultures communicated and reinforced the compact experience of participating in a cosmic reality in which the gods, the natural world, and society blended into one another.

Both the Hebrews and the Greeks expanded on this concept of a compactness of experiences making up a cosmic reality. Through differentiations of experience they became persuaded that the meaning of life is not finally rooted in the gods, the natural world, or society, or in a blend of all three. The life-orienting story that the Hebrews developed (sacred history) expressed the conviction that there is an ultimate other than man, society, or the cosmos. Greek tragedy pointed to fate, an impersonal cosmic order to which even the gods are subject. The Greek philosophers developed linguistic forms that expressed fundamental convictions without using narrative devices. A central stream of Greek philosophy based its logical constructions on the conviction that the proper ordering of life depends on attunement to eternal truth, beauty, and goodness. Yet, at the same time, the Hebrews and the Greeks responded to important aspects of the cosmological conviction and to the society-centered orientation to life that this conviction supported in the other Near Eastern cultures. The Hebrews were convinced that they were a special Covenant People, and the Greeks believed that in their distinctive type of city-state (especially in Athens) they had achieved the correct order of communal life. Thus, both peoples experienced a quality of ultimacy in and through the institutional patterns of their social order; at the same time, they experienced newly differentiated qualities of ultimacy that pointed beyond traditionally accepted ultimates such as the gods and the cosmos. Therefore, in Israel and in Hellas tensions that have profoundly influenced the religious heritage of the West developed between basic convictions and between rival loyalties and commitments.

The words "compactness" and "differentiation" have been introduced to describe certain constrasts between the experiences and convictions expressed in the traditions being considered. Unfortunately, these terms carry multiple connotations, and each can be interpreted in ways that conflict with the other. For example, the noted Near Eastern expert Thorkild Jacobsen believes that the compactness of the early Sumerian city-states, where the central temple contained all activities, supported a type of life that was far more free and creative than life in the much more highly differentiated society, controlled by imperial bureaucracies, of later centuries. Jacobsen interprets compactness to mean vital unity, and he sees differentiation as a movement toward either stultifying authoritarianism or empty fragmentation. On the other hand, many scholars—especially those convinced that the main force of human history has been man's struggle to escape from tradition-dominated social patterns into more open social structures—define compactness as static rigidity (bad) and differentiation as dynamic diversity (good).

No terms useful in the study of convictions are free from this problem of ambiguous or conflicting connotations. If the reader will accept compactness and differentiation as neutral terms he will be able to understand an important fact: even though all dimensions of experience that make human beings human have been present since Sumerian times, the actual range of symbolically expressed experiences has varied from culture to culture. Specifically, he will be prepared to approach the differences between Mesopotamia and Egypt, on the one hand, and Israel and Hellas, on the other, without prejudging the peoples who lived later in history as being superior to those who lived long before them. In addition, he will be prepared to approach myth, sacred history, and philosophy as equally valid in their original time and place, whatever conclusions he may reach concerning their religious significance today.

one

MYTH IN THE MESOPOTAMIAN TRADITION

THE term "Mesopotamia" refers to the lands bordering and lying between the Euphrates and Tigris rivers, from the Taurus Mountains in the northwest south to the Persian Gulf, and from the Great Syrian Desert in the west to the Zagros Mountains of southwest Iran.

The arts of grain cultivation and stockbreeding, the basic forms of economy necessary for supporting large-scale organized society, developed in this region of the world between 7500 and 5500 B.C.[1] Settled village life and an efficient barnyard economy came during the next thousand years, along with the arts of pottery-making, weaving, carpentry, and house-building. Two innovations in the field of the plastic arts between 4500 and 3500 B.C. were especially interesting precursors to important features of the earliest urban communities. One was the widespread practice of fashioning naked female figurines, small statuettes that undoubtedly represented the functions of fertility goddesses among the then well established peasantry. Recognition of a parallel between woman's life-bearing powers and the powers of the earth generated an image of Mother Nature. This image was expressed in a variety of types of figurines: woman standing pregnant, squatting as though in childbirth, holding one breast while pointing with the other hand to her genitals, standing on a lion, riding a bull, and so on.

When, about 4000 B.C., the Sumerians opened up a new culture area on the huge mudflats formed by the Tigris and the Euphrates rivers as they near the Persian Gulf, they translated the fertility imagery of the figurines into temple architecture. The lack of wood and stone in the delta area resulted in the invention of a new building material, sun-dried brick, and the impressive structures they built were the first large-scale temples erected anywhere by anyone. The temple towers, later called *ziggurats* (the Assyrio-Babylonian word for "top of a mountain"), were artificial mountains with a sanctuary at the summit, and their symbolic meaning was closely related to the religious significance of the figurines. The "mountain" towers joined Mother

---

[1] See Joseph Campbell's *The Masks of God* (New York, 1959) for a fuller summary of this period. Campbell believes that these arts originated in the Near East and spread from there to other parts of the world.

Earth with Father Sky, which were pictured as the primordial parents of all things. It may be that during this period their world-generating sexual union was already being reenacted annually in the summit sanctuaries, with the queen or princess of the town taking the role of the goddess and the king taking the role of the god.

The other development in the plastic arts was the invention of a totally new esthetic concept: the geometrical organization of a field around a center. On the pottery of the Halafian and the Samarran cultures, which flourished in the northern and central regions of the Mesopotamian valley, archeologists have found an abundance of graceful circular compositions that use geometric and other abstract stylized designs. This concept was used by the Sumerians not only in their ceramics; it was applied by them to town planning. They laid out their towns geometrically. By 3500 B.C., the larger market towns in Sumer were centered around the pivotal sanctum of a main temple surrounded by specialized circular zones, the *sars* praised by Gilgamesh in his description of Uruk in the closing lines of the Gilgamesh Epic (see page 58). This design of concentric circles, plus the further division of the entire town into quarters, was amazingly similar to the patterns found on some of the Halafian, Samarran, and Sumerian ceramics.

Archeologists have discovered that during the period from around 4000 B.C. to 3200 B.C. there was a notable expansion of the central temple areas. Apparently the priests spearheaded the movement toward a new kind of community organization that took account of the emergence of special functional classes of merchants, artisans, and peasants, as well as the formation of an elite class of professional priests. Both sociologically and psychologically, the problems of bringing these groups into an orderly relationship with one another must have been increasingly serious. The form of community that was developed was a type of city-state.

I

The Emergence of the Cosmological Conviction

The Sumerians also seem to have pioneered in the invention of writing and number systems. These contributed to a daringly imaginative correlation between areas of experience and concern seemingly unrelated to one another on the surface. This correlation between astronomical observation and social organization shaped the life orientation of Mesopotamian culture for more than two thousand years. With the aids of written language and written numbers the Sumerian priests recorded and refined their inherited mass of orally transmitted data concerning the cyclical movements of the sun, moon, and planets among the fixed stars. Then, somehow, their study of the heavens and their search for a meaningful ordering of human affairs in the new city-states interpenetrated each other, and from this union came a fundamental conviction that we shall call the *cosmological conviction.* It had at least five major facets: (1) there is a cosmic order that permeates every level of reality; (2) this cosmic order is the divine society of the gods; (3) the structure and dynamics of this society can be discerned in the movements and patterned juxtapositions of the heavenly bodies; (4) human society should be a microcosm of the divine society—it should be organized and governed like the macrocosm; and (5) the chief responsibility of priests and kings is to attune human order to the divine order.

The decisive belief about the cosmos was that it was the great society of the gods. Therefore, the Sumerians and their successors could express their convictions about the meaning and purpose of life by telling stories about the gods, especially "creation" stories describing the primordial establishment of cosmic organization in terms of activities of the gods and relationships they established. These stories did much more than present descriptions of the divine institutions, mores, and ritual patterns men were to imitate. They drew men into a deep awareness of participating in a sacred cosmic order, an encompassing framework and an ever flowing process in which man and his human world of problems, fears, meanings, hopes, purposes, and absurdities were not alien but had their allotted place. Such stories belong to the verbal symbolic form we are calling myth.

2

Mesopotamian Creation Myths

Biological images of creation

The word "birth" belongs to the language of beginnings, while the word "family" belongs to the languages both of social structures and of biological relationships. Since the Sumerians and their successors, notably the Babylonians and the Assyrians, believed that the birth of the cosmos was the same process as the birth of the gods, they found it convenient to use sexual imagery to describe their vision of the cosmic order. A Sumerian story, the Tilmun myth, shows how sexual motifs became associated both with creation and with the renewal of life every year through the cycle of the seasons. Ostensibly, the Tilmun myth explains how various plants originated through divine sexual generation, but its message actually focuses on the present rather than on the past and on human concerns rather than on information about the physical world.

The events of the myth take place "in the beginning" when the earth is being organized. Various areas are assigned to gods and goddesses as their property. Ninhursag, the goddess of earth, and Enki, the god of the fresh water that fertilizes earth, are given the island of Tilmun (modern Bahrain in the Persian Gulf). Tilmun is pure, fresh, bright—and empty. Sexual union between the couple is necessary before new living forms can appear. Neither animals nor men have acquired their familiar habits and characteristics; such evils as disease and old age have not yet come on the scene. Enki proposes to Ninhursag, and although there seems to be some tension between them which leads her at first to refuse, she finally accepts him. The first lines of the myth are directed to the divine couple:

> When you were dividing the virgin earth [with your fellow-gods]
> —you—the land of Tilmun was a region pure;
> When you were dividing the pure earth [with your fellow-gods]
> —you—the land of Tilmun was a region pure.
> The land of Tilmun was pure, the land of Tilmun was fresh,
> The land of Tilmun was fresh, the land of Tilmun was bright.
> When they lay down on the ground all alone in Tilmun—
> Since the place where Enki lay down with his spouse
> was a fresh place, a bright place. . . .
> The raven in Tilmun did not croak [as the raven does
> nowadays],
> The cock [?] did not utter the crow of a cock [as the cock does
> nowadays],
> The lion did not kill,
> The wolf did not seize lambs,
> The dog knew not [how] to make the kids crouch down,
> The donkey foal knew not [how] to eat grain,
>
> . . .
>
> Eye disease did not say, "I, eye disease,"
> Headache did not say, "I, headache,"
> The old woman there did not say, "I, old woman,"
> The old man there did not say, "I, old man," . . .[2]

This passage paints an impressive picture of the primeval "Garden of Eden" age when all was innocent and perfect. It has set the stage, and now the story unfolds rapidly. Ninhursag becomes pregnant and in nine days a daughter, Ninmu, is born. When Ninmu reaches puberty Enki impregnates her, and in nine days she gives birth to a daughter, Ninkurra (or perhaps Ninsig). Enki repeats the same process of impregnation once again with his granddaughter, and in one version of the story, with his great-granddaughter also. In both versions the last goddess born

---

[2] Translated by Thorkild Jacobsen in Frankfort's *Before Philosophy,* pp. 173-74.

is Uttu.[3] When she reaches marriageable age Ninhursag inserts a new factor into the situation. The documents (clay tablets) are badly damaged at this point, but the translators believe that Ninhursag advises Uttu not to cohabit with Enki unless he comes to her like a regular suitor, bringing the traditional gifts that Sumerian girls expected, cucumbers and apples and grapes. Enki becomes aware of this strategy, so he sees to it that when he approaches Uttu he is carrying the necessary gifts. Therefore Uttu does not hesitate to receive his advances and Enki impregnates her. But no daughter goddesses are born of this union. Instead, Ninhursag intervenes and, exercising her primordial role of Mother Earth, takes the semen from Uttu and uses it to bring into being eight different plants.

Once the eight plants have come into existence, the myth turns back to Enki and Ninhursag and develops the theme of their antagonism. Apparently Ninhursag thinks that she has the right to name the plants—that is, to announce what their qualities and functions shall be. But she discovers that Enki has eaten the plants in order to "know" them and to determine their fate. His action amounts to the claim that the power of plants belongs to him alone and that it owes nothing to the female principle. This final insult ignites a burning hatred in Ninhursag. She curses Enki, who is laid low by a terrible illness that completely incapacitates him. Because he is the god of water, fresh water disappears from the earth. The other gods become disturbed because fresh water

[3] Scholars do not agree in their interpretations of this highly stylized series of births of goddesses. Thorkild Jacobsen has constructed an interesting interpretation on the theory that this section of the myth explains the origin of various elements necessary for the making of clothing. He starts with the fact that scholars have learned from various sources that Uttu seems to have been a Sumerian deity whose activities had to do with clothing. Since she is the third or fourth in the biological line, Jacobsen reasons that the goddesses born before her may represent the plant fibers used in the weaving of linen, the vegetable dyestuff used in coloring cloth, and so on. S. N. Kramer is more cautious. According to him the available evidence indicates that Ninkurra was connected with stone-working and had nothing to do with clothing. (See note 5 of Kramer's introduction to his translation of the myth in James B. Pritchard's *Ancient Near Eastern Texts*, 2nd ed. (Princeton, 1955), p. 37.) He concludes that the motifs involved in the series of births are obscure, and therefore he does not try to construct a pattern that unifies the births around a single theme. Both scholars, however, generally agree in their interpretation of the remainder of the myth.

is essential to life; they call an emergency conference with Ninhursag, and eventually they persuade her to forgive Enki and also to heal him. She does so by joining herself sexually to Enki and by giving birth to eight deities, one for each ailing part of his body. These deities seem to represent a rebirth of the eight plants Enki swallowed, now born monogamously from the rightful goddess of earth and therefore no longer causing him trouble. The myth ends with the assigning of qualities and functions to these deities, and this time it is Ninhursag who gives them their names.

The curse sequence undoubtedly refers to the annual experience of summertime in Mesopotamia; the weather is so dry and hot that vegetation practically disappears. Wells go dry, and rivers also go dry or become trickling creeks. The life-giving fresh water (Enki) has disappeared. It is as though there were some kind of battle of wills going on in nature, with Enki the loser. He has been vanquished, cursed, incapacitated. But, just as the gods in the myth convince Ninhursag that she should relent and restore Enki to health, so the dread Near Eastern summer must give way to fall, and the rains return to nourish new plantings. The antagonism is resolved, and new life is generated. Thus, the myth not only describes an aspect of the birth of the cosmos but represents the seasonal renewal of nature.

To modern Westerners, the processes of nature are impersonal and objective; we are inclined to react against the personification of earth, water, and plants in the Tilmun myth. We are sure that personal and subjective faculties such as feeling, thinking, and conscious decision-making do not belong to weather or earth or water. In a story in which the physical phenomena of earth and water are homogenized with personality, the strange blending of impersonal and personal gives us a feeling of unreality or of make-believe. The story illustrates why most of us associate "myth" with what is fictitious, illusionary, or false. The Tilmun myth seems to be nothing more than a fanciful tale, a fumbling attempt to account for the beginnings of the physical universe. This impression is intensified by the fact that on the surface the myth is concerned primarily with events that occurred long ago. But when the motif of the annual renewal of life throughout the cosmos is introduced, the careful reader realizes that the main focus of the myth is applicable today—the conviction that what happens each year in the world of nature gives men confidence and hope as they struggle in the uncertain world of human concerns and problems. The myth is a way of representing through language a basic experience that makes persons aware of themselves and the physical universe as parts of an encompassing whole.

Since no man can get outside the encompassing whole, see it in its entirety, and thus understand with knowledgeable precision not only the "whole" but also his proper role within it, convictions rather than knowledge are decisive in shaping men's basic life orientations. The Tilmun myth expresses two motifs of the cosmological conviction that oriented and motivated the members of the Sumerian society; the sexual motif emphasizes the organic unity and interrelatedness of all things in the cosmos, while the seasonal renewal motif emphasizes the belief that men's deeply felt need for a periodic return to the sources of order and meaning in their lives is a need that can be fulfilled.

The most important single religious work in the large collection of materials unearthed by archeologists in Mesopotamia is a grandiose epic of creation that scholars call the "Enuma Elish." This title consists simply of the first two words of the Akkadian version, the earliest version available. The words mean "when above" or "when on high," referring to the heavenly realm of the gods in which creation took place. Since this is an economical term it will be used consistently in the present chapter. Although none of the texts recovered by archeologists is older than 1000 B.C., most experts assign the written composition to somewhere around 2000 B.C., when many of the most important elements of the earliest forms of Mesopotamian culture were first written down. They believe that most of the myths incorporated into the epic probably go back to Sumerian times. Because the epic brought together all the major motifs of the religious tradition, it played a central role in official Mesopotamian religious life for more than fifteen hundred years, especially in connection with the annual New Year's Festival during which it was always recited in its entirety. In the Sumerian-Akkadian version the hero creator-god was Enlil; in the Babylonian version it was Marduk; when the Assyrians took over the Mesopotamian valley they changed the name to Ashur; and finally the Persians called the god Bel. But throughout all these births and deaths of empires the basic structure of the Enuma Elish remained unchanged, and in each of the empires except the Persian it functioned as the core of the world view that oriented men to the society in which they lived and to the physical universe in which they believed their society was embedded.

The opening section of the Enuma Elish tells the story of creation in biological terms. Since the Babylonian version has been more completely reconstructed than any of the others, the following discussion uses the Babylonian names of the gods. In the beginning, three watery elements formed a kind of primordial trinity: Tiamat (the salt sea), Apsu (the fresh water), and Mummu (probably cloud banks and mist). The work begins:

> When a sky above had not [yet even] been mentioned
> [And] the name of firm ground below had not [yet even] been thought of;
> [When] only primeval Apsu, their begetter,
> And Mummu and Tiamat—she who gave birth to them all—
> Were mingling their waters in one;
> When no bog had formed [and] no island could be found;
> When no god whosoever had appeared,
> Had been named by name, had been determined as to [his] lot,
> Then were gods formed within them.[4]

The gods, who are the various powers of the physical universe, come into being through sexual generation and birth. Tiamat is the Primal Mother, and Apsu is the Primal Father. Their children are Lahmu and Lahamu, whose children, in turn, are Anshar and Kishar. These two pairs of gods and goddesses seem to represent the silt from which the delta mud flats were built up in southern Mesopotamia and the horizon created by the growing earth. Anshar and Kishar give birth to Anu (male), the sky; Anu begets Ea (male), the solid earth.

---

[4] Jacobsen in Frankfort, *op. cit.,* p. 184. The most important versions of the Enuma Elish, translated by E. A. Speiser, appear in Pritchard's *Ancient Near Eastern Texts.* Some portions have been included in Pritchard's paperback, *The Ancient Near East* (Princeton, 1965). The only complete version in paperback is Alexander Heidel's *The Babylonian Genesis* (Chicago, 1963), which is particularly interesting because the volume concludes with a lengthy chapter entitled "Old Testament Parallels." However, I prefer Jacobsen's translation of the opening sections of the epic. Therefore, this quotation and several succeeding ones are cited from *Before Philosophy.*

Here is a curious inconsistency. Sky and earth, both male, are presented in such a way that Ea has no mother. Probably the Sumerian version did proceed in the regular way with pairs of male and female deities, but the Babylonians seem to have broken the pattern in order to stress the male god Ea, whom they identified as the father of Marduk. Since Marduk emerges as the hero of the epic, this alteration is understandable. It also underscores the point that there is no effort to achieve scientific consistency in primitive creation myths.

Several references in Sumerian materials suggest that the primordial pair were An or Anu (sky, male) and Ki (earth, female). An and Ki give birth to Enlil and Ninlil, the god and goddess of air, wind, and storm. This provides a regular biological line, generation after generation, until all the features of the physical universe are brought into existence. The Sumerians also had an answer to the question of where An and Ki came from. In the beginning was Nammu, the primeval sea. The sea was nothing—*no thing*—it had no distinguishable shape. It was the formless, chaotic womb out of which all actual forms—*things*—issued. The first "thing" was the cosmic mountain whose base was Ki and whose summit was An—Mother Earth and Father Sky.

Incidentally, a clear echo of this picture of beginnings can be heard in the opening verses of the book of Genesis: "When God began to form the universe, the world was void and vacant; darkness lay over the abyss; but the spirit of God was hovering over the waters." [5] What waters could have been present before God created the world? Those of the primeval, formless sea. There is no sexual imagery; the cosmos is not formed through the birth of successive generations of gods and goddesses. Sex is created by God; it is not a divine power. Nor is the cosmos divine; it is created by a power other than itself and superior to it, however this otherness and superiority may be partially conceived and haltingly expressed in language. Nevertheless, the stories of creation in the book of Genesis are examples of the fact that the ancient Israelites made use of much older Mesopotamian traditions, adapting them to express their own distinctive convictions. In both traditions, however, the main focus of the creation narratives was on the present rather than on the past,

[5] Moffatt translation.

on meaningful existence today and tomorrow rather than on theories about how the physical universe was brought into existence.

Sociopolitical images of creation

The sexual pictures of reality presented in the Tilmun myth and in the brief opening section of the Enuma Elish gave the Mesopotamians an effective symbolic expression of their conviction that there is one order pervading every dimension of reality. All elements of the cosmos are finally related to one another as members of a single family that originated in the sexual union of Father Sky and Mother Earth. According to the Enuma Elish, however, there was no more peace and harmony in the family of gods than there was in human families. Most of the epic is devoted to stories of tension and open strife between generations of gods, and its imagery changes abruptly from sex to warfare.

Trouble breaks out between the primordial trinity (Tiamat, Apsu, Mummu) and the younger generations (Lahmu-Lahamu, Anshar-Kishar, Anu, and Ea). The newer gods are very lively.

> The divine companions thronged together
> and, restlessly surging back and forth, they disturbed Ti'amat,
> disturbed Ti'amat's belly,
> dancing within [her depth] where heaven is founded.
> Apsu could not subdue their clamour,
> and Ti'amat was silent . . .
> but their actions were abhorrent to her
> and their ways not good. . . .[6]

The generations are radically incompatible. Father Apsu decides that drastic action is necessary. He meets with Tiamat in council and declares:

> Abhorrent have become their ways to me,
> I am allowed no rest by day, by night no sleep.
> I will abolish, yea, I will destroy their ways,
> that peace may reign [again] and we may sleep.[7]

---

[6] Jacobsen in Frankfort, *op. cit.*, p. 188.
[7] *Ibid.*, p. 188.

When the clash comes, it is the younger gods who vanquish the older. The leader of the younger gods is Ea, the Earth. He places a spell of sleep on Apsu and after relieving Apsu of his crown and royal cloak kills him. Using the body as a foundation, Ea establishes his home on top of it. Then Ea locks up Mummu, passes a string through his nose, and sits holding him by the end of this nose rope.

Through this victory the younger gods become a permanent part of the cosmic order and their descendants own the various city-states. Anu, the god of the sky, is recognized as the head of the divine assembly, the Anunnaki.

During the ensuing temporary period of peace, the hero of the main part of the epic is introduced. Marduk is born in the dwelling (earth) that Ea has established on Apsu. While Marduk is growing up, the new order is threatened by a counterrevolution; the deposed gods are thirsting for revenge. Tiamat, the primordial mother, reappears on the scene accompanied by her second husband, Kingu. Soon the younger gods hear that all the forces of chaos are being mobilized by Tiamat, with Kingu as their commander-in-chief.

> Angry, scheming, restless day and night,
> they are bent on fighting, rage and prowl like lions.
> Gathered in council, they plan the attack.
> Mother Hubur [Tiamat] [8]—creator of all forms—
> adds irresistible weapons, has borne monster serpents,
> sharp toothed, with fang unsparing;
> has filled their bodies with poison for blood.
> Fierce dragons she has draped with terror,
> crowned with flame and made like gods,
> so that whoever looks upon them shall perish with fear,
> and they, with bodies raised, will not turn back their breast.[9]

Ea is the first god to discover the plot. He is so disturbed that he goes to his grandfather Anshar for advice and support. Anshar reminds Ea of his former victory over Apsu, and encourages him to bring Tiamat under the same spell that subdued Apsu. Ea fails. Anshar then turns to Anu, the head of the divine assembly,

---

[8] C.L.

[9] Jacobsen in Frankfort, *op. cit.*, p. 190.

who is sent out armed with the combined authority of all the younger gods but is unable to face Tiamat. He returns and asks to be relieved of his duty.

> Anshar grew silent, staring at the ground,
> he shook his head, nodded toward Ea.
> Ranged in assembly, all the Anunnaki
> lips covered, speechless sat.[10]

The situation is desperate. Finally, Anshar proposes that Ea's son, young Marduk, should champion their cause, and Ea is sent to put the proposal to Marduk. Marduk accepts the challenge, but only on condition that he be acknowledged the supreme god in place of Anu—in fact, that he be given greater power than Anu ever had. Ea reports back, and the call goes out for all the gods to gather in solemn assembly to consider Marduk's terms. In a mood of rejoicing, aided considerably by strong wine which dispels their fears, the gods decree the destiny Marduk demands. They make a princely dais for him and he sits down, presiding over the assembly. The gods then address him in chorus:

> "Thou art the most honored of the great gods,
> Thy decree is unrivaled, thy command is Anu.
> Thou, Marduk, art the most honored of the great gods,
> Thy decree is unrivaled, thy word is Anu.
> From this day unchangeable shall be thy pronouncement.
> To rise or bring low—these shall be [in] thy hand.
> Thy utterance shall be true, thy command shall be
> unimpeachable.
> No one among the gods shall transgress thy bounds!
> Adornment being wanted for the seats of the gods,
> Let the place of their shrines ever be in thy place.
> O Marduk, thou art indeed our avenger.
> We have granted thee kingship over the universe entire.
> When in Assembly thou sittest, thy word shall be supreme.
> Thy weapons shall not fail; they shall smash thy foes!
> O lord, spare the life of him who trusts thee,
> But pour out the life of the god who seized evil." [11]

---

[10] *Ibid.*, p. 191.

[11] At this point it is possible to pick up Speiser's translation as given in Pritchard's paperback, *The Ancient Near East* (Princeton, 1965), pp. 31-32.

Having conferred supreme authority on Marduk, the gods give him the insignia of kingship—scepter, throne, and royal robe—and arm him for the great battle with Tiamat. He takes bow, arrow, and club and holds lightning in front of his face. He makes a net to enclose the body of Tiamat and raises up the hurricane as his mighty weapon. His chariot is the storm, drawn by four powerful horses—"The Killer," "The Relentless," "The Trampler," and "The Swift." (These are the powers of Enlil, the Sumerian god of wind and storm, transferred to the sun-god of the Babylonians.)

The battle begins. Marduk's appearance is so threatening that Kingu and his host of chaotic powers are plunged into utter confusion. Only Tiamat stands her ground, taunting Marduk. He, in turn, challenges her to hand-to-hand combat.

> "[Why] art thou risen, art haughtily exalted,
> [Thou hast] charged thine own heart to stir up conflict,
> . . . sons reject their own fathers,
> Whilst thou, who hast born them, hast foresworn love!
> Thou hast appointed Kingu as they consort,
> Conferring upon him the rank of Anu, not rightfully his.
> Against Anshar, king of the gods, thou seekest evil;
> [Against] the gods, my fathers, thou hast confirmed thy
>   wickedness.
> [Though] drawn up be thy forces, girded on thy weapons,
> Stand thou up, that I and thou meet in single combat!" [12]

A terrific fight ensues. Marduk manages to envelop Tiamat in his huge net. When she opens her fearsome jaws to swallow him, he sends in the winds to hold her jaws open. The winds swell her body and open a corridor straight to her vitals. Marduk shoots in an arrow, pierces her heart, and kills her. When Kingu and his army try to escape, Marduk catches them in his net, and the victory is complete.

Marduk immediately proceeds to reorder the cosmos. He cuts Tiamat's body in two, and he lifts up one half of it to form the dome of heaven, leaving the other half as the sea on which Ea (earth) rests. He builds his home on top of the dome of the sky, making sure that it comes directly opposite Ea's dwelling to

---

[12] *Ibid.*, pp. 33-34.

form a "heavenly earth" as a counterpart to the "earthly earth." With great care he sets up constellations in the heavens and establishes their cyclical movement—three constellations for each of the twelve months—to determine days, months, and years. He gives particularly detailed instructions to the moon:

> "Monthly, without cease, form designs with a crown.
> At the month's very start, rising over the land,
> Thou shalt have luminous horns to signify six days,
> On the seventh day reaching a [half]-crown.
> At full moon stand in opposition[13] in mid-month.
> When the sun [overtakes] thee at the base of heaven,
> *Diminish* [thy crown] and retrogress in light.
> [At the time of disappearance] approach thou the course of the sun,
> And [on the twenty-ninth] thou shalt again stand in opposition to the sun." [14]

Many other innovations introduced by Marduk are lost to us because of a break in the text. When the materials become readable again, Marduk has conceived the brilliant idea of relieving the gods of the work needed to maintain the "earthly earth." He calls the gods to assembly, and he asks them who stirred up Tiamat to attempt the counterrevolution. Acting as a court, the gods convict Kingu. So Kingu is executed, and from his blood mankind is created. Marduk says:

> "Blood I will mass and cause bones to be.
> I will establish a savage, 'man' shall be his name.
> Verily, savage-man I will create.
> He shall be charged with the service of the gods
> That they might be at ease! . . ." [15]

Actually, Ea (earth) is the god who forms man, following Marduk's ingenious suggestions. Now that the gods have been relieved of the work of tending the earth, Marduk assigns them

---

[13] "At full moon": Akkadian prototype of the Sabbath insofar as injunctions against all types of activity were concerned. "in opposition": to the sun. Translator's notes—C.L.

[14] Speiser in Pritchard, *op. cit.,* p. 36.

[15] *Ibid.,* p. 36.

new duties. Three hundred are stationed in heaven to do guard duty, and three hundred are assigned to supervisory posts on earth. All of them are placed under the authority of Anu, but Marduk directs the total enterprise. Thus, all the divine forces are organized, and the cosmos is completed. It is a structure that must be renewed periodically, but it will never fail because the final victory has been won (although the assignment of half of the gods to guard duty makes one wonder).

Grateful for the creation of man, the gods resolve to build a sanctuary for Marduk, their last labor before turning over their toil to men. They mold bricks for a year and build Esagila, Marduk's temple and temple tower (ziggurat) at the center of Babylon. Then they meet in solemn assembly in Babylon to dedicate the temple and to confirm the eternal status of Marduk. His advancement from chief god of Babylon to head of the entire pantheon is signified by the conferring upon him of fifty names representing the power and attributes of all the major gods. Marduk has become emperor, and the entire cosmos is his empire.

3

Divine Rule and Human Rule

If by the term "creation story" we mean an account of how the physical universe came into being, only the brief opening section of the Enuma Elish fits the definition. The rest of the work deals with the emergence of Marduk as the savior of the gods, his battle with Tiamat, his reorganization of an already existing cosmos, and his glorification as the god above all gods. The point of the story, therefore, would seem to be a creation in the sociopolitical realm. It describes the establishment of kingship among the gods, first as a limited monarchy in which a semidemocratic assembly shared power with the king, and then as an absolute monarchy in which the assembly's powers were taken over by an emperor god. Interpreted in terms of the cosmological conviction, it is a mythicized account of two crises in Mesopotamian history when a new type of sociopolitical order was created: the transition from primitive communities and organized towns to kingly city-states and the transition from city-states to empire. During each of these two periods the Mesopotamians saw their sociopolitical structure as a human expression of the order already achieved by the divine society of the gods. To quote a most significant sentence written by the Sumerians as an introduction to a list of the earliest Sumerian kings, "When kingship was lowered from heaven, kingship was [first] in Eridu." [16] And the Enuma Elish, where Marduk's role as ruler of the earth is described, says there is to be "a likeness on earth of what he has wrought in heaven." [17]

Fortunately, this correlation of events among the gods with events among men can be considered from the point of view of men, especially some of the kings, as well as from the point of view of the gods, as described in the myths. There is Lugalzagesi, for instance, the Sumerian king who conquered a large part of the Mesopotamian valley and whose reign marked the beginning of the transition from city-state to empire. In about 2340 B.C. King Lugalzagesi erected in the city of Nippur a monument bearing the following inscription:

> "When Enlil king of the countries had granted to Lugalzagesi the kingship of the land; had turned the eyes of the land toward him; had prostrated the countries at his feet: then did he make straight his path for him, from the Lower Sea, by Tigris and Euphrates, to the Upper Sea [the Mediterranean].[18] From East to West Enlil nowhere allowed him a rival. Lugalzagesi gave the countries to rest in peace; watered the land with water of joy. . . . Then made he Uruk to shine in sheen of countenance; skyward, like a bull's, upraised the head of Ur; Larsa, dear city of the sun-god, watered with waters of joy; nobly exalted Umma, dear city of Shara. . . . May Enlil king of the countries prefer my prayer before his dear father An. May he add life to my life; cause the country to rest at peace with me. Folk as

---

[16] Translation by A. Leo Oppenheim in Pritchard's *Ancient Near Eastern Texts,* p. 265.

[17] Translation by Speiser in Pritchard, *op. cit.,* p. 69.

[18] C.L.

> numerous as scented herbs may he bestow on me with open hand; guide for me the flock of An [mankind];[19] look benevolently for me upon the land. Let the gods not change the good destiny that they have assigned to me. Shepherd, leader let me be forever!"[20]

The symbolism is clear. The divine assembly decided that Lugalzagesi was to be given control of a large territory. Anu announced the decision in the form of a divine decree; and Enlil proceeded to implement the decree by "making straight Lugalzagesi's path," which is to say that Enlil saw to it that Lugalzagesi defeated his rivals. Lugalzagesi, in turn, acknowledged that his success came to him because the gods had assigned him a successful destiny, and he prayed that this favorable attitude of the gods would continue.

The divine assembly is reminiscent of the city council, made up of the chief priests of the subordinate temples, in the early city-states. The roles of An and Enlil are interesting because they seem to represent two aspects of authority. An (or Anu) apparently symbolized the unapproachable majesty of ruling power, while Enlil symbolized this power in action. He carried out An's "great commands," which originated in the deliberations of the divine assembly. A modern parallel might be the passive authority of the British monarch, surrounded by pomp and circumstance, and the active authority of the prime minister. As kingship became more and more the center of active authority, both An and the assembly inevitably receded into the background, while Enlil became more and more important. This shift can be seen in Lugalzagesi's inscription. The king certainly paid homage to father An and to the assembly, but so far as the affairs of earth were concerned, Enlil had become the main link between heaven and earth. The impression that Enlil was becoming an "emperor god" is heightened when we learn that Nippur, Lugalzagesi's capital city, belonged traditionally to Enlil (as Babylon belonged traditionally to Marduk). When Nippur emerged as the seat of an empire Enlil's prestige also grew, al-

---

[19] Translator's note.

[20] Quoted by Jack Finegan in his *Light from the Ancient Past,* p. 37, from Patrick Carleton's *Buried Empires, the Earliest Civilizations of the Middle East* (London, 1939), p. 118.

though Lugalzagesi was exaggerating when he hailed him as "king of all countries."

Since the Mesopotamians believed that the gods could destroy as well as establish political units and leaders, Enlil appeared in human affairs as an agent of destruction as well as of construction. For instance, when barbaric hordes of Elamites swept into the kingdom of Babylon in 2025 B.C., smashing the city of Ur, which for a century and a half had been the capital of a sizable empire, the wild destructive power of the attack was identified as the work of Enlil. The invaders were likened to a storm that swept down on the city. When we remember that Enlil was "Lord Storm," we see that this picture is a remarkably direct way of saying that Enlil engineered the disaster. In a poem describing the fall of Ur, Enlil was presented as the divine destroyer.

> Enlil called the storm.
> The people mourn.
> Exhilarating winds he took from the land.
> The people mourn.
> Good winds he took away from Shumer.
> The people mourn.
> He summoned evil winds.
> The people mourn.
>
> . . .
>
> The storm ordered by Enlil in hate, the storm
> which wears away the country,
> covered Ur like a cloth, enveloped it
> like a linen sheet.
>
> . . .
>
> [Dead] men, not potsherds,
> Covered the approaches [to the city].
> The walls were gaping,
> The high gates, the roads,
> Were piled with dead.
> In the wide streets, where feasting crowds would gather,
> Scattered they lay.
> In all the streets and roadways bodies lay.
> In open fields that used to fill with dancers,
> They lay in heaps.

> The country's blood now filled its holes,
> like metal in a mould;
> Bodies dissolved—like fat left in the sun.[21]

There may have been an actual hurricane associated with the assault of the Elamites on Ur, but both storm and invaders were sent by Enlil, the divine executioner, carrying out the dread decision of the assembly of the gods. The most important point is that no change of sociopolitical structure among the gods (or among men) took place in such a situation. The divinely established institutional structures of monarchy and social organization were considered permanent; military upheavals took place *within* the structure.

By the time the Babylonians took over the Mesopotamian valley, around 1830 B.C., the imperial symbols had been developed more explicitly, with Marduk exalted to the position of emperor of the gods. The most illustrious member of the First Babylonian Dynasty was Hammurabi, who came to power in 1728 B.C. His immensely influential legal code began with this preamble:

> When lofty Anu, king of the Anunnaki, and Enlil, lord of heaven and earth, who determines the destinies of the land,
> Committed the Enlil function [lordship] over all the people to Marduk, the firstborn son of Enki, made him great among the Igigi,
> When they called Babylon by its exalted name ["Gateway of the Gods"],[22] made it surpassing in the world,
> When in its midst they established for him an everlasting kingdom whose foundations are firm as heaven and earth,—
> At that time Anu and Enlil called me, Hammurabi, the obedient prince, worshipper of the gods, by my name,

---

[21] Translation by Thorkild Jacobsen in Frankfort's *Before Philosophy,* pp. 154-55. This is a small section of the lengthy work "Lament for Destruction of Ur," which pictures also the goddess Nanna's vain efforts to convince Anu and Enlil that the city should not be destroyed. A complete translation by Samuel Noah Kramer is in Pritchard's *Ancient Near Eastern Texts,* pp. 455-63.

[22] C.L.

> To cause justice to prevail in the land, to destroy the evil and the wicked, to prevent the strong from oppressing the weak,
> That I [should] rise like the sun over the blackheaded people, to enlighten the land.[23]

Anu and Enlil are acknowledged, but the decisive "Enlil function" belongs to Marduk, originally the chief god of the city of Babylon. And just as the sun-god Marduk enlightens the heavens, so Hammurabi has risen "like the sun" to decisive power on earth.

Here we have strong echoes of the Enuma Elish, and there is a direct parallel between what happens to Marduk in the epic and what has happened to Hammurabi. At the same time, the continued presence of Anu and Enlil in the symbolism, and especially the retention of the significant term the "Enlil function," give ample evidence that the traditional myths had lost none of their power during the first thousand years of Mesopotamian history. A thousand years later, when the center of power had long since shifted to Assyria in the northern part of the Mesopotamian valley, the Assyrian emperor Tiglath-Pileser III (ca. 745-727 B.C.) was honored in an inscription which praised him as

> . . . the brave hero, who, with the help of Assur, his lord, smashed all who did not obey him, like pots, and laid them low, like a hurricane, scattering them to the winds; the king, who, advancing in the name of Assur, Shamash and Marduk, the great gods, brought under his sway the lands from the Bitter Sea . . . of the rising sun, and to the sea of the setting sun, as far as Egypt, . . .[24]

This sounds like Lugalzagesi's inscription (2340 B.C.), except that Assur, rather than Enlil or Marduk, now exercises the "Enlil

---

[23] Quoted by Eric Voegelin, *Order in History,* vol. I: *Israel and Revelation,* p. 24. A complete translation of the laws (but not the preamble), translated by T. J. Meek, is included in Pritchard's *The Ancient Near East,* pp. 138-67. The margins of this translation cite Biblical parallels by book, chapter, and verse.

[24] *Ibid.,* p. 26.

function." The conception of kingship as an office first established in heaven and then committed to earthly kings had remained substantially unchanged for two thousand years, since the First Sumerian Dynasty of Ur (ca. 2850 B.C.).

4

Cosmic Renewal: The New Year's Festival

Although sexual and sociopolitical symbols both appear in the Enuma Elish, images of sexual generation and of cyclical rebirth connected with the annual round of the seasons seem to be of secondary importance. Sociopolitical images dominate the drama, which culminates in the establishment of a stable cosmic empire. This fact suggests that the more primitive agriculturally based experiences of an intimate relationship between the rebirth of life in nature and a parallel renewal of vitality in human affairs were pushed into the background when urban-based empires emerged and the tribal past was considered out of date. It also suggests that the mythical tradition became divorced from the common life of most people and that the main function of the Enuma Elish during the period of the empires was to give the ruling dynasty an aura of legitimacy. But if the Enuma Elish is studied in the context of the annual Mesopotamian New Year's Festival, which was celebrated regularly from Sumerian times until the Persian emperor Xerxes discontinued it in 484 B.C., these suggestions will be misleading, even though they are partially correct. The Enuma Elish was always recited in its entirety during the New Year's Festival, but the course of events during its twelve days was much more than an acting-out of the creation story narrated in the epic. In fact, the elaborate series of rituals performed from day to day employed fertility symbols and actions as often and as prominently as they employed sociopolitical images and actions.

The heart of the New Year's Festival was a combination of belief in a cosmic order to which human existence should be attuned (the cosmological conviction); a profound awareness that unfortunately men had not successfully translated the divinely established models of attitude, relationship, and organization into their day-to-day living; and, finally, an equally profound experience of a triumphant passage from degeneration to regeneration, from the old year's threat of death to the new year's assurance of life. Both fertility symbolism and political symbolism could express the loss of vitality, the need for renewal, the longing and hope for a new beginning, and the jubilant experience of participating in the passage from the old year to the new, from the death of winter to the resurrection of spring, and from the guilt of the past to the innocence of the unspoiled present. Technically, the link between sexual (or fertility) symbols and sociopolitical symbols was present in the vision of the Sumerians from the beginning. They had become convinced that the predictable movements and configurations of the heavenly bodies revealed the models that men should imitate in ordering their society, for the placement in relation to the earth of these heavenly bodies also determined the biological cycle of seasonal fertility, maturation and death, and then fertility and new life again.

The Sumerians probably celebrated two New Year's Festivals, one in March/April and one in September/October, because in the Near East there are two growing seasons per year, each of which begins with the return of rain during these months. Sometime during the period after imperial organization had replaced the city-state, the festival came to be celebrated only once a year (March/April) and was held in a number of the old city-states that were traditional religious centers. When the Assyrians gained control of the Mesopotamian valley (ca. 1350 B.C.), the New Year's Festival was held only in the capital of the empire. Periodically, the emperor played the role of the hero-god Ashur (who had been Enlil for the Sumerians and the Akkadians, Marduk for the Babylonians); local governors were required to take turns playing the role in the intervening years. The emperor assumed the character of savior through his participation in the ritual reenactment of creation. For, although the main actors in the drama were believed to be the gods, representation of the human community, in the person of the king, was essential if the renewal of cosmic order achieved by the gods in their divine realm was to flow into the affairs of men.

The most complete accounts of the New Year's Festival available are Babylonian and Assyrian, although several documents from the period around 2000 B.C. have been discovered and shed some light on the celebration as it was held before the imperial period. Using these sources and the Babylonian materials, Henri Frankfort has reconstructed the scenario of the Babylonian celebration.[25] It was held during the first twelve days of the month of Nisan (March/April).

Nisan 1-4: Preparations and purifications. Marduk absent because imprisoned.

5: Day of Atonement for the king; the populace shares in various ways the suffering of the imprisoned Marduk and searches for him.

6: Several gods arrive by barge at Babylon, among them Nabu, the son and avenger of Marduk, who takes up residence in the main temple, Esagila.

7: Nabu, assisted by other gods, liberates Marduk by force from the "mountain" of the netherworld (probably symbolized by the base of the ziggurat tower of Esagila).

8: First Determination of Destiny. The gods assemble and bestow their combined power on Marduk.

9: Triumphal procession to the "House of the New Year's Feast" (the Bit Akitu) under the king's guidance. This represents the participation of the community in the victory taking place in nature and renews Marduk's creation of the present cosmic order.

10: Marduk celebrates his victory with the gods of the upperworld and netherworld at a banquet in the Bit Akitu and returns to his temple for the consummation of the sacred marriage that same night.

---

[25] Both the description and the interpretation in the following section are drawn largely from Frankfort's *Kingship and the Gods* (Chicago, 1948), chap. xxii. In the interests of brevity and clarity of presentation many of the significant passages quoted by Frankfort from original sources will not be quoted here.

11: The Second Determination of Destiny. The gods assemble to determine the destiny of society in the ensuing year.

12: The gods return to their own cities and to their own temples.[26]

The first five days of the festival focused on the need for renewal. The most obvious need could be seen and experienced directly: the desolate dryness of winter had killed off vegetation, had lowered or emptied streams and wells, and had raised the specter of eventual starvation for man and beast. A second need could also be observed: the heavenly bodies were on the point of completing their annual cycle, and their continuation into a new cycle could not be taken for granted. Their power must be replenished and their courses reestablished. A third need was experienced as guilt and estrangement: men had profaned life by departing from the divine models prescribed by tradition, and they longed to be reintegrated into the divine cosmic order.[27]

The rites in Esagila, Marduk's temple in Babylon, during the first five days were imbued with melancholy. Before the priests began their daily rituals, the high priest entered alone and prayed to Marduk and other gods. Curiously enough, inside the temple Marduk was still accessible to prayer, even though everyone knew that he was imprisoned in the "mountain" of the underworld. One of the prayers, sung before dawn on the second day, was called "The Secret of the Temple":

Lord without peer in thy wrath;
Lord, gracious king, lord of the lands;
Who made salvation for the great gods;

---

[26] *Ibid.*, pp. 317-18.

[27] Mircea Eliade writes: "The vast and monotonous morphology of the confession of sins . . . shows us that, even in the simplest human societies, 'historical' memory, that is, the recollection of personal events, . . . is intolerable. . . . [The] New Year scenarios in which the Creation is repeated are particularly explicit among the historical peoples, those with whom history, properly speaking, begins, that is, the Babylonians, Egyptians, Hebrews, Iranians. . . . These same peoples also appear to have felt a deeper need [than primitive peoples] to regenerate themselves periodically by abolishing past time and reactualizing the cosmogony." *Cosmos and History* (New York, 1959), pp. 74-75. Bracketed words added by C.L.

Lord, who throwest down the strong by his glance;
Lord of kings, light of men, who dost apportion destinies!
O Lord, Babylon is thy seat, Borsippa thy crown;
The wide heavens are thy body.
O Lord, with thine eyes thou piercest the Universese;

. . .

Lord of the lands, light of the Igigi,[28] who pronouncest
blessings;
Who would not proclaim thy, yea, thy power?
Would not speak of thy majesty, praise thy dominion?
Lord of the lands, who livest in Eudul, who takest the
fallen by the hand:
[Have pity] upon thy city, Babylon;
Turn thy face towards Esagila, thy temple;
Give freedom to them that dwell in Babylon, thy wards.[29]

On the evening of the fourth day the Enuma Elish was recited in its entirety. One commentary explicitly states that the reason for the singing of the epic was that Marduk was "bound." This is an interesting merging of biological and sociopolitical themes. The Enuma Elish says nothing about Marduk being imprisoned by the death-dealing powers of the netherworld. The gods need him to gain victory over Tiamat and Kingu and thus to maintain cosmic order. Why recite the story of Marduk's victorious rise to emperor when it is Marduk himself who needs liberation? One might even ask how the Lord of Creation got caught in the "dead" phase of the annual fertility cycle, since he is the one credited with organizing and renewing the forces of life. Such questions miss the point. We are dealing with an example of the compactness of experience and symbolization in Mesopotamian culture. The cosmological conviction affirmed the cohesion of all reality; therefore, Marduk had to be intimately involved in every cosmic need for renewal just as he was also acknowledged to be involved in every victorious achievement of renewal. The recitation of the Enuma Elish as part of the rites of passage from winter to spring brought into the ritual the most comprehensive of all Mesopotamian accounts of cosmic

[28] Igigi are the gods of heaven—C.L.
[29] Frankfort, *Kingship and the Gods,* pp. 318-19.

crisis and of cosmic victory; it cast the brightest possible ray of hope and confidence into the somber and anxious mood that dominated the first days of the New Year's Festival.

The first important dramatic element in the festival came on the Day of Atonement, Nisan 5, when the king was stripped of his power, humiliated, and finally reinstated to royal rule. Again, the early morning prayers on this day were of appeasement, offered especially to Marduk as manifested in the heavenly bodies.

> The white star [Jupiter] which brings omens to the world
> is my lord;
> My lord be at peace!
> The star Gud [Mercury] which causes rain is my lord;
> My lord be at peace!
> The star Gena [Saturn], star of law and order, is my lord;
> My lord be at peace! [30]

The temple was purified, offerings and incantations continued throughout the day, and the chapel of Nabu (Marduk's son, due to arrive the next day) was prepared. During these activities, the king was escorted to Marduk's chapel by priests and left there alone. Then the high priest came out of the Holy of Holies, where the statue of Marduk stood. He relieved the king of his scepter, ring, scimitar, and crown and took them back into the Holy of Holies, placing them on a "seat" in front of the statue. Then he returned to the king, struck him in the face, and ordered him to kneel to make a declaration of innocence:

> I have not sinned, O lord of the lands,
> I have not been negligent regarding thy divinity,
> I have not destroyed Babylon. . . .

The high priest immediately replied in Marduk's name:

> Do not fear . . . . what Marduk has spoken. . . .
> He [will hear] thy prayer. He will increase thy dominion . . .
> heighten thy royalty. . . .[31]

---

[30] *Ibid.*, p. 319.
[31] *Ibid.*, p. 320.

Then he went into the Holy of Holies, brought out the insignia of kingship (exactly as he had during the king's coronation), and gave them back to the king. Finally, he struck the king's face again in the hope of drawing tears, which would have been a favorable omen and proof of Marduk's goodwill.

Why did the king's confession, purification, and reinstatement as possessor of the Marduk-function on earth precede the dramatization, on Nisan 8, of Marduk's own exaltation to kingship over the gods, establishing the divine model of earthly kingship? The reason, no doubt, was that the king must become fit to officiate in the succeeding rites. His humiliation brought him into harmony with the desolateness of nature and the corresponding "captivity" of Marduk. An even more fundamental symbolism, however, was in the radical reversal to which the king was subjected. His imprisonment symbolized the envelopment of human society in extensive chaos. Even its summit was submerged, just as all levels of reality were considered dissolved into the shapeless, primordial "sea" as it was before creation. Then creation could be repeated and the structures of life renewed.

This precreation chaos was expressed not only in the temple ritual but also through various commotions and carnival activities inside and outside the city. People rushed around looking for Marduk, crying "Where is he held captive?" Apparently a condemned criminal was enthroned as a carnival king, a curious substitute for the imprisoned ("dead") Marduk. A late source tells of a temporary overturning of the entire social order, with slaves becoming masters for a day in their households and masters playing the role of servants. References to commotions outside the city near the "House of the New Year's Feast," which a few days later was to be the goal of the victorious procession of Marduk, suggest sexual orgies in which normal restrictions were suspended and the "oneness" of primordial confusion was reenacted.

Nisan 6 and 7 were devoted to the liberation of Marduk by his son Nabu, whose statue arrived by barge from nearby Borsippa on Nisan 6, accompanied by statues of the gods of many cities (Nippur, Uruk, Cuthah, Kish), each in its own elaborate barge. There was a triumphal procession from the landing platform to Esagila, where the gods were installed in their chapels. The ritual of liberation probably took place on Nisan 7, but unfortunately we do not know how it was represented.

Once Marduk had returned, the events of the Enuma Elish could be reenacted. On Nisan 8, the statues of the gods were brought together in the Chamber of Destinies in Esagila to elect Marduk king of the gods and to give him absolute power. The king of Babylon acted as master of ceremonies. Carrying a shining wand, he summoned each god in turn to leave his chapel and "taking his hand," guided the god to his appropriate position in the great hall. A hush of reverence fell over the entire city while the gods assembled. Evil influences caused by thoughtless acts and words had to be avoided. A late source, which includes a calendar of lucky and unlucky days, has an entry for Nisan 8 that reads: "Show no enmity at all."

Abruptly, on Nisan 9, the mood of the festival changed from somber and anxious waiting to joy and exuberance. Not only had Marduk returned, but he had been exalted to kingship, had vanquished Tiamat, and had created the cosmos. Some scholars claim that the battle between Marduk and Tiamat was dramatized in a mock battle between two groups of actors. Probably, however, the triumphal procession from Esagila to the "House of the New Year's Festival" represented the victory.[32] There is clear evidence that the procession was considered so important that its every detail was watched carefully and possessed the significance of an omen for the new year. The statues of the gods, accompanied by great numbers of priests and cheered by the populace, must have formed a brilliant and impressive parade as they were carried through the streets to the river's edge, loaded ceremoniously on their barges, and ferried across the Euphrates to the "House of the New Year's Feast" (the Bit Akitu).

The Bit Akitu of Babylon was undoubtedly similar to the one built later at Assur, which has been excavated. According to tradition, the outstanding feature of the Assyrian festival house was the richness of the gardens that surrounded it. Even the courtyard was filled with trees and shrubs. The excavations confirm the size and the careful planning of the gardens; they also show that a huge main hall, measuring twenty-five by one hun-

---

[32] Frankfort points out that apparently ritual acts were performed, such as the smashing of a pot (Marduk killing Tiamat) and the burning of a sheep (Kingu being overpowered). One would hardly expect a mock battle if the various steps in Marduk's triumph were represented by such rituals.

dred feet, extended the whole width of the building at the back. This was probably the banquet hall to which the king and the priests escorted the statues of the gods for the feast. A sumptuous banquet was served on Nisan 10; it was consumed spiritually by the gods and eaten joyously by their human servants.

On that same night, Marduk and the king returned to Esagila to participate in the sacred marriage with the goddess Sarpanit, a union reenacted by the king and a sacred female temple slave in a special "chamber of the bed" located someplace in the temple enclosure, perhaps at the summit of the ziggurat. One of the early documents mentioned at the beginning of this section, from the city of Isin, gives a picture of what went on:

> To guard the life-breath of all lands. . .
> To perform the rites correctly on the day the moon is invisible,
> Has on New Year's Day, the day of observances,
> A couch been set up for my lady.
> Grass and plants . . . cedar they purify there,
> Put it for my queen on that couch.
> On its . . . the blanket is arranged for her,
> A blanket delighting the heart, to make the bed good.[33]

Next follows a realistic account of the censing and bathing of both the goddess and the king and of their sexual union. The emergence of the couple from the bedchamber to an elaborate meal and entertainment brought the ritual to a conclusion.

> Around the shoulders of his beloved bride he has laid his arm,
> Around the shoulders of pure Inanna [the goddess of Isin][34]
> he has laid his arm.
> Like daylight she ascends the throne on the great throne dais;
> The king, like unto the sun, sits beside her.
> Abundance, pleasure, wealth are ranged before her,
> A sumptuous meal is placed before her.
> The black-headed people are [?] ranged before her.
> . . . . music . . . singers. . . .
> The king has reached out for the food and drink,
>
> . . .

[33] Frankfort, *Kingship and the Gods*, p. 296 (translated by Jacobsen).
[34] C.L.

The palace is in fest[ive mood], the king is glad,
The people are passing the day in abundance.[35]

The union of the god and goddess was in the final analysis an event in nature, and its immediate result was the restoration of the fertility of fields, flocks, and men after the stagnancy of winter. The sacred marriage marked the end of the period during which life in nature had been suspended. The Great Mother had been impregnated, and new life would come. The objective reality of this restoration was expressed with particular vividness in an early description ascribed to King Gudea of Lagash (about 2000 B.C.). Here the imagery of the dark storm that would bring back the rains permeated the account of the sexual union. The god in the Lagash myth and ritual was Ningirsu, and King Gudea said that Ningirsu entered his temple "like a rumbling storm" and "like a bird of prey descrying its victim." The goddess "approached his black side" and "entered between his black arms." [36]

The sacred marriage in Esagila, including its feast, was a powerful expression of biological renewal. But the symbolism of the banquet in the setting of the festival house was truly comprehensive. The elaborate fertile gardens outside and the royal gathering of gods, priests, warriors, and political leaders inside involved a complex interweaving of biological and sociopolitical symbols and completely expressed the universality of the cosmic renewal celebrated in the New Year's Festival.

Thus, by Nisan 11 the cosmos and society had been revitalized, but the future of human affairs had not yet been decreed. On Nisan 11 the gods met once more in solemn assembly to establish the destiny of mankind during the next twelve months.

---

[35] *Ibid.*, p. 296.

[36] *Ibid.*, p. 330. Frankfort points out in the same chapter that all three "living religions" that originated in the Near East—Judaism, Christianity, and Islam—have perpetuated the symbolism of death being vanquished at the beginning of the new year. In the Talmud, for instance, the raising of the dead is linked with rainstorms, which in turn are connected with the new year. In the Christian tradition the final resurrection has sometimes been expected at Epiphany, just after the turn of the year in January. In Moslem theology, as in the Jewish tradition, rain is connected with resurrection; it is said that rain will come down from heaven and mankind will germinate, just as the grains germinate.

This was their last official act. On the next day, Nisan 12, the statues of the gods were ceremoniously loaded onto their barges to be returned to their home cities; meanwhile, men began the work of the new year.[37]

5

The Power of the Myths

Myth was the special language form through which basic convictions were expressed in the ancient Near Eastern cultures. Myths presented the divine models of social and political attitudes, organization, and behavior that were authoritative for human existence in community. But the power of the sacred stories went beyond these functions. The Mesopotamian creation myths operated at the level where men's orientation to reality was shaped by the cosmological conviction and where they were motivated by a profound desire to experience harmony with the sacred world order. As the story was recited—and it was certainly told over and over again in every stratum of society and not merely in the ritual setting of the New Year's Festival—the hu-

[37] The Mesopotamian New Year's Festival is a classic example of what Theodore H. Gaster calls the Seasonal Pattern, a combination of myth and ritual that he believes is a worldwide phenomenon and that he has studied with special reference to the Egyptian, Babylonian, Hittite, and Canaanite cultures in the Near East. In his *Thespis: Ritual, Myth, and Drama in the Ancient Near East* (New York, 1961) Gaster insists that the public ceremonies by means of which societies usher in years and seasons are not arbitrary or haphazard or casual; he concludes that there is a standard pattern consisting of four major elements: mortification, purgation, invigoration, and jubilation. He presents an impressive collection of seasonal myths that not only supports his thesis but also documents the fact that what is called the cosmological conviction in this book was central to the life orientation of the early Near Eastern civilizations.

man and the divine, the mortal and the immortal, the secular and the sacred coalesced *here and now* for those who experienced the ultimate reality of which the myth spoke.

The reader may well ask how modern scholars know that such a statement is accurate when it presupposes that they have been able to penetrate the realm of living faith in cultures that died more than two thousand years ago. Although archeologists have been able to collect large numbers of myths committed to written form by the Babylonians and the Assyrians, they have not unearthed anything like an interpretive essay on "What the Enuma Elish Means to Me." The usual way of attempting to understand the experience of ancient civilizations is to draw parallels between documentary evidence about myth and cult (such as those summarized in this chapter) and the insights of cultural anthropologists who live as participant observers with contemporary "primitive" peoples to witness the functions of myth and cult in the context of their actual faith and life. For instance, Bronislaw Malinowski did field studies among the Trobriand Islanders of Melanesia, on the basis of which he reached the following conclusion:

> . . . I maintain that there exists a special class of stories, regarded as sacred, embodied in ritual, morals, and social organization, and which form an integral and active part of primitive culture. These stories live not by idle interest, not as fictitious or even as true narratives; but are to the natives a statement of a primeval, greater, and more relevant reality by which the present life, fates, and activities of mankind are determined, the knowledge of which supplies man with the motive for ritual and moral actions, as well as with indications as to how to perform them.[38]

Malinowski insists that in its living form myth is not merely a story told but a reality lived, which is precisely the claim made here concerning the significance of myth in the Mesopotamian tradition.

Nevertheless, cultural anthropologists have customarily ob-

[38] From an essay, "Myth in Primitive Psychology," writen some thirty years ago and included in Malinowski's *Magic, Science and Religion* (New York, 1954), p. 108. A significant and more recent treatment of myth is Adolf E. Jensen's *Myth and Cult Among Primitive Peoples* (Chicago, 1963).

served primitive tribal societies rather than highly developed civilizations, a fact that raises serious questions about the degree of directness with which analogies can be drawn between the power of myth in very compact primitive situations and in highly complex civilized situations. For the past generation anthropologists like W. Lloyd Warner have been studying American society with the same techniques used in field work among primitives, and Professor Warner suggests that Americans must take seriously significant continuities not merely between ancient primitive peoples and the inhabitants of the early Near Eastern civilizations but between primitives and us. He writes:

> In popular belief modern man seems far removed from his Stone Age kinsman of aboriginal Australia [the main locale of Warner's own field work];[39] but, despite obvious differences, the fundamental core of life of each is very much the same. Being a human being demands the same basic social and personal equipment in black Australia or in contemporary civilization. When he studies his own people, the social anthropologist who has had experience with primitive people soon loses his sense of strangeness, for he learns that they (and he) are very much like their primitive brothers. Perhaps at this present juncture of world affairs this is the most important thing we can learn about ourselves.[40]

This general statement says nothing about myth, but in the book Professor Warner illustrates one major component in the American counterpart of the cosmological conviction as well as some of the myths through which the core convictions that motivate our society are expressed.

According to Warner, the most important fact about our social system is that it rests on two seemingly opposite yet equally fundamental convictions. One is the equality conviction, and the other is the status conviction, which implies a definite element of inequality. The combination of these two is the American Dream—the vision, hope, and expectation that every person and his family will be able to rise in social status. The American

---

[39] C.L.

[40] From Warner's introduction to his *American Life: Dream and Reality* (Chicago, 1953), p. viii.

Dream functions like the Mesopotamian cosmological conviction in at least two respects: first, it provides a fundamental pattern for living; it is an orienting, directing, and motivating integrator in the life of the total society. Second, it derives its power not simply from custom or from the fact that historically it has worked well but from a conviction even more basic than the twin convictions of the Dream itself. Most Americans have believed and still believe that equal opportunity to "get ahead" according to native ability and diligent effort—a part of the right to life, liberty, and the pursuit of happiness—is somehow a part of the fabric of reality itself. This is the real meaning of the phrase in the Constitution, "We hold these truths to be self-evident." Without going into any philosophical or theological issues, it seems safe to say that in American culture the self-evident convictions presupposed by the Dream function as an ultimate in much the same manner as the divine society of the gods in the Enuma Elish functioned for the ancient Mesopotamian cultures.

Like the cosmological conviction, the American Dream is expressed most effectively through a special story form. The traditional and still unrivaled carrier of its convictions is the rags-to-riches success story. Innumerable examples could be cited, some crass and others noble, but the most powerful of these is the story of Abraham Lincoln. It is much more than a climb from rags to riches. Lincoln would not be the most powerful sacred symbol that has emerged thus far in the American tradition if the equality and status convictions were not exemplified in his career.

"Honest Abe Lincoln the railsplitter" expresses the equality side of the Dream. This slogan helped elect Lincoln to the Presidency when he was already a former congressman, a successful lawyer, and a close friend of many rich and powerful men. It did not reflect his current status, but it did reflect his own strong equalitarian sentiments, later expressed so memorably: "God must love the common people because he made so many of them;" and "Fourscore and seven years ago our fathers brought forth on this continent a new nation conceived in liberty and dedicated to the proposition that all men are created equal."

"From log cabin to White House" expresses the status conviction, the rags-to-riches motif. The common man can become the superior man, the man who does not inherit but who earns status. This is the Lincoln *of* the people who rose to power and who then acted effectively *for* the people.

A third motif was added when Lincoln was assassinated—the conviction that vicarious sacrifice is both tragic and noble. The manner of his death drew him inevitably into the orbit of the complex religious symbolism associated with the death of Jesus. Lincoln's life was considered a sacrifice on the altar of national unity climaxing a vicious civil war. Thousands of sermons and speeches have proclaimed that he, like the Jesus of Christian doctrine, died that all men might live as brothers. The conviction that individuals and groups must make sacrifices for the welfare of their society had always been present in the American tradition as a check on the dog-eat-dog implications of the social mobility ambition, but the death of Lincoln gave this conviction its distinctively American symbol. It lives today, and the tragic assassination of President John F. Kennedy in 1963 strengthened its power. "Ask not what your country can do for you—ask what you can do for your country."

Obviously, the story of Abraham Lincoln as outlined is not simply a chronicle of facts, nor is it fact embroidered with legend. It is a myth, and it functions as a myth. It is a conviction-expressing sacred story in which Americans see their "true selves." Lincoln is an archetype, an ideal model of the goal of the American Dream; both the Dream and Lincoln belong to the religious dimension of American culture.

There are other interesting examples of the power of myths in American life, but this example provides rather convincing evidence that, as Professor Warner says, modern men are surprisingly similar to their primitive and ancient brothers in significant sectors of their experience. This is especially true in what might be called the structural sector, wherein they all order their lives in terms of basic convictions. Thus, careful observation of the function of myths in modern cultures as well as in living primitive cultures suggests the way in which convictions expressed through myths exerted a powerful influence on the lives of the Sumerians, Akkadians, Babylonians, and Assyrians.

There is still another approach, however, which may supply some evidence. Although it does not analyze myths, it has the advantage of dealing with materials from the Mesopotamian tradition itself rather than appealing to primitive or modern parallels. It focuses on works that reveal how people responded to extreme suffering and tests the power (or lack of power) of the cosmological conviction. Did it or did it not provide a framework within which people were able to deal with suffering as a potentially meaningful, rather than an utterly meaningless, crisis? This approach indirectly tests the power of the myths that communicated the various facets of the cosmological conviction to members of the culture.

6

Suffering and the Cosmological Conviction

One of the most poignant Mesopotamian documents unearthed by archeologists resembles the Biblical book of Job and is known as "Ludlul bel nemeqi,"—"I will praise the Lord of wisdom." The hero of the poem believes himself to be completely righteous, but such serious evils have befallen him that he doubts the accepted belief that deviation from the divine norm brings suffering while obedience to the norm brings rewards of health, long life, honored standing in the community, many sons, and wealth. He even wonders whether the norm he has followed meticulously really is the correct norm.

> What is good in one's sight is evil for a god.
> What is bad in one's own mind is good for his god.
> Who can understand the counsel of the gods in the midst of heaven?
> The plan of a god is deep waters, who can comprehend it?
> Where has befuddled mankind ever learned what a god's conduct is? [41]

[41] Translated by Robert H. Pfeiffer in Pritchard's *Ancient Near Eastern Texts,* p. 435.

The sufferer describes his pitiable situation at great length; the following passage gives a good summary:

> My eyes stare without seeing.
> My ears are open without hearing.
> Faintness has seized my whole body.
> A stroke has fallen upon my flesh.
> Weakness has taken hold of my hand.
> Weariness has fallen upon my knees.
>
> . . .
>
> Wheat, even though putrid, I eat.
> Beer—life divine!—I have eliminated from me.
> Extremely long has lasted the distress.
>
> . . .
>
> My prison—that is what my house has become.
>
> . . .
>
> I spend the night in my dung, like an ox.
> I was soaked like a sheep in my excrements.
> My arthritis baffled the conjurer,
> And my omens confused the diviner.
> The enchanter has not determined the condition of my illness,
> And the time [of the end] of my malady the diviner did not give [me].
> No god helped, [none] seized my hand;
> My goddess showed no mercy, she did not come to my side.
> While the grave was still open they took possession of my jewels,
> Before I was dead the weeping [for me] was ended.
> All my land said, "How has he been mistreated!"
> My ill-wisher heard it, and his countenance shone [with joy];
> They brought the good news to the woman who was my ill-wisher, and her spirit was delighted.

In the next lines, however, a ray of hope appears, and the sufferer goes on to describe how hope was awakened in him:

But I know the day on which my tears will cease,
On which in the midst of the protecting deities their divinity will show mercy.

. . .

A dream in the morning [appeared] twice with the same meaning.[42]

In the first dream a man of superhuman stature approaches the sufferer and removes obstructions to his breathing, eating, hearing, speaking, and so on. In the second dream a certain man appears carrying a purification vessel. He pours water over the afflicted one and recites "the incantation of life." Then a third dream is reported in which the queen of life (Marduk's consort, Sarpanit) appears, promising that Marduk will help the sufferer and saying that she has been sent by Marduk to deliver the promise.

After a significant line, "He [Marduk][43] caused the wind to carry away my trespasses"—which are never specifically identified—the author announces that healing actually occurs:

Into the waves of the sea he sank the fever heat.
The root of the sickness he pulled out like a plant.
The unhealthy sleep, the spell of slumber,
As when the heavens are filled with smoke . . . ,
They were driven away, with the woe and pain . . . .

. . .

The torturing headache . . . .
He removed the running of my eyes and drove it from me.
[The blur] of my eyes, over which had spread the curtain of night,
A mighty wind blew it off and cleared their sight.
My ears, stopped and closed as in a deaf man,
He removed their obstruction, he opened my hearing.[44]

---

[42] *Ibid.*, pp. 435-36.

[43] C.L.

[44] Pfeiffer in Pritchard, 2nd ed., 1955, p. 437.

His description of the miraculous cure reveals the "true" source of the malady and the method of the cure.

> Out of [trouble], through deliverance, I came.
> The waters of Esagila though weary, I set forth in my hands.
> Into the mouth of the lion who was devouring me Marduk placed [a bit].
> Marduk removed [the incantation] of the one hounding me, turned back his lumps.
>
> . . .
>
> [Marduk] lifted high my head,
> He smote my smiter's hand;
> His weapon Marduk shattered.[45]

The illness was caused by sorcery, and the cure effected because Marduk broke the curse. The final section gives a full account of the elaborate ritual, including a splendid and impressive banquet, performed by the cured man in Marduk's great temple. The poem ends with the paean of praise that has given the work its title:

> "Who commanded it, who accomplished the vision of the deity?
> In whose mind is the going [freely] on one's way realized?
> Apart from Marduk, who revived his lifeless state?
> Besides Sarpanit, what goddess conferred life unto him?"
> Marduk is able to revive in the grave.
> Sarpanit knows how to deliver from destruction.
> Wherever the earth reaches, the heavens are spread out,
> The sun shines, fire glows,
> Water flows, the wind blows,
> [Wherever the beings] whose clay the goddess Aruru has nipped off,
> Creatures endowed with breath, stride rapidly,
> . . . as many as there are, [glorify] Marduk! [46]

This poem differs substantially from the Biblical book of Job because it is built on precisely the conviction that Job attacks:

---

[45] *Ibid.*, p. 437.
[46] *Ibid.*, p. 437.

if a man suffers he must have done something wrong, for suffering is always correlated with transgression, either ritual or moral. This is the conviction Job doggedly denies, but in the Mesopotamian poem the sufferer admits guilt. Apparently, he does not know exactly what it was that he did wrong, but the gods know, and he concludes that his transgression made him vulnerable to sorcery. To put it into language appropriate to the context of the cosmological conviction, Job is unwilling to agree that his existence is defined by certain social or cultural patterns identified as divinely established models; rather, he demands a hearing before the Almighty in which the sole issue is his own integrity as a person. He really does not hold the cosmological conviction. On the other hand, the sufferer in the Mesopotamian poem believes that his life is defined by archetypal models established by the gods and that somehow he has failed to conform sufficiently with these traditional patterns; he believes the cosmological conviction and therefore he is convinced that deviation from the norm means suffering. Suffering carries for Job a terrible threat of meaninglessness, whereas the cosmological conviction gives the Mesopotamian no basis to look upon suffering as without meaning or cause and therefore as intolerable. Writing about what he calls the "normality of suffering" in primitive and archaic cultures, Mircea Eliade says:

> Naturally, the motifs that yield a justification for suffering and pain vary from people to people, but the justification is found everywhere. In general, it may be said that suffering is regarded as the consequence of a deviation in respect to the "norm." That this norm differs from people to people, and from civilization to civilization, goes without saying. But the important point for us is that nowhere—within the frame of the archaic civilizations—are suffering and pain regarded as "blind" and without meaning.[47]

When one remembers that the basic convictions of every culture usually operate below the level of consciousness, the power of myths to bring the Mesopotamians in touch with the meaning-giving and confidence-creating cosmic order by giving

---

[47] Mircea Eliade, *Cosmos and History: The Myth of the Eternal Return* (New York, 1959), p. 98.

the cosmological conviction a concrete form of expression begins to be seen in its proper perspective. Any interpretation of the significance of the Enuma Elish myths or other myths *for the Mesopotamians themselves* is inadequate if it does not take into account the likelihood that for the majority of these people for more than two thousand years *myths* were the connecting link between their everyday living and the encompassing cosmic whole. They knew that their individual, family, and social existence was only a current phase of the whole and that the eternal order revealed the model patterns which gave even a limited span of life positive meaning.

7

The Revolt Against Death: The Gilgamesh Epic

One part of the mythical tradition, however, generated considerable resistance, especially when Mesopotamian life became complex, experience more highly differentiated, and trends toward individualism emerged. This theme that man had been created to be the slave of the gods was repeated every time the Enuma Elish was recited. After Marduk had assigned the various regions of the cosmos to specific gods he decided to allow them to manage the earth as absentee landlords, creating man to work in order that the divine owners might indulge themselves in the leisurely life befitting gods. Created originally of clay, man was destined to revert to clay when he died. Death meant annihilation of the individual person, or at best a meaningless, shadowy half-life in a dark region beneath the surface of the earth.

On the other hand, there were traditional legends concerning heroes and ancient kings who were divine or who won immortality. And, as always, there were sensitive individuals who were troubled by the curious phenomenon that although man shares with the animals the inevitability of having to die he *knows* that he has to die, and in this knowledge he seems to find an intimation that the ability to contemplate death prevents his annihilation by it. At any rate, a work that first appeared in written form around 2000 B.C. made use of many legends connected with Gilgamesh, a famous early king of the city of Uruk, and organized them into an unforgettable protest against death.

The epic begins and ends with a celebration of the greatness of the city of Uruk, which seems to function as a reminder that Mesopotamian culture was predominantly community-centered rather than individual-centered. In fact, to the exceptional individual who is acutely aware of being an individual, the prologue and the epilogue seem to reflect the traditional belief that even though man cannot hope to attain immortality, his society is an enterprise greater and more enduring than he. Fame, honor, remembrance in the traditions of one's society—what more should any man want? The main body of the epic reveals that Gilgamesh wanted much more.[48]

Gilgamesh is the son of the goddess Ninsun and a human father. He is an overwhelmingly energetic city-king who drives his subjects so hard that they cry out to the gods for help. The gods order the goddess Aruru to create a being who will divert the king's vitality into enterprises that will relieve the pressure on the citizens of Uruk. She "pinches off some clay" and fashions Enkidu, a powerful long-haired "primitive" who lives with the beasts. A hunter tells Gilgamesh about this human animal who protects game animals from hunters. Gilgamesh sends a sacred prostitute, Shamhat, from the temple of Anu and Ishtar to

---

[48] The most important versions of the Gilgamesh Epic (none are complete), translated by John A. Wilson, are available in Pritchard's *The Ancient Near East.* The presentation of the materials in Pritchard gives the reader a vivid picture of the actual complexities involved in translating ancient works. Except where noted, however, this account will cite Cyrus Gordon's translation as given in his *Before the Bible* (New York, 1962), which is more readable. A good paraphrased translation also is available in a Penguin paperback, N. K. Sandars' *The Epic of Gilgamesh* (Baltimore, 1964). Sandars includes Tablet XII, which does not seem to belong structurally to the epic but which is interesting because it recounts a tradition concerning the death of Gilgamesh.

"humanize" Enkidu and to bring him to civilization. One day when Enkidu comes to a water hole with some of his animal friends he finds Shamhat waiting for him.

> Shamhat exposed her breasts,
> Opened her bosom
> So that he took her charm.
> She didn't make off
> But accepted his love,
> He took off her clothes
> And lay upon her
> She treated him, primeval man, to woman's business.
> His love inclined over her.
> Six days, yea seven nights, Enkidu is in fine fettle and tups Shamhat.
> After he is sated with her charms
> He sets his face towards his beasts
> But the deer see him, Enkidu, and run off.[49]

Enkidu realizes that a fundamental change has taken place. Shamhat interprets the change:

> You are [wi]se, O Enkidu,
> You are become like a god.
> Why should you roam the field with the beasts?
> Come, let me lead you to the midst of walled Uruk
> To the holy house, the dwelling of Anu and Ishtar
> Where Gilgamesh, perfect in wisdom,
> Like a buffalo holds mighty sway over his people.[50]

Enkidu responds immediately and eagerly. He is ready to go to Uruk and even to challenge Gilgamesh.

Meanwhile, Gilgamesh has two dreams that are interpreted by his mother to mean he is going to gain a powerful friend who will never betray him. Enkidu arrives to fulfill the prediction. The two grapple with each other and so impress one another that they form a partnership devoted to wiping evil from the face of the earth. Evil means dragons, so the friends leave Uruk to look for the enemy. The good citizens of Uruk are happy to be relieved of Gilgamesh for a while.

---

[49] Cyrus Gordon, *Before the Bible,* p. 63.
[50] *Ibid.,* p. 64.

In their first exploit, Gilgamesh and Enkidu slay the evil dragon Humbaba. The hazards are so great that Enkidu wavers and tries to persuade Gilgamesh to look for a fight in which the odds are more even. Gilgamesh upbraids Enkidu for fearing death and praises the heroic ideal of leaving behind a name for bravery in the face of impossible odds. Enkidu agrees, and the two finally kill the dragon.

When the friends return from their victory, Gilgamesh celebrates by dressing very handsomely—so handsomely that the goddess Ishtar asks him to marry her. He refuses because she has a long record of marriages and infidelities and concludes, "You would love me, but you would treat me like them." Ishtar is enraged. She resolves to destroy Gilgamesh by getting permission from her father Anu, the king of the gods, to turn loose the fearsome Bull of Heaven. Anu reminds her that if a hero is killed there will be a seven-year famine. Ishtar replies that she has already stored a seven-year supply of food. Anu gives in; the Bull attacks Gilgamesh.

Enkidu joins Gilgamesh in the battle, and together they kill the Bull of Heaven, cut out its heart, and place the heart as an offering before Shamash, the god who detests evil. Ishtar complains bitterly that the victory was gained unfairly because Enkidu interfered, and in return Enkidu vulgarly tosses the right leg of the Bull in her face. This is a grievous insult, and it seals his fate. The gods decide that Enkidu must die. Enkidu curses his fate, and in particular curses Shamhat, who lured him into the career that is leading him to an early death. But the god Shamash rebukes him, reminding him that Shamhat has made him a hero and that it is no small honor to live and die a hero. Enkidu agrees and cancels the curse. A dream then gives him a preview of Irkalla, the dismal place underground where even heroes must spend a dreary eternity.[51]

The death of Enkidu fills Gilgamesh with almost uncontrollable grief. But much as he mourns for his friend, he dreads even more his own death. The heroic ideal of brave death in battle in the face of overwhelming odds seems empty now, and Gilgamesh resolves to search for eternal life. He has heard about a famous man who long ago had not only been saved from the

[51] This dismal place is the exact parallel to the Hades of Greek tradition and to the Sheol of Biblical writings.

Great Flood but had also won immortality by his actions during the emergency. He decides to seek out this man, Utnapishtim, and to ask him how a mortal can evade death. The journey is long and dangerous, but Gilgamesh is too deeply concerned to let any hazards deflect his resolve.

In his search, Gilgamesh is told again and again that his search for immortality is hopeless. The most interesting of these episodes takes place in a tavern run by Siduri, the divine ale-wife. He pours out his heart to her and asks her to help him:

> Enkidu, whom I loved so much . . .
> And who underwent all hardships with me,
> Has gone to the fate of mankind.
> Day and night I wept over him
> And gave him not over for burial . . .
> Seven days and seven nights
> Until the worm fell from his nose.
> Now that he is gone, I have not found immortality.
> I keep wandering like a hunter in the midst of the plain.
> Now, O ale-wife, I look at your face!
> Let me not see the Death that I dread! [52]

The tavern keeper tries to dissuade him from his wild-goose chase. She reminds him of the actual order of human life as established by the gods, and she recommends a conventional pleasure-loving life as an alternative to frustration.

> You will not find the immortality that you seek
> When the gods created mankind
> They ordained death for mankind
>   Immortality they kept within their own grasp.
> As for you, O Gilgamesh, let your belly be full
>   May you rejoice day and night
>   Establish gladness every day
>   Day and night dance and play
> May your clothes be clean
>   Your head be washed
>   May you be bathed in water

[52] Gordon, *op. cit.*, p. 73.

Watch the little lad who holds your hand
Let your wife rejoice in your bosom
This is the business [of mankind].[53]

Gilgamesh will not give up, and he insists that Siduri help him find the way to Utnapishtim. She gives directions for the perilous journey, including information about the Waters of Death over which Utnapishtim's boatman, Zur-Shanabi, will have to ferry him. Eventually Gilgamesh reaches the waters, crosses them in the ferryboat, and meets the legendary flood hero. Utnapishtim looks so "human" that Gilgamesh feels a tremor of hope. Utnapishtim proceeds to narrate the entire Flood story, however, in order to demonstrate that the circumstances which led the gods to confer immortality on him will never be repeated, since mankind will never again face the threat of complete annihilation by the gods.[54] Gilgamesh responds by asking, in effect, "Well, can't you do *something* for me?" The next section of the story pictures Gilgamesh trying to stay awake for a week, apparently because Utnapishtim has suggested that anyone who hopes to avoid the sleep of death ought to be strong enough to fight off ordinary sleep. Gilgamesh fails. He cries out:

. . . Where can I go?
The Snatcher has seized my [heart];
Death sits [in] my bedroom;
And wherever I set [my foot], there lurks Death.[55]

This poignant cry of despair evokes pity in Utnapishtim. He instructs Zur-Shanabi, the boatman, to let Gilgamesh wash off his grime in the waters and to give him a garment that will remain new and show no signs of wear until he reaches Uruk. When he leaves, Zur-Shanabi accompanies him on the long

---

[53] *Ibid.*, pp. 73-74.

[54] This Flood story is without doubt the source of the Biblical story in Genesis in which Noah is the main actor. The number of details taken over by the Biblical writers makes a point-by-point comparison easy. It is important to note, however, that in borrowing the story the Biblical writers placed it within their own religious tradition and shaped it so as to express the distinctively Hebrew convictions they wished to communicate.

[55] Gordon, *op. cit.*, p. 82.

journey home. Finally, as a going away present, Utnapishtim reveals to Gilgamesh the secret of a wondrous plant at the bottom of the sea. When this plant is eaten it brings back youth. It does not make a man immortal, but it is surely the next best thing. By tying stones to his feet Gilgamesh manages to dive to the bottom of the sea and to come up with the precious plant. He decides to take it back to Uruk with him and to save it until he is very old, but on the way home the plant is stolen by a snake, the "Lion of the Ground." Gilgamesh weeps bitterly as he pours out his heart to Zur-Shanabi:

> [For] whom O Zur-Shanabi, have my hands grown weary?
> For whom is my heart's blood spent?
> I have accomplished no good for myself
> But I have benefited the Lion of the Ground.[56]

Eventually Gilgamesh pulls himself together and the two travelers complete their journey to Uruk. The epic ends as it began, with a celebration of the greatness of the city, but this time it is Gilgamesh himself who speaks the words of praise:

> Go up, Zur-Shanabi, walk on the wall of Uruk.
> Examine the terrace
> Look at the brickwork
> To see whether its bricks are not baked
> And whether the Seven Sages did not lay its foundations.
> One [sar] is city, one [sar] is garden, one [sar]
> is meadow; [plus] the area of Ishtar's Temple.
> Uruk is composed of three [sars] and the temple area.[57]

Are these final lines an expression of resignation? Perhaps. But without doubt the protest against death was what made the Gilgamesh Epic probably the most widely known and most influential literary work in the Near East by 1500 B.C.

The theme of the Gilgamesh Epic, as well as the engaging manner in which it was presented, caused it to be copied over and over again, to be translated into numerous languages, and to become influential in the formation of the literary conventions

---

[56] *Ibid.*, p. 84.
[57] *Ibid.*, p. 85.

of cultures other than its own. But its spirit of protest and its implicit attack both on the cosmological conviction and on the traditional myths through which the conviction was communicated apparently did not permeate the culture at large. It was a significant form of religious criticism but never received encouragement or implementation in any culture in the Mesopotamian valley—so far as we know—prior to the reform of the Persian religious tradition by Zoroaster. For most of the people most of the time the cosmological conviction was effective, and the myths united men with the ultimate reality to which the cosmological conviction referred.

Recommended Paperbacks

Frankfort, Henri. *The Birth of Civilization in the Near East.*
Garden City, N.Y.: Doubleday Anchor Books, 1956.

An excellent brief survey, including a helpful introductory discussion of methodology, and also an appendix that deals with the question of how much the Egyptians borrowed from the Mesopotamians.

Frankfort, Henri, *et al. Before Philosophy.*
Baltimore: Penguin Books, 1949.

Both the introductory chapter by Frankfort and the chapter on Mesopotamia by Thorkild Jacobsen are especially useful because they cover topics and materials not included in the present volume.

Gaster, Theodore H. *Thespis.*
Garden City, N.Y.: Doubleday Anchor Books, 1956.

A particularly valuable study of the seasonal pattern expressed in ritual, myth, and drama in the ancient Near East; includes typical examples and a section on literary survivals of the seasonal pattern in Biblical and classical poetry.

Kramer, Samuel Noah. *History Begins at Sumer.*
Garden City, N.Y.: Doubleday Anchor Books, 1959.

The best brief survey of the remarkable rediscovery of Sumerian civilization. It covers a wide range of topics and is written in a popular style.

Kramer, Samuel Noah (ed.). *Mythologies of the Ancient World.* Garden City, N.Y.: Doubleday Anchor Books, 1961.

Kramer's survey of Sumerian and Akkadian myths is particularly interesting because it includes many translations of primary materials.

Malinowski, Bronislaw. *Magic, Science and Religion.* Garden City, N.Y.: Doubleday Anchor Books, 1955.

A classic study by one of the most influential pioneers of modern anthropological field study methods. The essay on "Myth in Primitive Psychology" is especially relevant to the present study.

Pritchard, James (ed.). *The Ancient Near East.* Princeton, N.J.: Princeton University Press, 1965.

A selection of materials from Pritchard's standard reference work, *Ancient Near Eastern Texts Relating to the Old Testament.* An indispensable introduction to actual works of various types produced by the cultures studied in this book. The pictorial illustrations are excellent and instructive.

two

MYTH IN THE EGYPTIAN RELIGIOUS TRADITION

UNLIKE Sumerian civilization, early Egyptian civilization never disappeared from view. The pyramids alone, the greatest of which had already been built by 2600 B.C., took care of that. But the rapid transition from primitive agricultural communities to a magnificent imperial civilization, with no traceable evolution from villages to city-states to empire as there was in Mesopotamia, even today baffles scholars, who can do no more than form reasonable guesses concerning the circumstances that favored such an extraordinary development. The fact that almost every easily recognizable trait of Egyptian culture evolved during the five or six hundred years from around 3100 B.C. to 2500 B.C. has led to widely divergent interpretations of the inner character of the entire three thousand years of ancient Egyptian history. Since this "inner character" involves the basic convictions that shaped the Egyptian way of life, a brief account of the fluid state of scholarship will be given to establish certain assumptions on which this chapter rests.

I

Rival Interpretations of Egyptian History

Most interpreters agree on the following outline of Egyptian history:[1]

3100-2615 B.C.	Protodynastic Period (including Dynasties I-II)

[1] Except where otherwise noted the dates in this chapter are cited from the chronology prepared by David Noel Friedmann and published in *The Bible and the Ancient East,* G. E. Wright (ed.) (New York, 1961), pp. 220-24.

2615-2175	Old Kingdom (Dynasties III-IV)
2175-1991	First Intermediate Period (Dynasties VII-XI) Internal disintegration
1991-1786	Middle Kingdom (Dynasty XII)
1786-1570	Second Intermediate Period (Dynasties XIII-XVII) Invasion from outside by the Hyksos
1570-1065	New Kingdom, or Empire Period (Dynasties XVIII-XX)
1065-525	Post-Empire Period (Dynasties XXI-XXVI)
525	Persian Conquest

Most scholars also agree that although there were two extended periods of crisis that shook Egyptian society to its foundations during the six hundred years between 2175 and 1570 B.C., the full course of more than three thousand years following the early flowering of the civilization appears to have been unusually stable and amazingly resistant to change. But at this point some scholars begin to disagree rather violently.

One view, represented by Arnold Toynbee, is that Egyptian civilization reached its zenith very early and then, instead of dying a natural death, continued in a petrified state of life-in-death for more than two thousand years. He writes:

> If we examine the history of the Egyptiac Society, we find that little more than a quarter of its vast time-span of four millennia was a period of growth. The impetus which manifested itself first in the mastery of a peculiarly formidable physical environment—in the clearing, draining, and cultivation of the jungle-swamp that originally occupied the lower valley and the Delta of the Nile to the exclusion of Man—and which then displayed its increasing momentum in the precocious political unification of the Egyptiac World at the end of the so-called Predynastic Age, reached its climax in the stupendous material performances of the Fourth Dynasty. The Age of the Fourth and Fifth Dynasties was the zenith of Egyptiac history, by whatever criteria we measure the curve of its progress and decline.

> It was the zenith in the characteristic achievement of the Egyptiac Society: the co-ordination of human labour in great engineering enterprises ranging from the reclamation of the swamps to the construction of the Pyramids. It was also the zenith in the spheres of political administration and of art. Even in the sphere of religion, where wisdom is proverbially born of suffering, the so-called "Pyramid Texts" testify that this age likewise saw the creation, the collision, and the first stage in the interaction of the two religious movements—the worship of the Sun and the worship of Osiris—which came to their maturity after the Egyptiac Society had gone into its decline.[2]

Toynbee believes that the mobilization of all economic and political resources during the period of the Old Kingdom was an effort so tremendous that the structure of the society was irreparably overstrained and that this overstrain led to the internal disintegration of Egypt during the First Intermediate Period. Politically and economically, the united kingdom fell apart. The Seventh through Eleventh Dynasties were unable to prevent or to overcome the Balkanization of the country. It fell to the Twelth Dynasty, which came to power in about 1991 B.C. and ruled for two hundred years, to reestablish the unity of the country and the preeminence of divine kingship as the institutional form through which national unity was once again maintained. This Middle Kingdom Period (1991-1786 B.C.) does not impress Toynbee. He looks on the invasion of Egypt around 1786 B.C. by Semitic groups, the Hyksos, as the natural termination point for the old Egyptiac society and as the natural starting point for a new society in which, ideally, the energy of the foreign Hyksos and the rich heritage of the native Egyptians should have fused to provide the matrix for creative economic, political, artistic, and religious achievements. What actually happened was that after two hundred years the Egyptians regained their independence, reasserted their belief in their traditional institutions, and entered a restoration period (the New Kingdom or Empire Period), which lasted from 1570 to 1065 B.C. Toynbee's comment is that this was "the old tree's dead trunk artificially re-erected." [3]

---

[2] Arnold J. Toynbee, *A Study of History* (New York, 1935), vol. I, pp. 136-37.
[3] *Ibid.*, p .139.

Directly opposed to Toynbee's analysis is the view held by Henri Frankfort and the equally eminent Egyptologist John Wilson. Commenting on Toynbee's evaluation of the Empire Period as a state of life-in-death, Frankfort writes:

> Reading this, one would not suspect that the five centuries following the expulsion of the Hyksos are the most brilliant epoch of Egyptian history. One would also not assume that after about one thousand years of this "life-in-death," religious texts glorifying Amon-Re were written which in profundity of thought and literary splendour belong to the greatest in Egyptian literature.[4]

Frankfort and Wilson believe that, despite the seemingly changeless character of Egyptian history, the "tree" was by no means a "dead trunk" in 1000 B.C., much less in 2000 B.C. Their position is that although the distinctive form of the civilization was created very early, this form was varied, endangered, regained, and further developed throughout Egyptian history without loss of vitality or identity.

The disagreement between these scholars regarding the effects of the economic and political disintegration and the social distress of the First Intermediate Period on religious convictions and practices has a particularly direct bearing on the present chapter. Toynbee believes that a new form of religiousness appeared among the lower classes when the life of the country became disrupted. By this, he does not mean merely a yearning among large numbers of people for the immortality available to kings and nobles through their worship of the sun, and the subsequent spread of the conviction that ordinary men could participate in a life beyond physical death through worshiping Osiris. He means, rather, the emergence, among the dispossessed lower classes, of a religious movement that eventually would have taken over the dying Egyptian civilization during the Second Intermediate Period, as Christianity took over the Greco-Roman civilization. He believes this would have happened if national unity had not been restored artificially through the rallying of all Egyptians against the Hyksos invaders. The most

[4] Henri Frankfort, *The Birth of Civilization in the Near East* (New York, 1956), p. 19.

important element in this national reunification was an amalgamation of the official aristocratic sun-god religious tradition, which Toynbee describes as dead, with the popular Osiris movement centered around beliefs concerning personal immortality, which Toynbee identifies as a living force and as the potential creative core for a new civilization. He paints a vivid picture of the unfortunate outcome of this combination:

> The religious result of the Restoration was a permanent syncretism in which the Osirian religion was taken up by the priesthood of the dominant minority and was sterilized. The priests were prudent enough not to rob the internal proletariat of their hard-won Osirian immortality, but they were also shrewd enough to exploit the popular craving by making it easier to satisfy. Professional ingenuity was exercised—as of old, for a consideration—in teaching Man how to make up for deficiencies in righteousness by magical methods of taking the kingdom of Osiris by storm; and the magic was adroitly purveyed in guaranteed formulas at popular prices. The immortality which had once been bought by Pharaohs for the price of pyramids was now brought within the reach of every man for the price of a few texts written on papyrus rolls.[5]

Frankfort and Wilson find absolutely no evidence during the First Intermediate Period of an emerging religious movement among the dispossessed that gave promise of forming a nucleus independent of the old traditions regarding the divine kingship and that could thus offer a new foundation for political, social, and cultural life. They argue convincingly that Toynbee insists on the presence of such a movement simply because his general theory of the growth and decay of civilizations (based on the Greco-Roman model) calls for the emergence of a movement of this type at this particular point in Egyptian history. Once having decided that such a movement existed, he must account for the fact that it did not take over the "dead" civilization and become the creative core of a new one. This leads him to his theory of a fatal combination of the democratic Osiris movement with the aristocratic sun-god tradition and also to his notion of two thousand years of a state of "life-in-death," which Frankfort and Wilson believe does great injustice to the artistic,

---

[5] Toynbee, *op. cit.*, p. 144.

intellectual, and religious achievements of the New Kingdom (1570-1065 B.C.).

Even though his "church" of the dispossessed is a fiction, however, Toynbee seems to be correct in sensing that the breakdown of the imperial order around 2175 B.C., which inaugurated the First Intermediate Period, was more than institutional. It shook the foundations of the Egyptian way of life so thoroughly that it created an experiential climate pregnant with new religious possibilities. Here the interpretations of Frankfort and Wilson are less satisfactory, because they treat certain differentiations of experience and their linguistic expression as insignificant in comparison with the massive continuity of Egyptian civilization. This author believes that, although they did not lead to any organized movement with political impact, these differentiations must be taken seriously in any effort to understand the full range of Egyptian religious achievement. Therefore, after a survey of the Egyptian form of the cosmological conviction and representative Egyptian creation myths, special attention will be given the variety of religious explorations undertaken by Egyptians during the First Intermediate Period and during the succeeding periods as well.

2

The Distinctiveness of Egyptian Convictions

Like the Mesopotamians, the Egyptians believed the order of their society was part of the cosmic order. Their basic convictions were not inspired by an awareness of the cosmic order, as revealed in the heavens, fused with a vigorous search for a new way of organizing an increasingly complex society. Instead, the distinctive features of Egyptian convictions seem to have been rooted in the primitive East African matrix from which Egyptian civilization emerged. The transition from primitive village communities to an imperial civilization was so sudden that manifestations of the gods in kings and animals continued to be a central religious element instead of disappearing in a gradual process of political evolution, as they did in Mesopotamia. This is only one of several theories, none of which is completely convincing. But it is certain that from the very beginning of the First Dynasty (ca. 2850 B.C.) the king of Egypt was believed to be the god Horus, who was also embodied in the image of a seated or standing falcon. He was also identified with the sun or with a star as "the heavenly Horus," the "lord of heaven." The core of the beliefs that formed the Egyptian cosmological conviction lay in experiences of ultimacy associated with the divine kingship. Thus, while the Egyptians shared with the Mesopotamians the conviction that there is a universal order permeating every level of reality, other dimensions of their cosmological conviction were quite different. They believed that the creator of the cosmos had chosen Egypt as his own, that he had brought the divine ordering power (Maat) directly into Egyptian society by manifesting himself as the god Horus in the person of the Pharaoh, and that the presence of a god-king on the throne generation after generation guaranteed that Egypt would exist securely without falling prey to the world's evils.

This personal link between eternal divine order and Egyptian society made irrelevant any myths about the society of the gods except as they described the method of continually reestablishing divine kingship. The Egyptians did not see the total cosmos as a state, nor did they look upon their society as a small-scale replica (microcosm) of the society of the gods (macrocosm). Furthermore, although Egyptian myths included stories of hatred and strife among the gods, they did not seem to emphasize the belief that kingship was an Enlil function (or Marduk function) originally established in the realm of the gods and subsequently delegated to human kings for the sake of order in human affairs.

They did focus on Maat, the divine creative power mediated by the god-king. Maat was the power of being, the "substance" that lives in gods, in the world, in kings, and in societies—the power that unites all levels of reality. As the Maat of the cosmos it meant order—biological, astronomical, geographical. As the Maat of society it meant good government and justice. As the Maat of an adequate understanding of the proper place for everything in the order created and maintained by the gods, it meant truth.

Maat, in all these meanings and in others we can scarcely capture in our vocabulary, was centered in the king but achieved effective power throughout Egyptian society by means of royal administration—a bureaucracy. In the early days, the mediation was accomplished biologically; relatives of the king, or of former kings, held administrative posts as far down on the scale of importance as the available personnel would permit. By 2565 B.C. (Fourth Dynasty), a prince of the blood was still needed for the chief office, the post of vizier, but commoners participated in the royal Maat by receiving appointments to positions in the government. Later, even this remnant of biological transmission of power was often abandoned. Maat continued to be conceived of, however, as present in every official who derived his charge from the king.

The meaning of transmission was given memorable expression by Rekhmire, the vizier of Thutmose III (1490-1436 B.C.), in his autobiography:

> I was a noble, the second of the king . . . . It was the first occasion of my being summoned. All my brothers were in the outer [office]. I went forth . . . clad in fine linen. . . . I reached the doorway of the palace gate. The courtiers bent their backs, and I found the masters of ceremonies clearing the way [before me]. . . .
>
> *After the ceremony:* My abilities were not as they had been: my yesterday's nature had altered itself, since I had come forth in the accoutrements [*of the vizier,* . . .] to be Prophet of Maat. . . .
>
> *The Pharaoh says:* ". . . Would that thou mightest act in conformance with what I may say! Then Maat will rest in her place."
>
> *The account concludes:* [I acted] in conformance with that which he had ordained. . . . I raised justice to the height of heaven; I made its beauty circulate to the width of earth . . . . When I judged the petitioner, I was not partial. I did not turn my brow for the sake of reward. I was not angry [at him who came] as [a petitioner], nor did I rebuff him, [but] I tolerated him in his moment of outburst. I rescued the timid from the violent. . . .[6]

[6] Translated by John A. Wilson in Pritchard's *Ancient Near Eastern Texts,* p. 213.

Thus the Maat of the cosmos filtered down from the gods, through the god-king and his administration, into the existence of the humblest Egyptian, both as a demand for justice and as a gift of the power to be just.

This dependence on the Pharaoh as the link with cosmic order accounts for the fact that the Egyptians did not correlate renewal of their sociopolitical order with the annual cycle of the heavenly bodies and of the seasons as closely as did the Mesopotamians. They associated sociopolitical renewal primarily with the death of an old king and the accession and enthronement of a new king, but, since kings did not die every year, the ritual celebration of sociopolitical renewal was periodic rather than annual. The coronation of a new Pharaoh, however, seems to have been scheduled to occur at the spring or fall—the turning point in the year when nature was moving from "death" to new "life." Interestingly enough, the need for the renewal of royal power *during* the reign of a Pharaoh was not only felt but was given special expression in the Sed Festival. Traditionally it was said to have been celebrated every thirty years, though actually certain Pharaohs repeated the ritual every six or even every four years.

The distinction between periodic and annual renewal does not imply a split between the sociopolitical and the biological motifs in Egyptian convictions regarding the divine kingship. The god-king was intimately involved annually with the agricultural cycle. For instance, the king went every year at harvest time to cut a sheaf of grain and to dedicate it to the god Min (Min-Horus the Vigorous). In the ceremony the king went in procession, accompanied by a white bull (symbol of vigorous fertility), the queen, statues of the royal ancestors, and the statue of the god Min (depicted with an erect phallus, again a symbol of fertilizing power). On reaching a field of ripe emmer, the king cut a sheaf and offered it to the bull. The succeeding rites are obscure, but there are hints that the king and queen had intercourse: a priest chanted, "Hail to thee, Min, who impregnates his mother! How mysterious is that which thou hast done to her in the darkness."

The mystery is that of conception and birth. Was it merely Min who was renewed or was it at the same time the god in the king preparing the renewal of his incarnation by begetting an heir? The concluding rites of the festival indicate that indeed the kingship was involved. At the end of the ceremony, the king returned from the shrine of Min crowned with the double crown of the Two Lands (northern and southern Egypt) and holding some of the stalks of grain that had been cut and consecrated. Four birds were released to carry the following proclamation to the four corners of the earth: "Horus, the son of Isis and Osiris, has assumed the Great Crown of Upper and Lower Egypt." Since no coronation was actually involved, the meaning must have been a reaffirmation of the harmonious interlocking of nature and society in the person of the Pharaoh.[7]

The comprehensive unity of the Egyptian cosmological conviction can also be illustrated by the so-called Mystery Play of the Succession, which includes both the sociopolitical and the biological motifs. Archeologists have found an extraordinary document, a large roll of papyrus that is the actual script of a play performed at the accession of Seostris I (1971-1928 B.C.). Many elements of it undoubtedly go back to the Old Kingdom. The king is referred to as "the king who will rule," and there are indications that the play was performed at several cities along the Nile during the transition period after the death of the old king but before the official coronation at Memphis of the new. The agricultural cycle also enters here, for the coronation—as well as the final burial of the old king—took place either in the spring or in the fall. Frankfort has provided a careful and detailed account of this mystery play in Chapter Eleven of *Kingship and the Gods*. For our purposes, we shall refer only to examples of unification of biological and sociopolitical elements in the figure of Osiris, who appears in the play both as the dead father of Horus (the new king) and as the dead grain that, in the form of beer and bread, plays an important part in the ceremonies.

For instance, in an early scene barley is threshed by bulls and male asses, which are driven over it to trample out the barley kernels.

The text runs:

---

[7] See Frankfort, *Kingship and the Gods*, pp. 187-90.

> It happened that barley was put on the threshing floor.
> It happened that male animals were brought to trample it.
> That means Horus avenging his father. . . .
> Horus speaks to the followers of Seth: "Do not beat this my father."
> *Beating Osiris; cutting up the god—barley.*
>
> Horus speaks to Osiris: "I have beaten for thee those who have beaten thee." [8]

The ritual is interrupted by a most remarkable scene in which the new king takes over the sacred powers of his father:

> It happened that beer was brought.
> This means Horus weeps because of his father and turns to Geb.
> Horus speaks to Geb: "They have put this father of mine into the earth."
> *Osiris—loaf of bread.*
> Horus speaks to Geb: "They have made it necessary to bewail him."
> *Isis—Mistress of the house—beer.*
> A loaf of bread; a jug of beer.[9]

The king bewails his father's death, but the bread and beer indicate that the son's loss is his people's gain. Now that he is the dead Osiris the former Pharaoh somehow becomes one with the cosmic powers that provide sustenance to men, here symbolized by the grain whose "death" is necessary for the making of both bread and beer. No text could illustrate better how intimately the notions of kingship and of nature's generative force were related in Egypt. As might be expected, the play ends with the crowning of the new king, a preview of the official coronation that occurred in Memphis after the final burial of the dead Pharaoh.

---

[8] *Ibid.*, p. 127.
[9] *Ibid.*, p. 136.

3

Representative Creation Myths

The two main sources of myths that expressed the Egyptian version of the cosmological conviction are the Pyramid Texts, incised on walls in the interior of pyramids prior to 2175 B.C., and the Coffin Texts, inscribed on coffins during the succeeding centuries. This change from the one medium to the other indicates a critical turning point during the First Intermediate Period. The Pyramid Texts consist mainly of rituals, incantations, and hymns referring to the funeral and transfiguration of a Pharaoh who has died, while the Coffin Texts appear to be mainly literary elaborations on traditional myths, designed for the deification and eternal life of commoners who could afford to have them inscribed on their coffins. Neither the Pyramid Texts nor the Coffin Texts contain a connected story comparable to the Enuma Elish, but some myths are alluded to so often that the origin of the gods and of the cosmos (signifying also the birth of a united Egypt under a god-king) can be reconstructed with considerable confidence. The great creation story of Heliopolis (Cairo, "The City of the Sun"), which originated during the First Dynasty, became the standard view throughout Egyptian history. The story ran as follows:

First, there were the primeval waters, out of which arose the primeval hill (as the earth reappears every year after the inundation of the Nile). The primeval hill was the creator-god Atum, who proceeded to engender the first male-female pair of gods, Shu and Tefnut, through sexual self-impregnation.[10] Shu was the

[10] Some scholars refer to this act of Atum as masturbation or self-pollution, which misses the point entirely and unfortunately suggests that the Egyptian imagination was perverted. How can the mystery of beginnings be described in sexual imagery, the ancient and unrivaled traditional symbolism, unless somehow the twoness of male and female is overcome by imagining a primordial oneness from which twoness originates? Some notion of self-impregnation is inevitable, and it is a profound image even though when taken literally it may seem morally questionable. C.L.

air and moisture that carry the sky, and Tefnut was his female supplement. The children of Shu and Tefnut were Geb (earth) and Nut (sky). Father Shu raised Nut up from Geb and so separated the sky from the earth. A quarrel about the kingship in Egypt broke out among the sons of Geb and Nut: Seth (the desert and murderous heat) and Osiris (vegetation, the growing grain, the dead king), with their female counterparts, Isis ("the throne") and Nephthys ("that which rules in the House"). Seth killed Osiris and took the throne, only to be vanquished by Horus, the son of Osiris and Isis. The victory of Horus was acclaimed by the gods who made up the divine court of Heliopolis, and he was crowned as the successor of his father Osiris and as the true king of Egypt. The myth of Osiris, Isis, and Horus was not only the most significant of the Egyptian myths but was also immensely popular with the Egyptians, even though scholars doubt that it was ever written down in a single comprehensive tale. Apparently it was handed down orally in the Egyptian tradition and only alluded to in writings of various kinds.[11]

Anthes has pointed out that this myth is more concerned with proving the divine character of the king of Egypt than it is with giving an account of how the cosmos and the kingship came into being. This statement makes sense, since the core of the Egyptian cosmological conviction is the unbreakable link that the Pharaoh provides between the divine and the human realms. Having noted that a routine of ceremonial questioning appears frequently in the Pyramid Texts as a method of identifying a god, Anthes has created an imaginary series of questions and answers that illustrate what the myth means when the main point is taken to be the identification of the son of a deceased Pharaoh with Horus and therefore with the creator-god Atum.

The son of the deceased king appears before the court (the Ennead) claiming that he is the god Horus.

> *Question on the part of the court:* You are a human being. It is your father who is Horus.
>
> *Answer on the part of the crown prince:* I am the god Horus because my father, the Horus, has died. He has become Osiris for his body is buried in the earth as a grain and his spirit rises to heaven as vegetation.

---

[11] See Anthes in Kramer (ed.), *Mythologies of the Ancient World,* pp. 68-90.

Q. How did it come to pass that Horus, the god, died?

A. The death of the god could not be effected but by murder. It was the only equal of Horus, his brother Seth, who was powerful enough to kill him.

Q. You have said that your father who thus has become Osiris is buried in the earth and at the same time lives in heaven. What does this mean?

A. The king who was Horus and is now Osiris originated in the primeval beginning, in eternity, and he has gone back to where he originated, that is, to his parents. Geb, the earth, is his father, and, Nut, the sky, is his mother.

Q. Eternity is oneness, but Geb and Nut are separated from each other. How can they possibly be the parents of Osiris?

A. One who was more powerful than they separated them: their father, Shu, who raised Nut up from Geb.

Q. Are you claiming that Shu is your first ancestor?

A. The pair, Shu and Tefnut, are the children of the One who existed by himself in the primeval beginning, Atum. I am one with my father, Atum.[12]

In this fictitious court hearing the divine lineage of the god-king is made clear, and the king, like Atum, is revealed to be "older than creation." He is one with the primeval god who was present before heaven and earth, gods and men, and everything else came into existence. This belief is precisely what was affirmed by the Egyptians; it is the basis upon which the Pyramid Texts were composed. We might ask, then, why a genealogy of five generations was needed to prove the ultimacy of the king's divine status. The answer is that the several generations systematically "cover" the entire cosmos and thus emphasize the cosmic universality of the power of Horus and therefore of the god-king.

Another version of the creation story describes the primeval chaos out of which Atum arose. Chaos consisted of eight elements: the waters and the sky over them, the boundless and the formless, darkness and obscurity, the hidden one and the concealed one. Atum ("the one who has been completed by absorbing others") emerged from this primeval group of elements, and as the sun-god he ordered the cosmos.

---

[12] *Ibid.*, pp. 40-41.

Both of these myths were employed by the authors of what has come to be called the Memphite Theology. This work was composed very early to justify Memphis as the symbolic center of Egypt, because the official royal residence was located there, across the river from Heliopolis.[13] It gives a fascinating picture of the way Egyptian sages dealt with myths in a constructive, consciously interpretative manner. Like the Enuma Elish, it dealt at the same time with the birth of the gods, the birth of the cosmos, and the birth of a particular sociopolitical order; but apparently it was never organized in connected epic form. It brought together mythical histories, mystery plays, pieces of speculative construction, and even a theory about the formation of symbols on the basis of sense experience.

The unification of Egypt was described in a myth similar to the story associated with the Heliopolis creation story. The earth-god Geb judged the rival claims of his younger son Seth and his grandson Horus (the son of Geb's first-born, Osiris) to rule over Egypt. He gave Seth Upper Egypt and Horus Lower Egypt. But then he had second thoughts and decided to award Horus rulership of the whole of Egypt. Strangely enough, Seth was a good loser. Harmony was restored, and as a sign of this harmony two plants symbolic of the Two Lands were planted at the gate of the temple of the god Ptah in Memphis.

Since Osiris was identified not only as the father of Horus but also as the dead king—the Osiris whom every Horus became when he died—it seemed important to the sages to bring Osiris into direct relationship to Memphis, the seat of kingship. Accordingly, they concluded their work with a mystery play which included the following episodes: the dead Osiris was seen floating toward Memphis on the Nile; Isis and Nephthys, who made the discovery, informed Horus, who told them to keep the body from floating on past Memphis; they rescued the body, which was then buried in the royal castle; Osiris became Earth (the god Ptah) and also became the eternal companion of the sun god Re in his daily circuit across the heavens. Meanwhile, Horus had ascended the throne. The document ends with these words:

---

[13] In Pritchard's *Ancient Near Eastern Texts,* p. 4., John A. Wilson writes: "The extant form of this document dates only to 700 B.C., but linguistic, philological, and geopolitical evidence is conclusive in support of its derivation from an original text more than two thousand years older."

> Thus Osiris became earth in the Royal Castle on the north side of this land which he had reached. His son Horus appeared as king of Upper Egypt and as king of Lower Egypt in the arms of his father Osiris in the presence of the gods that were before him and that were behind him.[14]

The symbolism in this dramatized myth of Osiris is compact and very complex. The fertility imagery (Osiris as vegetation, associated with the Nile and with earth Ptah), the biological and political imagery (Horus, the living king, in the embrace of his father Osiris, the dead king), and the cosmic imagery (the sun god Re) all refer simultaneously to a human historical dimension and to a divine eternal dimension of reality. They express the distinctively Egyptian way of experiencing the intimate interpenetration and final unity of every level of reality in the all-embracing cosmos. This experience supported the conviction of the Egyptians that they and their society were a special part of the cosmic order, because their god-king participated in every level of reality and personally brought the creative power of Maat into Egyptian life. Undoubtedly the cosmological conviction, in turn, helped to produce repetitions of the experience of unity.

One particular section of the Memphite Theology has attracted much attention because it pictures the god Ptah's method of creating the cosmos in images that resemble those in the accounts of creation in the Biblical Book of Genesis, and because it includes an outline of the theoretical model for these images that resembles philosophical speculations, which are usually thought of as a Greek innovation. Ptah breaks with the traditional biological method; he does not originate anything through sexual generation:

> [Something] in-the-form-of-Atum became, in the heart, and became, on the tongue [of Ptah].
>
> . . .
>
> It so happens that heart and tongue prevailed over all other members of the body, considering,

[14] Quoted by Frankfort in *Kingship and the Gods,* p. 32.

> that the heart is in every body, and the tongue is in every mouth,
> of all gods, all men, all cattle, all creeping things, and whatever else lives;
> [Ptah prevails] by thinking [as heart] and commanding [as tongue] everything that he wishes.[15]

Thus the cosmos originates in the mind and imagination (heart) and through the command (tongue) of Ptah. This passage is strikingly similar to the first chapter of Genesis: "And God said, 'Let there be light'; and there was light." (verse 3, Revised Standard Version) But in the Bible God is conceived to be beyond his creation as well as continuously active within it, while Egyptian religious convictions never lead to a clear-cut distinction between the gods and the cosmos. Nor is Ptah the one and only god of the Egyptians; they never hear him say, as the Israelites hear God say, "You shall have no other gods before me." (Exodus 20:3, RSV) The world Ptah calls into being is full of gods, beginning with the primordial Atum and his family and continuing through all levels of the cosmic order. Surveying the results of his creative activity, Ptah finds that he has made the gods, the cities, and the districts of Egypt. He has put the gods in their shrines and given every god a body of wood or stone or clay. In other words, the Memphite Theology's description of the dynamics of cosmic order in terms of imagery drawn from the human practice of combining thought and action to accomplish a purpose is a remarkable development *inside* the range of cosmological experience.

The model for the description of Ptah's method of creating the cosmos is given in a kind of footnote, which is inserted in the middle of the creation account.

> The sight of the eyes, the hearing of the ears, the air-breathing of the nose
> they report to the heart. It [the heart] causes every thought to come forth,
> and the tongue announces what the heart thinks.
> Thus are done all works and all crafts, the action of the arms, the movement of the legs, and the action of all other members, according to the command which the heart thought,

[15] As quoted by Voegelin, *Order and History,* vol. I, pp. 91-92.

> which came forth from the tongue, and which makes the dignity [or essence, worth] of everything.[16]

It is evident from the preceding passage that as early as 2700 B.C. some Egyptian sages were making psychological and speculative observations about human knowledge, evaluation, and decision making. The passage also suggests that men who could intersperse their sacred myth of creation with deliberate indications of the principles they were using in selecting their imagery were infinitely more sophisticated and reflective than most of us imagine anyone could have been forty-five hundred years ago. But great as they were, these men were not formulating Greek philosophy two thousand years before Plato. The same type of comment that was made about the Biblical tradition is relevant here. Greek philosophy rested on a range of experience and conviction that was different from the cosmological basis of Egyptian speculation. The Egyptians never experienced the kind of "natural" order that is central to the world view that was the basis of both Greek tragic drama and Greek philosophy. They were never gripped by the conviction that the world is a process of birth, growth, and death that is closed to the gods and that can be interpreted by human reason in terms of impersonal (though still divine) forces. This was a Greek and not an Egyptian conviction, a Greek differentiation of experience that generated new images expressed in new symbolic forms.

4

The Career of the Sun God

Since the divine kingship was the core that provided the greatest continuity in the Egyptian orientation to life for nearly three thousand years, it will be useful to give special attention to

[16] *Ibid.*, p. 93.

the sun god, who under various names was the greatest of the gods and therefore the true father of the Egyptian god-kings. The oldest sun god was probably Re. Although Atum was considered the creator in the creation story of Heliopolis, Re proved himself capable of taking over the role of creator and of assimilating to himself the Horus tradition of the divine kingship. As Re-Atum he was the father of all, the king of gods and men; as Re-Harakhty he was Horus in his heavenly aspect, the Horus of the Horizon, the rising sun.[17] Accordingly, the Pharaohs became "Sons of Re." This development occurred prior to 2300 B.C., in the Old Kingdom.

During the Middle Kingdom Re penetrated into the cults of local or regional gods, becoming more and more the national god. His assimilation of the god Amon of Thebes under the name Amon-Re proved to be especially important, for in about 1600 B.C. Thebes became the royal residence. It later became the first permanent capital of Egypt. The role of Amon-Re in relation to the divine kingship followed the traditional pattern established during the early dynasties of the Old Kingdom. In about 1450 B.C., Thutmose III, who extended the frontiers of the Egyptian Empire and laid the foundations of a long period of stability, expressed the character of his rulership in these words:

> . . . [The god Amon]—he is my father, and I am his son.
> He commanded to me that I should be upon his throne, while I was [still] a nestling.
> . . . He made all foreign countries [come] bowing down to the frame of my majesty. . . .
> He has given victory through the work of my hands, to extend [the frontiers of Egypt] . . .
> He is rejoicing in me more than [in] any [other] king who has been in the land since it was [first] set apart.
> I am his son, the beloved of his majesty. . . .
> I repay his good with [good] greater than it, by making him greater than the [other] gods.
> The recompense for him who carries out benefactions is a repayment to him of even greater benefactions.

---

[17] Combining names of gods was standard procedure. The newer, less established god was placed ahead of the older god in the compound name. When Re had become the established god who was assimilated by a new supreme god, Amon, he moved to the rear; thus the compound name, Amon-Re. C.L.

> I have built his house with the work of eternity, . . .
> I have extended the places of him who made me.
> I have provisioned his altars upon earth. . . .
> I know for a fact that Thebes is eternity, that Amon is everlastingness, . . .[18]

The section that expresses the king's indebtedness to the god and describes his many efforts to repay, even to over-repay, his debt is interesting in the light of what scholars have learned about the increasing power of priestly groups during the later centuries of Egyptian history. Thutmose III was indebted to the Amon-Re college of priests in Thebes who chose him to be king. The Pharaohs of the Empire Period were far less independent of the military, civil, and priestly bureaucracies than earlier kings had been; as Thebes consolidated its control over the entire country the Amon-Re college of priests consolidated its control over the entire bureaucratic structure.

The only revolt against these priestly kingmakers of Thebes was the so-called revolution engineered by the famous Pharaoh Akhenaton (1364-1347 B.C.), who has often been credited with being the founder of the first genuine monotheistic faith. More accurately, he was the last Pharaoh who tried to reestablish the ancient role of the god-king as the one and only link between the divine and the human realms. Akhenaton's original name was Amenophis IV; when he founded the cult of Aton, equipped it lavishly with land grants, and moved his capital from Thebes to a brand-new city farther north, he repudiated his Amon name and assumed the Aton name. Aton was an old word that designated the sun disk in its physical appearance. It was not used as a name of the sun god until a generation or so before Akhenaton exalted it to supremacy. Akhenaton acknowledged only the sun god Re (Re-Harakhty, the sun rising on the horizon) and taught that Re appeared only in the sun disk, the Aton. He made no use of the ancient myths of creation and simply referred to himself as the son of Re and Aton. The exclusiveness of Akhenaton's claim to be the sole mediator of divine power can be seen in such passages of his Aton hymns as the following:

---

[18] Translated by Wilson in *Ancient Near Eastern Texts,* pp. 446-47 (selected portions).

Thou art in my heart,
And there is no other that knows thee,
Save thy son [Akhenaton].
For thou hast made him well-versed
In thy plans and in thy might.[19]

When the Amon-Re priests resisted the "revolution," the king divested them of their immense wealth and sent gangs of henchmen throughout the land to erase the name of Amon from inscriptions wherever the name appeared. Unquestionably, the institutional overthrow was successful only because Akhenaton had the army on his side. The king also tried to redirect the personal religiousness of his people so that it would focus on him as the god on earth. He did this by proclaiming that the only way his subjects could participate in the ultimacy of divine reality was through unquestioning obedience to him. He tried to enforce this demand by suppressing the cult of Osiris, which linked men with divinity through its promise of personal rebirth in eternity. Neither the official nor the popular facets of Akhenaton's movement outlasted his reign. His son, Tutankhaton, capitulated to Thebes and became Tutankhamon. The god Amon-Re regained his primacy.

But Akhenaton was more than a reactionary. In his hymns, preserved through inscriptions in the tombs of his nobles, we hear a new voice:

Thou dawnest beautifully on the horizon of the sky,
Thou living Aton, the beginning of life!
Thou art gracious, great, glistening, and high over every land,
Thy rays encompass the lands to the limit of all that thou hast made.

All cattle rest upon their pasturage,
The trees and the plants are flourishing,
The birds flutter from their nests,
Their wings uplifted in adoration to thee;
All beasts spring up on their feet,
All creatures that fly or alight,
They live when thou hast risen for them.
The ships sail up-stream and down-stream alike,

---

19 Quoted by Voegelin, *Order and History,* vol. I, p. 109.

Every high-way is open at thy appearance.
The fish in the river dart before thy face;
Thy rays are in the midst of the great green sea.

The Aton is the creator-god:
O sole god, like whom there is no other!
Thou didst create the world according to thy desire,
While thou wert alone.

The countries of Syria and Nubia, the land of Egypt,
Thou settest every man in his place,
Thou suppliest their necessities:
Everyone has his food and the time of his life is reckoned.
Their tongues are divers in speech,
And their forms as well;
Their skins are distinguished,
As thou distinguishest the foreign peoples.[20]

This king was a truly extraordinary individual, a mystical esthete who expressed his convictions concerning the cosmos, as well as his delight in the beauties of nature, with great poetic power. He was convinced that all men shared a common humanity in spite of their racial, linguistic, and cultural differences, and he was convinced that Aton was the god of all men. He almost broke through the limits of the cosmological experience of the unity of all reality to the experience of an ultimate otherness in the divine, which the cosmological framework of his orientation could not contain. Yet he never abandoned this orientation. He still appealed to the old solar deities as supporters of his interpretation of the kingship, and he did not attack other gods the way he attacked Amon-Re. It is not surprising, however, that some scholars who have compared the Aton hymns with the Bible have concluded that there might have been a connection between Akhenaton's faith and the faith of the Israelites who migrated from Egypt toward their Promised Land a century or so after his reign.

Actually, the Amon-Re tradition produced even more profound expressions of the experience of ultimacy and of the mys-

---

[20] *Ibid.*, pp. 107-08. This is only about a fourth of the famous hymn. Wilson's translation of the entire extant document is included in Pritchard's paperback anthology, *The Ancient Near East*, pp. 226-30.

tery of the ultimate than anything achieved by Akhenaton. The best extant documentary evidence is an extract from a long document written in praise of Amon-Re, dated to the reign of Ramses II (1290-1224 B.C.), the period during which most scholars believe that the Israelites made their Exodus out of Egypt under the leadership of Moses. This section of the document is a hymn that explores the implications of the name Amon, which meant "the hidden one" or "the invisible one." In it the poet demonstrates that he is aware of the inability of human language to express directly the experience of ultimacy and of the mystery of the ultimate. Furthermore, the poet makes conscious use of two indirect types of expression, which are as significant today as they were then.

> The first to come into being in the earliest times,
> Amon, who came into being at the beginning,
> so that his mysterious nature is unknown. . . .
> Building his own egg, a daemon mysterious of birth,
> who created his [own] beauty,
> the divine god who came into being by himself.
> All [other] gods came into being after he began himself.
>
> . . .
>
> Mysterious of form, glistening of appearance,
> the marvelous god of many forms.
> All [other] gods boast of him,
> to magnify themselves through his beauty,
> according as he is divine.
>
> . . .
>
> One is Amon, hiding himself from them,
> concealing himself from the [other] gods, . . .
> He is far from heaven, he is [absent from] the Underworld,
> [so that] no gods know his true form.
> His image is not [displayed] in writings.
> No one bears witness to him . . .
> He is too mysterious that his majesty might be disclosed,
> he is too great that [men] should ask about him,
> too powerful that he might be known.
> Instantly [one] falls in a death of violence
> at the utterance of his mysterious name, unwittingly or wittingly.
>
> . . .

All gods are three: Amon, Re, and Ptah,
and there is no second to them.
"Hidden" is his name as Amon, he is Re in face, and his body is Ptah.
Their cities are on earth, abiding forever:
Thebes, Heliopolis, and Memphis unto eternity.[21]

On the one hand, Amon is invisible, formless, and nameless. Note that all three adjectives are negative. This attempt to describe the god by saying what he is *not* employs a linguistic technique that has survived to the present day in the religious traditions of the West. In the Christian tradition it has been called the *via negative* (the negative way). It exalts the mysterious "otherness" of God. On the other hand, Amon is "the marvelous god of many forms." He is Amon, the wind; insofar as he has a body, he is Ptah, the earth; and insofar as he has a face, he is Re, the sun. The attempt to describe the god by drawing analogies with things that men know through sense experience employs another linguistic technique, which in the Christian tradition has often been called the *analogia entis* (the analogy of being). It exalts the "presence" of God while presupposing his otherness. Incidentally, the last section of the hymn makes it clear that the trinity of Amon, Re, and Ptah is not an anticipation of the Christian Father, Son, and Holy Ghost. There is no mystery in this; it allows the powerful rival cities of Heliopolis and Memphis to participate on equal terms in the divinity of Amon of Thebes.

The universality of Amon-Re stands in marked contrast to the exclusiveness of the creator-god Atum some thousand or more years earlier, as reflected in what may be the earliest extant hymn to the sun:

Greetings to thee, eye of Horus [the land of Egypt],[22] which he [Atum] adorned with his two hands completely.
He does not make thee hearken to the West;
he does not make thee hearken to the East;
he does not make thee hearken to the South;
he does not make thee hearken to the North;

---

[21] Translated by Wilson in Pritchard's *Ancient Near Eastern Texts*, pp. 368-69.
[22] C.L.

he does not make thee hearken to those who are in the middle
of the land;
but thou hearkenest to Horus.

. . .

The doors stand fast upon thee like Immutef;
they open not to the West; they open not to the East;
they open not to the North; they open not to the South;
they open not to those who are in the middle of the land;
but they are open to Horus.[23]

The focus is on Egypt and Egypt alone. There is no cosmopolitan awareness.

A movement toward what we call universal monotheism is unmistakable in the hymn to Amon-Re, yet the poet-priest still moves within the compactness of the cosmological myths that express the unity of all reality and the divine ultimacy of the cosmos. The hiddenness of Amon is a concealment *within* the cosmos and not an otherness experienced as a concealment *beyond* the cosmos that makes the cosmos less than all-embracing, subject to a reality more ultimate than itself. Nevertheless, the ability of human language to deal with the quality of ultimacy in human experience and also with the mystery of the ultimate, which is believed to appear in human experience but to transcend it infinitely, is still a live issue in every major religious tradition in the world today. In the Christian tradition these limitations of language have never been overcome; in fact, the same negative and analogical techniques of expression used by the ancient priest from Thebes have come to be taken for granted in the common piety of Christians.

The words of a Christian hymn written less than a hundred years ago provide a convenient example. Notice how many negatives there are (*not* mortal, *not* visible, *not* resting, *not* wanting), and notice also how many positive analogies with space-time objects and sense experiences there are. Otherness and presence are intertwined in such a way that both are affirmed simultaneously and equally.

Immortal, invisible, God only wise,
In light inaccessible hid from our eyes.

---

[23] Quoted by Voegelin, *Order and History*, vol. I, pp. 70-71.

Most blessed, most glorious, the Ancient of Days,
Almighty, victorious, Thy great Name we praise.

Unresting, unhasting, and silent as light,
Nor wanting, nor wasting, Thou rulest in might;
Thy justice like mountains high soaring above
Thy clouds which are fountains of goodness and love.

To all, life Thou givest—to both great and small;
In all life Thou livest, the true life of all;
We blossom and flourish as leaves on the tree,
And wither and perish—but naught changeth Thee.

Great Father of Glory, pure Father of Light,
Thine angels adore Thee, all veiling their sight;
All praise we would render; O help us to see
'Tis only the splendor of light hideth Thee! [24]

5

Trends Toward Individualism

The first section of this chapter pointed out that especially during the First Intermediate Period (2175-1991 B.C.) the pressure of events created an experiential climate favorable to the exploration of new religious possibilities. One of these possibilities was the development of a type of ethical sensitivity that led certain individuals to launch prophetic criticisms against the Pharaohs themselves, even though there seem to have been strong taboos against criticizing the god-kings. A good example is the prophetic text known as "The Admonitions of Ipu-Wer." Here a certain Ipu-Wer confronted the Pharaoh and condemned

[24] *The Hymnal,* Presbyterian Board of Christian Education (Philadelphia, 1944). Hymn 66. The author was Walter Chalmers Smith.

the past and present administration of Egypt. He appeared as a reporter in the early portion of his description of the anarchy that had disrupted the land, but by the end he denounced the king for evading his responsibilities:

> Authority, Perception, and Justice are with thee, [but] it is confusion which thou wouldst set throughout the land, together with the noise of contention. Behold, one thrusts against another. Men conform to that which thou hast commanded. If three men go along a road, they are found to be two men: it is the greater number that kills the lesser. Does then the herdsman [the Pharaoh] [25] love death? So then thou wilt command that a reply be made: "It is [because] one man [loves] and another hates. [That is, their forms] are few everywhere." [This really means that thou hast acted] to bring such [a situation] into being, and thou hast spoken lies.[26]

Ipu-Wer sounds like the Biblical prophet Nathan confronting King David with the charge: "You are the [guilty] man!" (II Samuel 12:7) But no Egyptian prophetic movement with political implications and consequences developed as it did in Israel. For some individuals, neither the god-king nor Egypt united under him could supply the creative image for constructive thinking. One extraordinary Coffin Text from around 2000 B.C. suggests that a few sensitive Egyptians found a new image in a vision of society as ideally a community of equals. They attributed the evils of inequality of rank and of wealth to "the heart of man." The text opens with the sun god receiving into his heavenly rest persons who have died. He bids them peace, his peace. In order that they may participate in it he tells them how he won his peace at the time of creation by disengaging himself from the coils of the serpent of iniquity. His "heart" did for him the following four good deeds:

> I made the four winds that every man might breathe thereof [like his fellow] in his time. That is [one] deed thereof.
>
> I made the great inundation that the poor man might have rights therein like the great man. That is [one] deed thereof.

---

[25] C.L.

[26] Translated by Wilson in *Ancient Near Eastern Texts,* p. 443.

I made every man like his fellow. I did not command that they do evil, [but] it was their hearts which violated what I had said. That is [one] deed thereof.

I made their hearts to cease from forgetting the West, in order that divine offerings might be given to the gods of the nomes. That is [one] deed thereof.[27]

These "deeds" imply a Garden of Eden innocence or a once-upon-a-time Golden Age, and they justify the ways of the god to man by placing the responsibility for evil squarely on man. Furthermore, they imply that the restoration of goodness will come when men suppress the chaos that is in their "hearts" and find their peace in obedience to the creative commands of the god. This hope seems to go far beyond the normal hope of Egyptians in troubled times, which was that unity under an effective god-king would be restored. Unlike the Osiris religiousness, which Wilson has described as "mortuary," the orientation toward equality could have become the basis for a new type of human community. No such equalitarian community emerged. In fact, only one copy of this text has been found and scholars are not able, at the present time, to place the work in its original context and to solve the enigma of its appearance in the Egyptian tradition.

A much more popular development was the so-called Osirian religiousness, the spread of the conviction that immortality was not a prerogative of gods and god-kings but a reward for the kind of virtuous life that could be achieved by any man. For the kings, transfiguration after death traditionally had been pictured as an eternal circuit of the heavens with the sun god Re. This view contradicted the prehistoric belief, never abandoned in Mesopotamian civilization, that the dead descend into a shadowy netherworld beneath the earth. At first only the Pharaohs participated in immortality, and then this privilege was gradually extended to nobles, who were allowed to build their tombs near the royal tombs. The state theology continued to picture a solar hereafter, often identifying it with a place—the northern region of the sky where the circumpolar stars "prove" their immortality by never disappearing below the horizon. In this view Osiris was the dead king who was transfigured either into the heavenly

[27] *Ibid.*, pp. 7-8.

companion of Re or into a companion of the circumpolar stars.

During the First Intermediate Period, however, the earthy aspect of Osiris, the vegetation aspect that could easily be correlated with the annual cycle of the seasons and the yearly rise and fall of the Nile, became more and more prominent. Convictions and experiences related to the confidence that in the world of nature life always reasserts itself and conquers death seem to have encouraged belief in what might be called the inevitable immortality of every man. Belief in a subterranean kingdom of the dead now included a decisive new element, the conviction that every man faces a last judgment on the other side of death and that if he is acquitted of religious impiety and moral guilt he will enter into eternal joy. In popular piety Osiris became the lord of the realm of the dead beneath the earth. His yearly death and rebirth in the agricultural cycle formed the basis for the conviction that he was not the lord of a kingdom of corpses but rather the lord of human beings who had been reborn to eternal life. In this context the role of Horus, the king who sees to it that his dead father (Osiris) is properly buried in order to make possible his rebirth, was adapted also to the popular belief. Every son of a deceased Egyptian became a Horus. Like the royal Horus he was responsible for seeing to it that mortuary rites were performed properly and that the family tombs were provided with perpetual care.

The classical description of the trial in the afterworld dates from about 1600 B.C., when the Coffin Texts were replaced by the so-called Book of the Dead, similar in literary materials to the Coffin Texts but written on papyrus rolls rather than inscribed on coffins. The myth of the trial told the story of judgment in terms of a well-conducted earthly court trial. The court consisted of the Divine Council and was presided over by Osiris. The god of wisdom, the ibis-headed Thoth, was the public attorney. He made the god Anubis weigh the heart of the deceased person on a double scale, where it was supposed to balance the weight of an ostrich feather, the symbol of Maat. He also made the deceased testify for himself. Finally, he made a judgment and presented it to the court for a verdict. Curiously enough, the records say nothing about the possibility that the verdict might be negative, except that the story mentions the amemet-beast waiting for his prey. The only recorded verdicts, however, read as follows: "The *amemet*-beast, 'the devourer,' shall not have power over him. He shall be given the food yielded to Osiris and a permanent [share of an] acre in the Field of Satisfaction."[28] Since the inclusion of the myth of judgment in the Book of the Dead was undoubtedly aimed at helping deceased persons obtain a favorable verdict by stating that this is what they would receive, the absence of accounts of individuals being consigned to hell or to extinction is understandable.

The test of virtue, of course, was obedience to the standard patterns of Egyptian attitude and action. The Egyptians expressed their sensitivity to qualities of personal and group relationships in a sizable literature. We will cite three examples dating from widely separated periods of Egyptian history in order to indicate the continuity of mortal values, beginning with "The Wisdom of Ptahhotep" (Fifth Dynasty, about 2500 B.C.):

> Do not let your heart become proud because of what you know;
> Learn from the ignorant as well as from the learned man.
>
> . . .
>
> It is true that one may become rich through doing evil,
> But the power of Truth and Justice is that they endure
> And that a man can say of them: "They are a heritage from my father."
>
> . . .
>
> Let your face shine during the time that you live . . .
> It is the kindliness of a man that is remembered
> During the years that follow . . .[29]

Almost five hundred years later, about 2070 B.C., we find these words in "The Wisdom of the Pharaoh Kheti":

> Be not ruthless, for it is fine to be generous;
> Act in such a way that your work will endure because it is endearing.
> Speak the truth in your house

[28] Anthes, in Kramer (ed.), *op. cit.,* pp. 56-57.

[29] Quoted in Audrain and Samivel's *The Glory of Egypt* (New York, 1955), translated by J. E. Manchip-White, p. 67.

So that the great ones who rule the land will hold you in respect . . .
It is the inside of the house that compels outward admiration.

. . .

The virtue of a man whose heart is just is more acceptable to God
Than the choice bull of a man who commits iniquity.[30]

More than fifteen hundred years later, during the eighth century B.C., the "Wisdom of Amenemope" had this to say:

The man who respects the poor is beloved of God.

Be not covetous of wealth.
You can swallow down a fat morsel,
But you may vomit it up
And be emptier than you were before . . .

. . .

Do not say: "I have found a powerful patron . . .
Now I can play a dirty trick on someone I dislike."
No. Remember that you do not know what is in the mind of God,
And that you cannot know what may happen tomorrow.
Rest still in God's arms
And your silence will confound your enemies.

. . .

Leave no one behind you at the river crossing
While you are lolling in the ferry-boat.[31]

These examples suggest the kinds of values and personal qualities that the Egyptians believed were significant during their

---

[30] *Ibid.*, p. 68.

[31] *Ibid.*, p. 70. The final two lines are an amazing forerunner of both the image (ferry-boat) and the message of Mahayana Buddhism, which criticized Theravada Buddhism precisely because, in the eyes of the Mahayanists, it was willing to leave most people behind at the river crossing from which the "big ferry-boat" (Maha-yana) proposed to carry all men, eventually, across the river to the opposite bank where salvation awaited them (Nirvana). C.L.

lifetimes and that would be the criteria by which they would be judged individually and rewarded or punished after they died. The degree of continuity from century to century and from millenium to millenium is impressive. Without question, the application of the Osiris myth to men's concern about an eternal personal destiny heightened the dimension of individual responsibility in Egyptian life. This is true in spite of the Coffin Texts that tell about more and more elaborate magical attempts to insure a favorable decision in the Last Judgment.

The same pressure of events during the First Intermediate Period—which led some individuals to formulate prophetic criticisms in the name of Maat and the divine kingship tradition, or to dream of a new organizing center of meaning in convictions concerning human equality, or to seek meaning in a moral life that would be rewarded with eternal blessedness in the hereafter—pushed still other individuals toward radical skepticism. The most impressive example of this type of response was "A Song of the Harper," a tomb inscription for a king that dates, once again, from the period around 2000 B.C.

> How weary is this righteous prince;
> The goodly fortune has come to pass! [death] [32]
> Generations pass away since the time of the god,
> [but] young people come in their place.
> The gods who lived formerly rest in their pyramids,
> The beatified dead also, buried in their pyramids.
> And they who built houses—their places are not.
> See what has been made of them!
> I have heard the words of Ii-em-hotep and Hor-dedef,
> With whose discourses men speak so much.
> What are their places [now]?
> Their walls are broken apart, and their places are not—
> As though they had never been!
> There is none who comes back from [over] there,
> That he may tell their state,
> That he may tell their needs,
> That he may still our hearts,
> Until we [too] may travel to the place where they have gone.
>
> Let thy desire flourish,
> In order to let thy heart forget the beatifications for thee.

---

[32] C.L.

Follow thy desire, as long as thou shalt live.
Put myrrh upon thy head and clothing of fine linen upon thee,
Being anointed with genuine marvels of the god's property.
Set an increase to thy good things;
Let not thy heart flag.
Follow thy desire and thy good.
Fulfill thy needs upon earth, after the command of thy heart,
Until there come for thee that day of mourning.
The Weary [of Heart] hears not their [mourn]ing,
And wailing saves not the heart of a man from the underworld.

REFRAIN: Make holiday, and weary not therein!
Behold, it is not given to a man to take his property with him.
Behold, there is not one who departs who comes back again! [33]

The key to this skeptical poem lies in its attack on the pyramids, the traditional symbols of everlastingness. Ii-em-hotep was the architect of Djoser, the creator of stone masonry on a large scale and builder of the terraced pyramid of Sakkarah, the oldest still surviving. Hor-dedef was the son of Cheops, the builder of the greatest of the pyramids (about 2600 B.C.). The legendary fame of these men was still known in 2000 B.C., but their tombs were no longer the glorious monuments they had once been. The neglect of the pyramids, worn with age, and the plundering and destruction of minor tombs must have made a deep impression. Also remembered were the tremendous trust funds that had been set up for the perpetual care of the tombs and the elaborate priestly apparatus that had been established to carry on the proper rituals generation after generation. But these were only vague memories. Trust funds, priests, rituals—all had vanished. It comes as something of a shock to realize that in 2000 B.C. the man who wrote "A Song of the Harper" was as far away historically from the building of the pyramid of Cheops as we are from the construction of the cathedral of Chartres. He looked back over the centuries, and in his eyes they added up to futility. He looked ahead to his remaining years of life and to the question

[33] Translated by Wilson in Pritchard's *Ancient Near Eastern Texts,* p. 467. The first four lines are from a version found in the tomb of Nefer-hotep. The rest of the song is from a manuscript of about 1300 B.C.

"What then?" and in his eyes they were equally futile. He saw no evidence that encouraged him to hope for eternity beyond his time-space existence. The result was a pleasure-seeking orientation that was too world-weary to be exuberant, that required too much effort to be joyful.

The fact that this poem was copied over and over again during the centuries that followed its composition indicates that a deep skepticism was incorporated permanently into the range of differentiated experience available to sensitive and critical Egyptians. The number of such individuals, however, was never large enough to undermine the predominant social experience of order. The conviction that Egyptian society was an integral part of the divine cosmic order because the divine creative power of Maat was directly present in Egypt in the person of the god-king and effective through the imperial bureaucracy underlay the civilization from its beginning to its end. Despite the difficulties modern scholars have in reconstructing an adequate picture of the dynamic functioning of sacred stories in the Egyptian orientation to life, there seems to be no question that the special language form through which the basic convictions of that orientation were carried in the living tradition was myth.

Recommended Paperbacks

Frankfort, Henri, *et al. Before Philosophy.*
Baltimore: Penguin Books, 1949.

John A Wilson's chapter on Egypt is very useful, although it does not have the scope of his *The Culture of Ancient Egypt.*

Kramer, Samuel Noah (ed.). *Mythologies of the Ancient World.*
Garden City, N.Y.: Doubleday Anchor Books, 1961

Contains the best brief treatment of Egyptian mythology, written by Rudolph Anthes.

Pritchard, James B. (ed.). *The Ancient Near East*
Princeton: Princeton University Press, 1965.

Selections from the classic source book, *Ancient Near Eastern Texts,* edited by the same scholar. The sections of texts included are not as relevant to the present study as those that come from the Mesopotamian tradition, but the pictorial illustrations are superb.

Wilson, John A. *The Culture of Ancient Egypt.* Chicago: University of Chicago Press (Pheonix series), 1951.

An excellent account of Egyptian life and culture, placed in an interpretive historical framework.

three

SACRED HISTORY AND THE PEOPLE OF ISRAEL

TODAY the word "Israel" has a precise meaning; it refers to a nation-state located at the eastern end of the Mediterranean Sea. Throughout the past three thousand years, however, the term has functioned in a number of different ways. According to the Jewish scriptures, which Christians call the Old Testament, Israel was originally a title bestowed on a man named Jacob by his god. This title was perpetuated by Jacob's descendants, the so-called twelve tribes, who are said to have migrated into Palestine and eventually occupied the entire country. Modern archeological studies suggest that the occupation began late in the fourteenth century B.C. and was completed by about 1100 B.C.

The tribal confederation calling itself the People of Israel is the first "Israel" that can be studied as a living historical reality. All reports about the historical evolution preceding the occupation of Palestine belong to the traditions of the various tribes or groups of tribes (such as the "Leah" and the "Rachel" groups) who eventually united to form the People of Israel. Soon after 1100 B.C. it became clear that the loose, decentralized organization of the tribal confederation could not cope with political and military threats to its continued existence. An age of considerable political and military power was ushered in by King David and was later presided over by his son, King Solomon. The people of Israel became the Davidic Empire, which existed for scarcely eighty years. Then the northern region seceded from the southern region of the country and took the name of Israel, while the south took the name of its traditionally most powerful tribe, Judah. With respect to the term Israel this complicated matters considerably, because the kingdom of Judah shared the religious and cultural traditions of the north, and the Judahites still considered themselves members of the People of Israel. In fact, after the kingdom of Israel was destroyed by the Assyrian empire the kingdom of Judah became the repository of the total Israelite tradition and preserved its continuity. Over the years the word Israel functioned more and more as a symbol of the life-orientation and sense of historic mission inherited from the past, which provided meaning and motivation in ever-changing circumstances. For the social group that would carry this tradition, the future lay with Judah and with the name Jew.

New complications arose when the early Christians claimed the term Israel for the Christian church. They believed that the church was the true people of Israel and that the Jews had forfeited their right to this title. Yet today, nearly two thousand years later, a high point in the worship of Jewish congregations every Friday evening in every part of the world is the proclamation: "Hear, O Israel, the Lord our God is One." To these rival claims might also be added the belief of Islam that it represents the authentic line stretching back to the original People of Israel. Thus, "Israel" is intertwined in a persistent and peculiar way with the religious history of the West. This chapter will concentrate on the People of Israel during the period between about 1100 B.C. and 300 B.C. The date 300 B.C. has been chosen because by that time the distinctive narrative form called sacred history had become a highly organized written tradition, had withstood tremendous threats to its integrity, and had finally emerged as the core of the collection of documents commonly known as the Old Testament. The date 1100 B.C. has been chosen because the Old Testament tradition itself does not recognize any earlier People of Israel than the union of twelve tribes living in Palestine and because modern scholarship suggests that the occupation of the country by the tribal confederation was completed about 1100 B.C.[1]

I

The Traditions of the Tribal Confederation

In Mesopotamia and in Egypt creation myths told the story of how the existing order of life was established by the gods. In the Enuma Elish the emergence of the empire in Mesopotamia was the earthly counterpart of the emergence of Enlil (or Marduk, or Ashur) as emperor of the gods and organizer of the

[1] cf. Martin Noth, *The History of Israel* (New York, 1960), pp. 80-81.

cosmos. The imperial unification of Egypt was enshrined in the myth of divine kingship, in which the elevation of Horus in the divine realm and his designation as true king of Egypt was at the same time the establishment of the earthly pharaoh's rule. The traditions of the People of Israel were radically different. Their story of how the present order of life was established said nothing at all about certain events in the divine realm which were duplicated on earth. A particularly good example is chapter twenty-four of the Book of Joshua, which tells the story of the formation of the Israelite tribal confederation.

> Joshua assembled all the tribes of Israel at Shechem, summoning the elders of Israel, their leaders, judges, and officers. When they had presented themselves before God, Joshua said to all the people, "Thus says the LORD, the God of Israel: 'In days of old your fathers lived beyond the River, namely, Terah, the father of Abraham and Nahor, and served alien gods; but I took your father Abraham from beyond the River, and I had him range the whole land of Canaan, and made his descendants numerous. I gave him Isaac, and to Isaac I gave Jacob and Esau. I gave the highlands of Seir to Esau to occupy, whereas Jacob and his children went down to Egypt. Then I sent Moses and Aaron, and I smote Egypt with what I did in her midst. After that I brought you out; I brought your fathers out of Egypt, and when you reached the sea, the Egyptians pursued your fathers with chariotry and cavalry to the Red Sea; but when they cried to the LORD, he put darkness between you and the Egyptians, and brought the sea over them, and engulfed them. You saw with your own eyes what I did in Egypt. You lived for a long time in the desert, and then I brought you to the land of the Amorites who lived beyond the Jordan. They fought with you, but I delivered them into your power, so that you took possession of their land, since I exterminated them from your way. Then Balak, the son of Zippor, king of Moab, appeared, and fought against Israel. He sent for Balaam, the son of Beor, to curse you; but I would not listen to Balaam, so he had to bless you, and thus I saved you from his power. Crossing the Jordan, you arrived at Jericho, and the citizens of Jericho fought against you, as well as the Amorites, Perizzites, Canaanites, Hittites, Girgashites, Hivvites, and Jebusites; but I delivered them into your power. I sent leprosy ahead of you to drive the two Amorite kings out of your way; it was not done by your sword nor your bow. I gave you a land on which you had never labored, and cities in which you settled without having built them, vineyards and olive groves from

which you eat without having planted them.' Therefore, stand in awe of the LORD, and serve him faithfully and loyally; remove the gods whom your fathers served beyond the River, and in Egypt, and serve the LORD. However, if you can find it obnoxious to serve the LORD, choose today whom you will serve, either the gods whom your fathers served who are beyond the River, or the gods of the Amorites in whose land you are living; but as for me and my house, we will serve the LORD."

The people in reply said, "Far be it from us that we should forsake the LORD to serve alien gods; for it is the LORD our God who brought us and our fathers up out of the land of Egypt, out of a state of slavery, and performed those great signs before our eyes, and took care of us all through the journey that we made, and among all the peoples through whom we passed; the LORD also drove out of our way all the peoples, namely, the Amorites, who inhabited the land, so we too will serve the LORD; for he is our God."

Then Joshua said to the people, "You may not serve the LORD and foreign gods as well; for being a holy God and a jealous God, he will not forgive your transgression nor your sins. If you forsake the LORD, and serve foreign gods, he will turn and do evil to you, and annihilate you, after having done you good."

"No," the people said to Joshua; "it is the LORD that we would serve."

So Joshua said to the people, "You are witnesses against yourselves that you have chosen the LORD as the one to serve."

"We are witnesses," they said.

"Remove, then, the foreign gods that are in your midst, and turn your hearts to the LORD, the God of Israel."

The people said to Joshua, "The LORD our God we will serve, and his injunctions we will heed."

So Joshua made a covenant with the people that day; he made statutes and ordinances for them at Shechem, and Joshua wrote these regulations in the book of the law of God; and taking a large stone, he set it up there under the oak that was in the sanctuary of the LORD. Then Joshua said to all the people, "See, this stone shall be a witness against us; for it has heard all the words that the LORD has said to us; so it shall be a witness against you, lest you deny your God."

Then Joshua dismissed the people, each to his heritage.[2]

JOSHUA 24:1-28

[2] The translation is by Theophile J. Meek in *The Bible: An American Translation,* edited by J. M. Powis Smith (Chicago, 1939). All scriptural passages

This account is a historical narrative rather than a myth. But it is not a mere recital of events, for it functions as a religious confession concerning the ultimate source and contemporary meaning of the events it recalls. It is sacred history, combining event and interpretation, confrontation and response, experience and expression. The emphasis of the story is on exclusive loyalty to one specific god, Yahweh,[3] on the making of a solemn and binding covenant with that god that calls for obedience to him alone, and on the proclamation of statutes and ordinances that are to be obeyed. Scholars see in this story a collection of cult legends reflecting the ritual scenario of one of the major annual festivals of the People of Israel, during which the tribes gathered at Shechem to make a united profession of faith in Yahweh, to reenact the making of the covenant with Yahweh, and to receive up-to-date instruction about the will of Yahweh.

For the Israelites, both the deepest convictions about the order and purpose of life and the cultic expression of these convictions through worship were historically oriented. Cult legends arranged in capsule history form appear very clearly in a ritual confession, which many scholars believe goes back to the early period of the Israelite conquest of Canaan (Palestine). The prayer

---

cited in this chapter will be quoted from this volume unless otherwise indicated. The typographical distinctions of the word Lord have been retained.

[3] The name Yahweh may be strange to some readers. Jehovah is undoubtedly more familiar, but this name was born of misunderstanding in the fourteenth century and is actually an artificial construction. Ancient Hebrew had no written vowels, but in the seventh century A.D. Jewish scholars constructed a system of vowel signs to make sure that the scriptures would be read properly, and in the case of the name of God this involved a problem. Long, long before that time the name Yahweh had become so sacred that no one was allowed to pronounce it; instead, the reader of scripture was supposed to substitute the word "Adonai" (Lord) whenever the consonants JHWH (or perhaps YHWH) appeared in the text. The scholars who inserted the vowel signs did not use the original vowels of Yahweh but put in the vowel signs of Adonai to remind readers that this was the term they should use. The fourteenth-century Christian scholars constructed the hybrid Jehovah because they did not understand the origin and purpose of combining the consonants of Yahweh with the vowels of Adonai. In this chapter we shall adopt Yahweh as the distinctive term for the god of Israel as worshiped by the People of Israel. The Biblical quotations from the so-called Goodspeed modern version employ the more general terms of Lord and God, but the reader should remember that the People of Israel called their god by a personal name, Yahweh.

was recited by the worshiper when he brought a basket of the first fruits of his harvest to the altar of his god:

> "A nomad Aramean was my father; he went down to Egypt to reside there, with a small company, and there he became a nation, great, mighty, and numerous; the Egyptians treated us harshly, oppressed us, and imposed hard servitude upon us; but we cried to the LORD, the God of our fathers, and the LORD heard our cry, and seeing our affliction, our toil, and our oppression, the LORD brought us out of Egypt, with a strong hand and an outstreched arm, with great terrors, signs, and portents; and bringing us to this place, he gave us this land, a land abounding in milk and honey. And now see, I have brought the first of the produce of the soil, which thou, O LORD, hast given me!"
>
> DEUTERONOMY 26:5-10

Once again, actual events in time and space are remembered as definitive disclosures of the creative power and purpose of the One who is being worshiped. Note that in this confession, just as in Joshua's speech, past and present merge into one. The prayer refers to the ancestors as "us," and Joshua continually uses the word "you" even though he is recalling events that were actually experienced by previous generations. Superficially there might seem to be a parallel with the myths of Mesopotamia and Egypt, where various ways of reenacting the divine drama of cosmic renewal enabled participants in the annual festivals to share in the divine drama of creation. The fact, however, that for the Israelites the divine disclosure was located in a time and space progression of events rather than in an eternal realm of the gods meant that participation in the covenant with Yahweh and obedience to his will could not be simply an endless repetition of patterns already established, of divine commands already fully articulated. The fact that public religious observances were not as important to the Israelites as they were to their neighbors points in this direction. Recently discovered Ugaritic texts have disclosed that in comparison with documents derived from the Canaanite world surrounding Israel the Old Testament reveals surprisingly little interest in purely cultic procedures and problems. The heart of the Israelite traditions lay in the dynamics of sacred history. Nevertheless, the cult festivals that brought together all the Israelite tribes were undoubtedly the vehicle through which continuity of the sacred history traditions was maintained. Four major themes formed the core of the religious heritage: the ancestors, the Sinai revelation and covenant, the divine law, and the Exodus.

The ancestors

The ritual prayer quoted above identifies Israel's ancestors as Arameans, seminomadic people from the upper Mesopotamian valley. A striking feature of the opening sentence of Yahweh's speech as presented by Joshua is the disclosure that there was a time when Yahweh was not the god of Israel's ancestors, that he entered their life at a definite point in time. Some scholars believe that more survived in Israelite tradition than the mere memory that at one time the ancestors worshiped gods whose primitive designations still survive in the Book of Genesis as the "God of your father Abraham," "the Awe of Isaac," and "the Mighty One of Jacob." [4]

Some features of the ancestral gods may well have been foreshadowings of the Yahwism of the future. Scholars have found inscriptions attesting the worship of gods similar to Yahweh in certain ways among the Nabataeans, who, like the Israelite ancestors, moved from the wilderness to the arable land east of the Jordan. Even though the Nabataean migration took place a thousand years or more after the migration of the Israelite ancestors, the parallels between their nomadic religion and reports in the Old Testament are striking enough to merit attention. One feature was that the cult of the Nabataean gods was not attached to any specific place. This feature is reminiscent of the tabernacle (tent) and of the portable ark (wooden chest symbolic of the divinity's presence) of Israelite tradition, and it is in sharp contrast to the cults of the Canaanites, which were connected with the soil. The Nabataean gods were invariably connected with a particular group and with that group's fortunes, and the worship of gods placed strong emphasis on the relationship between God and man, especially between God and a group of men. This is similar to the special way the Israelites remembered their ancestors. Abraham, Isaac, and Jacob were credited with being the

[4] Genesis 26:24; 31:42; 49:24.

first who received the revelation of a deity who promised them arable land and pledged himself to care for them and their posterity and to whom he would relate himself in a special way. It would seem, then, that certain features characteristic of the religious convictions and practices of seminomadic groups in the ancient Near East flowed into the stream of Israelite traditions concerning the particular deity worshiped by these tribes.

The Sinai revelation and covenant

Yahweh himself was always connected with vivid memories of a mountain called Sinai, where he had revealed himself in a special way. The actual location of the mountain has never been established. Some scholars believe that it was Jebel Serbal in the peninsula of Sinai, which according to Nabataean inscriptions was still a holy place in the third century A.D., attracting pilgrims from far and near. Whatever the location, the Israelite traditions make it plain that even though the tribes who encountered Yahweh there did not stay long, the experience they underwent there was of incalculable significance for the later Israel. According to tradition it was at Sinai that Yahweh embraced them, took them into a covenant bond that demanded exclusive loyalty to him, and convinced them so deeply of the permanence of this covenant relationship that when these tribes entered Palestine they brought their brother clans into the same covenant. If our interpretation of the Shechem assembly is correct, the original event that was later celebrated and reenacted in an annual festival was an hour, filled with drama, in which those tribes who had made the Sinai experience of Yahweh the core of their tradition simply forced on the rest of the tribes a decision for or against Yahweh. The tribal confederation was formed on the basis of the agreement Joshua won in this showdown. The clan league had no direct political functions. It was a sacral community, uniting the twelve tribes in the worship of Yahweh and in the care of the common sanctuary.[5] Politically, the con-

---

[5] The number twelve was not especially distinctive. Similar sacral communities existed nearby and in other parts of the ancient world, such as Greece and Italy. Six-member societies were also common; in fact, it has

stituent groups had to look out for themselves, except when the confederation itself was endangered or when one of the members faced annihilation. The real unity of the confederation was promoted by regular pilgrimages to the common sanctuary for the great religious festivals. It was on these occasions that their common convictions were expressed in ritual and in the recital of the stories that provided them with a common heritage.

The divine law

The great annual festival that commemorated the Sinai event and reenacted the making of the covenant with Yahweh (probably a fall New Year's festival) also included the proclamation of Yahweh's statutes and ordinances. There is evidence that a particularly solemn celebration took place every seven years at the central shrine, in which the reading of the divine law played a leading part. The importance of this law in the life of the tribal confederation is evident in the fact that the only office for all Israel explicitly mentioned in the oldest tradition was judicial rather than priestly and also in the fact that the only exact and obviously authentic chronological information for the period before the founding of the Israelite monarchy is contained in Judges 10:1-5 and 12:7-15, where a list of "judges" is given with their tenure of office. Martin Noth's conclusions regarding this material are worth quoting:

> The fact that this information was recorded officially and transmitted to posterity can probably only be explained by the fact that in the earliest period of Israel's history dates were based on the period of the judges' years of office. If that is so, it follows that this was the central office in the Israelites' twelve-tribe association and that the law played a decisive role in this association.[6]

---

been suggested that the "Leah tribes"—Reuben, Simeon, Levi, Judah, Zebulum, and Issachar—constituted an association that was the forerunner and basis of the twelve-tribe association. The numbers six and twelve had to do with upkeep of the common shrine. Each tribe assumed responsibility for a month or two months in rotation.

[6] Noth, *op. cit.*, p. 102.

The distinctiveness of the Israelite confederation did not consist of a particular form of worship; apparently the forms and festivals indigenous to agrarian life in Palestine were adopted and more or less adapted to Yahwist convictions. The distinctiveness lay in the fact that Israel was subject to a divine law which the settlers brought with them and which set definite limits on their assimilation into Canaanite society, even though it took over many elements of Canaanite legal codes in order to deal with practical problems of everyday life.

That Israelite traditions insisted a certain distinction be maintained is reflected clearly in the classic formulation known as the Ten Commandments. The first command, "You must have no other gods beside me" (Exodus 20:3), involved a cultic intolerance that was unique in the history of religion. We have already pointed out in the case of the confession connected with the harvest festival how the Israelites historicized what was previously a purely agrarian celebration, and we have suggested that the covenant renewal ceremony historicized the Canaanite New Year's festival. But the most astonishing phenomenon connected with Yahweh's invasion of Palestine was the exclusion of sex from Israel's cult. In the Canaanite cult, as in Mesopotamia and Egypt, sex was a sacral mystery. Copulation and procreation were so central in the mythical tradition that the religious atmosphere was saturated with sexual imagery. Sex was a divine reality. But as far back as traditions concerning Yahweh went, Yahweh stood absolutely beyond the polarity of sex. For Israel, therefore, sex belonged purely and simply to the human realm. It must not be divinized and it must not be considered an avenue for participation in the creative power and purpose of Yahweh except in historical terms—that is, in terms of the progression of human generations toward a divinely intended historical goal.

Given the central role of sexual images in ancient Near Eastern festivals, which were believed to be indispensable to agriculture, the removal of sex from the sacred rites implied that in the long run the legitimacy of Canaanite cults would have to be questioned and that a struggle for supremacy between the fertility gods (symbolized by the term Baal) and Yahweh would be inevitable. On the other hand, given the belief that Yahweh was beyond sex, and thus somehow beyond the traditional Near Eastern cosmos of gods and men, Yahwism was open-ended. Because it was not bound by myths of a divine cosmos and a corresponding human order established by the gods in all essentials,

Yahwism had a potential for development in the midst of changing historical circumstances that was unique among the religious traditions of the ancient Near East.

The Exodus

No other event was celebrated by the later Israel with greater praise or persistence than the deliverance of some of their ancestors from Egypt and their rescue at the Red Sea. As Gerhard von Rad has said:

> In this event, quite insignificant by the standards of secular history, those who were delivered experienced something which in its significance far transcended the personal fate of those who at the time shared in it. The deliverance from Egypt and the rescue at the Red Sea found their way into Israel's confession of faith—indeed, they actually became Israel's earliest confession, around which the whole Hexateuchal history was in the end ranged.[7]

Exactly which sections of the later Israelite tribes migrated into the Delta region of Egypt we do not know, but the tradition is firm that they were conscripted by the Egyptians for labor on large building projects, that they decided to escape, that they were pursued, and that the chariot division pursuing them became mired in a "sea." Tradition is also firm in the conviction that the Exodus was a revelatory occasion of overwhelming power. The almost unbelievable escape and rescue were experienced as "mighty acts of God," in and through which the participants became convinced that they had been chosen for a divine purpose. Throughout Israelite history the Exodus story was not only celebrated regularly in the cult but was recalled with particular vividness whenever a historical crisis called for another mighty act of deliverance.

Interestingly enough, the cult festival devoted to the Exodus theme—Passah (Passover) and Matzoth, the associated feast of unleavened bread—was held in spring and made use of the ancient cosmic renewal rites familiar in the Near East. The Passah

[7] *Old Testament Theology,* translated by D. M. G. Stalker (New York, 1962), vol. I, p. 13.

rites included the sacrificial slaughtering of a lamb or kid whose flesh was eaten and whose blood was sprinkled on doorposts to ward off evil. This was a part of the dramatization of the victory of the divine forces of fertility over the dark forces of death and disorder. But among the Israelites Passah came to be a historical commemoration of the Exodus event. The fertility theme, with its sexual connotations, was suppressed.

Another phenomenon with important implications for the future was the power of the Exodus to enter contemporary history again and again in the form of a fervent expectation of divine intervention in situations that under any normal system of calculation would be disastrous. An example from the period of the tribal confederation immediately comes to mind. A coalition of Canaanite princes was formed under a general named Sisera, and it posed such a serious threat to certain of the Israelite tribes that their situation became a matter of sheer survival. The politically unorganized tribes had to be united for military action on a much larger scale than ever before. In the crisis a charismatic personality, the prophetess Deborah, mobilized and crystallized public opinion among the clans, instigated an outstanding warrior named Barak to organize the warriors, and announced that Yahweh had already delivered the enemy into their hands—provided the tribal warriors would execute Yahweh's decision with courage and vigor.

The Canaanites had horses and chariots; yet in spite of their technological superiority they lost the main battle near Megiddo at the river Kishon. A violent thunderstorm put their chariots out of action, and when they tried to retreat over the river, which had suddenly changed from a trickle into a torrent, they suffered heavy losses. General Sisera got away, but within a few hours he was murdered by Jael, a Kenite woman in whose tent he sought refuge. The amazing victory was complete. The acknowledged victor was Yahweh. Barak returned home; his leadership was temporary, and it ended when the crisis had been met.

This story indicates the ambiguous relationship of Yahweh to the political life of the Israelite tribal association. The divine will, as it was rehearsed in essentials and revised in details at the festival gatherings, did not include any model of a political structure. A second example is the story of another charismatic leader, Gideon, who also stepped in during a crisis caused by a foreign group called the Midianites and who was reported to have won a victory against impossible odds because Yahweh fought for his people. In fact, Gideon was required to reduce his fighting force to a ridiculously small size so that no one could doubt the victory was Yahweh's and Yahweh's alone. The final episode in the narrative as recorded in the Book of Judges (Chapters 6-8) reads:

> Then the Israelites said to Gideon, "Rule over us, you, then your son, and then your grandson; for you have saved us from the power of Midian."
>
> But Gideon said to them, "I will not rule over you, nor shall my son rule over you, since the LORD rules over you."[8]
>
> JUDGES 8:22-23

These stories show that one of the serious problems posed by the Exodus-Sinai core of the Israelite tradition was whether Yahwist convictions could be related positively to the cosmologically oriented city-state institutions of Palestine. Yahweh was not regarded as an aggressive war god, urging the spread of his power by the sword. The occupation of Palestine by the Israelite tribes was much more a process of peaceful infiltration than a dramatic series of successful military campaigns. The crucial point was that Yahweh only came to the assistance of the tribal confederation politically when it was endangered by aggression and oppression.[9] Eventually, the question of a stable political

---

[8] Translated by Theophile J. Meek.

[9] This means that the general picture given in the Book of Judges is more accurate than the impression given by the Book of Joshua. Also, it means that the picture painted by the authors of the Book of Deuteronomy, which describes the wars involved in the conquest of Palestine as an instrument for exterminating everybody in sight who did not believe in Yahweh, was a fictional innovation. These authors rewrote Israel's history of the conquest with streams of imaginary blood because they were fiercely concerned with religious issues of their own time. They were engaged in a "holy war" of their own against all who would not commit themselves to full-fledged and exclusive obedience to what they believed was the true version of the divine law.

One point must be granted, however. The ancient Israelites did subscribe to the notion of a holy war. An important ritual aspect of those military operations organized in moments of mortal danger by charismatic individuals (the so-called "great judges" for whom the Book of Judges was named) was the *ban*. No Israelite was allowed to benefit from Yahweh's victories. All gold and silver loot went into the treasury at the central sanctuary, and all living beings were slaughtered as a sacrifice in Yahweh's honor.

organization would have to be faced. Soon after 1100 B.C., a threat appeared that forced the issue, and the traditions that have been preserved concerning that crisis indicate how difficult it was for the Israelites to bring their basic convictions into focus when a centralized monarchy became the only practical means by which to insure their continued existence as a people.

About 1200 B.C. there was an influx of landseeking groups from the Mediterranean region into the civilized areas of the Near East. Some of those who came by sea settled in the southern part of the coastal plain of Palestine. The Old Testament tradition calls them Philistines and describes them as a federation of five city-states: Gaza, Askalon, Ashdod, Akkaron (Ekron), and Gath. They developed a vigorously expansive military dominion in Palestine and confronted the Israelite tribal association with the prospect of being subjugated if not annihilated. Samuel was the charismatic leader who came forth to help the tribal association meet the first of several Philistine crises. Just as Joshua at Shechem had welded disparate tribes into a cultic confederation generations earlier and had paved the way to the occupation of Palestine, so now Samuel welded them together and paved the way to monarchy. The Philistines seem to have been able to invade Israelite territory almost at will until Samuel called all the tribes together for a solemn assembly at Mizpeh. Then Yahweh, the Exodus Yahweh of mighty acts, intervened once again. The story is recounted in the seventh chapter of First Samuel.

> So they assembled at Mizpeh, and drew water and poured it out before the LORD, and fasted on that day, saying, "We have sinned against the LORD."
>
> Samuel also judged the Israelites in Mizpeh. And when the Philistines heard that the Israelites were assembled together at Mizpeh, the city rulers of the Philistines went up against Israel. And when the Israelites heard of it, they were afraid of the Philistines.
>
> Then the Israelites said to Samuel, "Cease not to cry out to the LORD our God for us, that he may save us from the power of the Philistines."
>
> Accordingly Samuel took a sucking lamb and offered it up as a whole burnt-offering to the LORD. And Samuel cried out to the LORD in behalf of Israel, and the LORD answered him. For just as Samuel was offering up the burnt-offering, the Philistines came on for an attack upon Israel; but the LORD thundered

> with a mighty voice that day against the Philistines, and threw them into confusion and they were overcome before Israel. And the men of Israel went forth from Mizpeh and pursued the Philistines and harassed them until they were below Bethcar.
>
> Then Samuel took a stone and set it between Mizpeh and Yeshana and called its name Ebenezer, for he said, "Hitherto the LORD has helped us."
>
> Thus the Philistines were humbled and came no more into the territory of Israel. The hand of the LORD was against the Philistines all the days of Samuel. Also the cities which the Philistines had taken from Israel were restored to Israel from Ekron even to Gath; and Israel rescued their territory from the power of the Philistines.[10]
>
> I SAMUEL 7:6-14

Whatever the actual details may have been at Mizpeh, however, the victory was temporary. The tribal confederation was still in mortal danger. In the next chapter of First Samuel it is reported that all the elders of Israel met with Samuel and asked that a monarchy be established. Samuel is pictured as resisting the demand on the ground that it represented a failure of loyalty to Yahweh. Not long afterward, however, Samuel gave in. The eleventh and twelfth chapters of First Samuel contain two separate accounts of the founding of the monarchy. The editors who arranged the materials as we read them today suggest that Samuel summoned all the tribes to Mizpeh, where the man he believed Yahweh had chosen—Saul—was presented to the people and was hailed with the shout, "Long live the king!" But then the story goes on to say that certain sections of the tribal association did not accept Saul as king, and the entire association united under his leadership only after Saul had demonstrated unusual military prowess in a subsequent engagement with Ammonite enemies. The editors introduce the second account of the founding of the monarchy, this time at Gilgal, by having Samuel say, "Come, and let us go to Gilgal and *renew* there the kingdom" (I Samuel 11:14),[11] as though Saul had been crowned king already and was going to be crowned a second time. This is doubtful, especially since the closing section of the Gilgal account strongly emphasizes the theme of a covenant renewal with Yahweh (I

---

[10] Translated by Leroy Waterman.

[11] Italics added—C.L.

Samuel 12:20-25), and thus seems to lie directly in the orbit of the annual Israelite festival whose ritual included a covenant renewal ceremony, and perhaps later, a renewal of the kingship.

Both versions include capsule histories similar to those cited earlier in the chapter, and both reflect the fact that adoption of the new form of political organization caused tensions in the realm of religious convictions. As recited in these summaries of the past, sacred history began with the Exodus event, continued with allusions to Yahweh's having given his people their Promised Land, and ended with the charge that in view of all the wonderful deeds of Yahweh in their behalf the people were being disloyal to him by asking for a king. Yet, taken in their entirety, both stories about the founding of the monarchy affirmed that the new structure was established with Yahweh's blessing even though tradition could give no precedent for it. In later years this founding of the monarchy was added to sacred history as another link in the series of crucial events through which Yahweh had revealed himself. Words attributed to Samuel in the version of the story emphasizing covenant renewal illustrate how the event was assimilated into the Exodus-Sinai traditions.

> Now therefore see the king whom you have chosen and whom you have requested; for the LORD has now set a king over you. If you will fear the LORD and serve him and listen to his voice, and not rebel against the commandment of the LORD, and both you and the king who reigns over you follow the LORD your God, it is well. But if you will not listen to the voice of the LORD, but rebel against the commandment of the LORD, then shall the hand of the LORD be against you and your king to destroy you.
>
> I SAMUEL 12:13-15

These words sound quite simple and straightforward. They remind us of Jesus' words: "Give unto Caesar that which is Caesar's and unto God that which is God's." But what if there was at the core of the religious tradition an ineradicable conviction that everything belongs to God, while at the same time political realities dictated that God's will for the community must be committed into the hands of a king and his policy advisers? Did this mean that the divine purpose of Yahweh for his Chosen People should be identified with the institutionalized purposes of a political organization and that the mighty miracles performed by Yahweh in the past should be identified with military successes planned and executed by a king's professional army? Or was Yahweh still the mysterious, free, history-making Lord of the Exodus-Sinai traditions?

The fact that the stories about Samuel and King Saul became fixed in such a way that they voiced serious doubts about the appropriateness and adequacy of monarchy is most significant. It indicates what later history disclosed, that full agreement on answers to such questions as these was never reached. The most convincing answers in favor of monarchy as a permanent capstone of sacred history were developed by King David and the dynasty he founded. But the sovereignty of this dynasty soon became limited to the southern part of the country. The David-Zion tradition was fostered in Jerusalem and Judah, while in the much larger northern part of the country (the kingdom of Israel) the Exodus-Sinai traditions lived on, both in the sense that kingship was viewed more in terms of charismatic leaders than in terms of a single legitimate dynasty and in the sense that there came a time when Yahweh was experienced once again as a Lord who could repudiate monarchical structures as well as establish them.

2

The David-Zion Tradition

Historically, the monarchy that Samuel established with Saul as its king brought the northern and southern tribes together, but it could not cope successfully with the military and political crisis. The Philistine threat was wiped out by David, who not only imposed a new order on the tribal association but also proceeded to build an Israelite empire that went far beyond the dreams of any of the tribal leaders. By Mesopotamian and Egyptian standards it was rather small, but it was the nearest approach in ancient times to the unification of the entire buffer zone between the great powers of East and West. Thus, David's model was neither the sacral association nor the Palestinian city-state but the empires of Mesopotamia and Egypt.

The initial step was taken when Saul (a northern tribesman who had ruled from the north) was killed in battle. Saul's son, Ishbaal, was crowned king of "all Israel." This territory included Judah, the southern region of Palestine, which Saul had brought into his kingdom with considerable difficulty. But David and his men took over Hebron, the old capital of the southern region, and before long he was hailed as "King of Judah." The second step was a war between the clans of Saul and of David, which ended with the murder of Ishbaal by some of his own kinsmen, who realized that David was certain to emerge victorious. The northerners had to surrender, but David showed his sensitivity to the Exodus-Sinai tradition, as well as his shrewdness, by arranging to make a covenant before Yahweh with the "elders of Israel." Apparently it included a formal declaration that Yahweh had already ordained David to be shepherd and prince of Israel (the north) while Saul was king, which officially removed the stain of illegitimacy and usurpation. David was crowned a second time, becoming king of north and south, of Israel and Judah. The third major step was the brilliant one of establishing a capital in a region and a town that was neither Israelite nor Judahite, the Jebusite city of Jerusalem located strategically on Mount Zion near the territory controlled by Judah. It was located in the south where David was most certain of support, and yet it was in a real sense a neutral city that the northerners could accept as the capital of the kingdom. David conquered Jerusalem. It became his personal possession and his base for empire building.

The symbols of kingship and of empire that were developed under David and his successors were closely connected with Jerusalem. *Jeru-Shalem* meant "a creation of Shalem" (an old west-Semitic god); the Hebrew word *shalom* meant "prosperity, success, harmonious situation, peace." In David's time the town was the seat of the high god, El Elyon, a god of *zedek* (righteousness). The program of empire building that emanated from Jerusalem after David took over was legitimized as a righteous (*zedek*) policy of establishing a dominion of peace and prosperity (*shalom*), with these qualities now attributed to Yahweh. The king of Jerusalem was a priest-king like the kings of the ancient Sumerian city-states. He was the point of contact through which the divine power of El Elyon entered human affairs. The Davidic kingship claimed for itself this cosmologically derived function, even though David and his successors did not take over the specific *office* of cultic high priest. Along with the former Jebusite priests of El Elyon the priests of Yahweh became ministers of the royal cult.

Without question, Mount Zion, the sacred mountain, carried with it the symbolic overtones of the "cosmic mountain," the link in Mesopotamian tradition between heaven and earth, gods and men. Mount Zion became the mountain of God, his chosen dwelling place and the locus from which his universal sovereignty flowed into the affairs of men. The nomadic Yahweh of Mount Sinai thus settled down on a new mountain not originally associated with him at all.

The most dramatic impetus to this symbolic transfer was given by David himself when he moved the "ark of the covenant" to his royal city. Throughout the centuries the ark had stood for the presence of Yahweh among his people; now it belonged to the king and rested on Mount Zion. The transference of the ark made Jerusalem the common sanctuary for all the clans of Israel. When Solomon built his famous temple and installed the ark in it he was establishing both a royal chapel and a temple of the empire. Therefore, the cult developed in the temple affected the religious life of the broad mass of the people in spite of the fact that Jerusalem stood completely apart from any earlier traditions connecting it with Yahweh. The accounts of the reception of the ark in the temple in First Kings, Chapter 8, and in Psalm 132 indicate that the ark figured in an annual festival celebration commemorating the founding of the sanctuary, Yahweh's choice of Mount Zion as the home of the Davidic dynasty, and the covenant of Yahweh with David through which the dynasty itself had been founded.

The appropriation of Canaanite forms and concepts was intensified by the more intimate contacts that David's conquests made inevitable. Foreign cults from neighboring empires also began to exert a stronger influence. The Jerusalem temple itself illustrated what was happening. As Voegelin has pointed out:

> And what we know of Solomon's Temple, with its orientation toward the rising sun, the pylons channeling the rays of the sun into the interior, the Babylonian "brazen sea" on the

> twelve bulls, oriented in groups of three toward the four cardinal points and its various other equipment and decoration, looks more like a connoisseur's collection of Near Eastern cosmological symbols than the sanctuary of the Yahweh who led his Chosen People from the Sheol of civilization into the freedom of his realm.[12]

Turning to the cult as practiced in the temple, certain liturgical psalms offer succinct and vivid examples of the adoption of themes and images from the Mesopotamian and Egyptian traditions. Psalms 93, 97, and 99 open with the same phrase: "The LORD is king!" and each develops this proclamation in both cosmic and imperial images. The following two excerpts are typical.

> The LORD is King; he is clothed with majesty.
> The LORD is clothed, he is girded with strength.
> Indeed, the world is established immovable.
> Thy throne has been established from of old;
> Thou art from remotest antiquity.
>
> The floods have lifted up, O LORD,
> The floods have lifted up their voice;
> The floods lift up their roar
> Above the sound of many waters.
> Mightier than the breakers of the sea,
> The LORD on high is mighty!
>
> PSALMS 93:1-4 [13]

This psalm shows that Yahweh could be praised through Egyptian and Babylonian images of the birth of the gods and the cosmos from a watery chaos. The cosmos is firmly established, but under the earth the roaring of the primordial sea can still be heard. Yahweh emerges victorious. This echoes the Enuma Elish drama.

> The LORD reigns; let the earth rejoice!
> Let many shores be glad!
> Clouds and darkness are around him;
> Righteousness and justice are the foundation of his throne.

---

[12] Eric Voegelin, *Order and History* (Baton Rouge, Louisiana, 1956), vol. I, p. 320.

[13] All translations of the psalms are by J. M. Powis Smith.

Fire goes before him,
And blazes around his steps.
His lightnings illuminate the world;
The earth beholds and trembles.
The mountains melt like wax before the LORD,
Before the LORD of all the earth.
The heavens proclaim his righteousness,
And all the peoples see his glory.
All who serve wrought images are put to shame,
They who prided themselves on their nonentities.
Worship him, all you gods!

Zion hears and rejoices,
And the daughters of Judah exult,
Because of thy judgments, O LORD.
For thou, O LORD, art the highest over all the earth;
Thou are exalted high above all gods.

PSALMS 97:1-9

Yahweh is no longer simply the god of Israel who demands exclusive loyalty from Israel. He is the divine world ruler, whose cosmic order is righteous and just. More than that, he is the ruler of the gods. There are echoes here of the divine assembly which was central to the myths of Egypt and Mesopotamia. At least one psalm, 82, makes explicit use of the conception of the divine assembly.

God takes his stand in the divine assembly;
In the midst of the gods he gives judgment
"How long will you judge unjustly,
And show partiality toward the wicked?

"Give justice to the weak and the fatherless;
Do right by the afflicted and wretched;
Set free the weak and needy;
Rescue them from the hand of the wicked."

They have neither knowledge nor sense;
They wander about in darkness;
All the foundations of the earth shake.

I say "You are gods,
And all of you sons of the Most High!
Yet you will die as men do,
And fall like any prince."

Arise, O God, judge the earth!
For thou wilt take possession of all the nations.

In the David-Zion conception of human kingship we find a similar affirmation of continuity with the Exodus-Sinai Yahwist tradition, while at the same time symbols belonging to Egyptian and Mesopotamian imperial institutions were being adopted. The point of confluence between the Exodus-Sinai tradition and the David-Zion tradition can be seen clearly in the report of a message (oracle) from Yahweh communicated to David by the prophet Nathan:

> Thus has the Lord of hosts said, "I took you from the pasture, from following the sheep, that you should be a leader over my people, over Israel; and I have been with you wherever you have gone, and I have destroyed all your enemies from before you, and I will make for you a great name like the name of the great who are in the earth. And I will appoint a place for my people Israel, and will plant them, that they may dwell in their own place, and they shall be disquieted no more, and the perverse shall no more afflict them as formerly, from the day that I decreed judges over my people Israel.

"And I will give you respite from all your foes.
And the Lord declares to you
That he will make you a house.
And when your days are finished,
And you are laid with your fathers,
I will raise up your heir after you,
Who shall be born of your body;
And I will establish his kingdom.
He shall build a house for my name,
And I will establish the throne of his kingdom forever.

"I will be his father,
And he shall be my son;
When he goes astray,
I will chasten him with the rod of men,
And with the stripes of the sons of Adam.
But my lovingkindness shall not depart from him,
As I withdrew it from him who was before you.

Your house and your kingdom shall be confirmed before me
forever;
For all time your throne shall be established."[14]

II SAMUEL 7:8-16

Yahweh has made a covenant with David and David's successors. Not only has this new covenant superseded the covenants made with Israel's ancestors, with the tribal association, and lately with Saul, but it is the final covenant. The monarchy ruled by the Davidic dynasty "shall be established forever." The same point is made in the poetic oracle called "the last words of David" (II Samuel 23:1-7), which includes the lines:

Although he has decreed for me an eternal covenant,
Set forth in all things and sure . . . .

The Nathan oracle identifies the king as the specific point of contact between Yahweh and his people, and it hails him as Yahweh's adopted son. A striking feature of Psalm 2 is the appearance of the adoption theme in words that seem to be a direct quotation of a coronation formula encountered again and again in Egyptian materials.

Wherefore do the nations rage,
And the peoples plot in vain?
The kings of the earth stand up,
And the princes also take counsel,
Against the LORD and against his anointed:
"Let us burst their bonds asunder,
And cast their cords from us."
He that sits in the heavens laughs;
The Lord makes sport of them.
Then will he speak to them in his wrath,
And terrify them in his fury:
"I, indeed, have anointed my king,
On Zion, my holy hill."

Let me tell of the decree of the LORD:
He said to me, *"You are my son;*
Today have I begotten you.

---

[14] Translated by Leroy Waterman.

Ask of me, and I will make the nations your inheritance,
And the ends of the earth your possession.
You shall break them with an iron rod;
You shall crush them like a potter's vessel."

Be cautious, therefore, O kings;
Take warning, O rulers of the earth.
Serve the Lord with fear,
Kiss his feet with trembling,
Lest he be angry and you perish in the way;
For his wrath is soon kindled.
How happy are they who take refuge in him! [15]

The italics probably preserve the formula used in a coronation liturgy prepared for the Davidic dynasty. The sentence, "I, indeed, have anointed my king, on Zion, my holy hill," also seems to be quoted directly from a coronation liturgy.

Another interesting parallel between the cosmological traditions and Psalm 2 is the use of the term *decree:* "Let me tell of the decree of the Lord." Yahweh's decree recalls the myths that picture the divine assembly of the gods making decisions and issuing their "unalterable decrees." We are reminded of the Mesopotamian assembly decreeing Marduk's emperorship and of the heavenly courtroom trial in which Horus, rather than Seth, is decreed to be the true heir to the throne of Egypt. We are reminded also of the inscriptions of Lugalzagesi and of Hammurabi concerning the divine decree that conferred imperial power on them. There is a decisive difference, of course. No myths about Yahweh's process of decision making in response to events in the divine realm lie behind the psalmist's choice of the word *decree,* just as no myth of the divinity of the Davidic king lies behind the phrase, "this day have I begotten thee."

The question of "foreign influences" can now be brought into sharper focus. Did the David-Zion tradition capitulate at all to the mythical orientation of the great Near Eastern empires in which history was subordinated to the eternally recurring cycles of nature? Eventually, in a way, it did. A study of the new spiritual and cultural processes created by the success of David and Solomon indicates that Israel achieved a remarkable new

---

[15] Italics added—C.L.

understanding of itself precisely through the unique quality of its religious heritage, which made commemoration of historical origins and reflection on them the characteristic form by which fundamental convictions were expressed.

The court at Jerusalem fostered an intellectual and cultural upsurge that opened the way to new and creative dimensions of life. Within the course of a few generations three major historical works were written, which mark the era as not simply innovative in a local sense but as the occasion of a momentous advance in man's understanding of himself. One was the history of David's rise to power (I Samuel 16:14-II Samuel 5:12). The second was the history of Solomon's succession to the throne (II Samuel 6:12-I Kings 2:46). The third was the so-called Yahwist's narrative, which presented a connected account of the entire prehistory of the monarchy. This document began with the creation story in Genesis, Chapter 2, covered the period of the patriarchal ancestors, the sojourn of the Hebrew tribes in Egypt and their exodus under Moses, the Mount Sinai covenant making, the successful penetration into Palestine under Joshua, the period of tribal association with its recurrent crises, and the establishment of the first monarchy under Saul.[16]

Until this time, the old historical traditions consisted of events that were more or less episodic and isolated. The great revelatory events, those celebrated in the cult legends, were miracle stories. They could stand on their own wherever they were recited; their original context had been forgotten long ago, even though there was no doubt that they were rooted in actual historical occurrences. As Gerhard von Rad has said of the era ushered in by David and Solomon:

---

[16] The term "Yahwist's narrative" is a modern designation. Literary analysis of the Pentateuch (the first five books of the Old Testament) has convinced scholars that several sources were combined and intertwined by the editors who brought the documents to their final form. Style, content, concepts, vocabulary, and other distinctive features have been used as evidence. The systematic use of Yahweh as the name for God proved to be a major feature of what has come to be considered the earliest comprehensive document. Thus the label "Yahwist." The document is also commonly called the J-source, following German scholars who transliterated the Hebrew letter with a J rather than a Y.

One of the best summaries of the results of documentary analysis is that by E. A. Speiser in his introduction to his Anchor Bible commentary on the Book of Genesis. See *Genesis* (New York, 1964).

> What was new was that Israel now found herself able to shape history into great complexes; that is, not merely to call to remembrance isolated events basic to the history, or to string such data more or less connectedly together for the purposes of cultic recital, but really to present the history in its broad historical connexions, including all the many events which cannot be made to fit with complete consistency into any teaching, and taking in also its reverses, and, above all, its terrible and splendid humanity.[17]

From the point of view of the composition of the Old Testament as we know it today, the comprehensive Yahwist narrative of Yahweh's purposeful dealings with men and his choosing of Israel as his special agent in human history is the most significant of the three documents. If the unknown author we call the Yahwist had not preserved and rearranged the information about the early ages in Israel's past that had been preserved in various forms, the very basis of sacred history as it was recast in several later versions might well have been lost beyond recovery. Von Rad has gone so far as to say that

> If, at the end of the period of the Judges in the time of Samuel and King Saul, or indeed even later, in the time of David, Israel had vanished from the political scene because of a catastrophe in her history, as little would have been preserved about her for posterity, in spite of her wealth of historical traditions, as has been preserved in the case of the Ammorites and the Moabites, who, no doubt, had their specific traditions too; only they never found their way into such a large-scale view of history.[18]

More will be said about the Yahwist narrative and later comprehensive histories in the next section. As to the question whether the David-Zion conception of kingship compromised the historical orientation of the Exodus-Sinai convictions in favor of the mythical orientation of the great Near Eastern empires, the document that legitimated Solomon's succession to the throne of David indicates that at least initially the historical orientation remained decisive. This superbly integrated narrative was prob-

---

[17] Von Rad, *op. cit.*, p. 49.
[18] *Ibid.*, p. 50.

ably written about 950 B.C., during the period of Solomon's reign before the serious troubles beset him that led to civil war almost as soon as he relinquished the throne to his son. It covered the imperial portion of David's career after his rise to power, his successful conquests, and his establishment of Jerusalem as his capital, and it ended at the point where Solomon consolidated his power (II Samuel 6:21-I Kings 2:46).

The Nathan oracle, quoted above, appears early in the story. But before its author allows the promise of a never-ending dynasty to be delivered to David, he introduces as a prologue an episode connected with bringing the ark of the covenant to Jerusalem. It seems that Queen Michal was shocked and disgusted by the fact that David whirled with all his might in the joyful procession. When he came home after the ceremonies she said,

> "How dignified was the king of Israel today as he stripped himself in the sight of the maidservants of his retainers, as a common rake exposes himself!"
>
> But David said to Michael, "It is before the LORD that I dance. Blessed be the LORD, who chose me rather than your father and rather than any of his house to appoint me as a leader over the people of the LORD, over Israel, therefore I will disport myself before the LORD and I will be yet more abandoned than that and I will be vile in your eyes. But of the maidservants to whom you have referred I shall indeed be held in honor."
>
> And Michal the daughter of Saul had no child to the day of her death.
>
> II SAMUEL 6:21-23

The final laconic sentence introduces the single great historical tension around which the entire subsequent narrative is built. Nathan's oracle concerning the continuation of the Davidic dynasty follows immediately, and it thrusts into the foreground the question, "Who will David's successor be?" The question becomes ever more insistent as the complicated course of events in the new empire and in the royal house unfolds in a series of diverse yet well-arranged scenes. David stands at the center, a genius as a warrior and statesman, but a man driven by his passions to such an extent that he can even plot the death of Uriah in order to steal his wife Bathsheba. As he grows old he has to face the fading of his splendor and the transferring of his popularity to his sons. His attachment to his sons is so strong that he is guilty of blind indulgence, and this brings his throne to the brink of ruin.

The oldest son, Amnon, falls victim to licentiousness. He violates his half-sister Tamar and is killed in revenge by Absalom, Tamar's full brother. Later, Absalom falls victim to his ambitious schemings to seize the throne. He is killed in the course of an unsuccessful military coup. The next in line, Adonijah, seems to be on the point of taking over, but at the last minute he is bypassed. In the midst of an almost intolerably tense situation Solomon's mother, Bathsheba, and the prophet Nathan induce the now senile David to name Solomon officially as his successor. David's choice is honored by both the people and the army. Solomon manages to have Adonijah assassinated and the narrative ends with the empire "completely established in the hand of Solomon." (I Kings 2:46)

This work uses a new literary technique of historical narration, which had no parallel in the ancient Near East. The political connections are portrayed consecutively and according to their historical causes. The freedom with which the historian treats the king is also unique. The first word spoken by Israel about Yahweh and his adopted son in Jerusalem is absolutely unmythological and utterly realistic. Whereas the kings of Mesopotamia and Egypt remained hidden behind the symbols of their sacral office, David is acknowledged to be Yahweh's chosen one; yet he is depicted as the person he actually was, both great and fallible, courageous and weak, wise and foolish, vital at the beginning of his reign and senile at the end. Whereas the kings in Mesopotamia underwent a ritual humiliation annually as a part of the cultic ceremonies connected with the New Year's Festival, David experienced an actual humiliation when Absalom almost took over his throne. (II Samuel 15:17ff.) Stripped of his royal insignia, leaving his palace and his throne and even the ark of the covenant, "David went up the ascent of Olivet, weeping as he went, with his head covered and walking barefoot, and all the people who were with him covered each his head, and they went up, weeping as they ascended." (verse 30) These sufferings were not the acting out of cultic or ritual conventions, but they had a profoundly religious dimension; David understood the crisis in his kingdom to be a judgment of Yahweh upon him.

The narrator discloses his own interpretive point of view on the crisis in an episode that occurred soon after David, climbing the Mount of Olives in flight from Jerusalem, learned that even his most trusted adviser, Ahithophel, had joined Absalom. David prayed: "O LORD, I pray, turn the counsel of Ahithophel to foolishness." (II Samuel 15:31) Upon reaching the summit, "where one worships God," David met another of his close advisers, Hushai, and it occurred to him that he ought to send this loyal man back to Jerusalem to join Absalom as a spy. He did not know at the time that Hushai was Yahweh's answer to his prayer. The story continues:

> Then Absalom and all the men of Israel came to Jerusalem, and Ahithophel with him. Now when Hushai the Archite, David's friend, came to Absalom, Hushai said to Absalom, "Long live the king, long live the king!"
>
> And Absalom said to Hushai, "Is this your loyalty for your friend? Why did you not go with your friend?"
>
> Then Hushai said to Absalom, "No! for whom the LORD and this people and all the men of Israel have chosen, his will I be and with him will I remain. And secondly, whom should I serve? Should it not be his son? As I served your father, so will I serve you."
>
> Absalom also said to Ahithophel, "Give your counsel. What shall we do?"
>
> And Ahithophel said to Absalom, "Go in to your father's concubines, whom he has left to keep the house; and all Israel will hear that you are in bad odor with your father and the hands of all who are with you will be strengthened."
>
> So they pitched a tent for Absalom upon the roof; and Absalom went in to the concubines of his father in the sight of all Israel. And the counsel of Ahithophel, which he gave in those days, was as if one consulted an oracle of God—so was all the counsel of Ahithophel regarded both by David and by Absalom.
>
> Moreover Ahithophel said to Absalom, "Let me, I pray you, choose out twelve thousand men, and let me arise and pursue after David tonight; thus I will come upon him when he is weary and exhausted and I will throw him into a panic and also all the people who are with him; and I will strike down the king alone. And I will bring back all the people to you as the bride returns to her husband. You seek only the life of one man, and all the people shall be at peace."
>
> And the plan pleased Absalom, and all the elders of Israel.
>
> Then Absalom said, "Call now Hushai the Archite also, and let us hear likewise what he has to offer."
>
> And when Hushai came to Absalom, Absalom said to him,

as follows, "Thus Ahithophel has spoken; shall we carry out his plan? If not, speak out."

Then Hushai said to Absalom, "This time the counsel that Ahithophel has given is not good."

And Hushai said, "You know your father and his men, that they are tried warriors and thoroughly aroused, like a bear in the open robbed of her cubs. Furthermore your father is an expert campaigner and will not spend the night with the people. Even now he has hidden himself in one of the caves or in some other place. And in case he falls upon the people at the first, whoever hears the report will say, 'there has been a slaughter among the people who follow Absalom.' Then even the valiant man whose heart is like the heart of a lion, will utterly lose courage; for all Israel knows that your father is a skilled warrior, and those who are with him are valiant men. But I counsel that all Israel be surely gathered together to you, from Dan to Beersheba, as many as the sand that is by the sea, with you yourself marching in their midst. And we will come upon him in some place where he has been located, and we will light upon him as the dew falls upon the ground; and of him and of all the men who are with him there shall not be left even one. But if he withdraws into a city, then all Israel will bring ropes to that city and we will drag it into the valley, until not even a pebble can be found there."

And Absalom and all the men of Israel said, "The counsel of Hushai the Archite is better than the counsel of Ahithophel."

II SAMUEL 16:15-17:14

This event marked the turning point in the rebellion. If he had followed Ahithophel's advice Absalom would have successfully seized the throne. But he believed Hushai and lost his life as well as his chance to be king. The author speaks explicitly of Yahweh and divine intervention only three times during the entire story, and this is one of them. The important point is that here, as in the other instances, Yahweh's activity is covert. David did not send Hushai to Jersusalem with instructions to confuse the advice Ahithophel would be giving to Absalom. He sent him to be a spy, and Hushai simply responded to the occasion that developed when he joined Absalom's company. Yet it is obvious that the narrator sees Yahweh at work, answering David's prayer and averting the danger to his throne.

This view of history marked the change to a new concept of

Yahweh's mode of revealing himself. It expressed the conviction that instead of manifesting himself intermittently through charismatic leaders like Moses or Deborah or Samuel, through catastrophic events like the Egyptian disaster at the Red Sea or the Midianite disaster at the brook of Kidron, or through sacral institutions like the holy war that functioned only during critical situations, Yahweh was continuously active in all departments of life, especially in men's attitudes, insights, impulses, thoughts, and resolves. The people involved in the events being narrated were not "religious characters." They pursued their own aims passionately and doggedly. But the author is convinced that in and through the working out of their several destinies, these very people were participating in Yahweh's historic purpose for his people.

Under immensely changed social and cultural circumstances the author gave effective expression to the distinctive Israelite conviction that Yahweh revealed himself historically rather than mythically. He built his story on the traditional pattern of a divine promise moving toward fulfillment, in this case Yahweh's promise to David and the tortuous but nevertheless inevitable road that led to the first instance of the promise being fulfilled. In the long run, the ability of the Davidic dynasty to maintain its continuity generation after generation led to a situation in which the David-Zion tradition functioned quasi-mythically, in the sense that no new chapter of sacred history was expected. As the gods had established the institutional pattern of the Egyptian and Mesopotamian empires "forever," so Yahweh had established the Davidic dynasty "forever." Nothing really new needed to happen.

Beyond Yahweh's covenant with David and his choice of Mount Zion as his permanent dwelling place Israel never recognized any further event capable of producing traditions. Even though the anonymous poet known as Second Isaiah hailed the return to Jerusalem of some exiles from Babylonia around 529 B.C. as another mighty saving act of Yahweh in history, the restored Jerusalem community did not append this event to the earlier series that ended with David and Zion. The expectation of a readiness for such events seems to have vanished. This was true of the "Israel" in the north (the kingdom of Israel, 930-721 B.C.) as well as the "Israel" in the south (the kingdom of Judah, 930-587 B.C.), except that in the north the series ended with Yahweh's giving Israel the land of Canaan, because the northern kingdom did not accept the David-Zion tradition. In both kingdoms a tremendous amount of literary work went on, however, which was predicated on the conviction that all the old tribal traditions, even the most sketchy and obscure ones of a small clan, had to do with one entity, Israel and the people of Yahweh, and therefore belonged to the total picture of Israel's history. According to von Rad,

> For Israel, especially the Israel of the later monarchical period, the saving history had come to a leisurely end. The consciousness of being herself involved at the centre of a history created by Jahweh had vanished (Isaiah 5:19; Zephaniah 1:12). The conservative circles of Jahwism concentrated all the more on making themselves at home in the long-hallowed traditions of God's mighty acts, and on formulating these traditions ever more carefully.[19]

This unique historical and literary effort indicates that no matter how close the parallels to a mythical orientation were in the David-Zion tradition, and no matter how generously both the Southern and the Northern kingdoms took over patterns from Mesopotamia and Egypt, the fact remains that the sacred history traditions continued to provide a core of conviction and meaning.

3

Disagreements over the Meaning of Sacred History

Despite the preservation of traditions of the past, however, tremendous tensions undoubtedly developed over the interpretation of sacred history and its significance for contempo-

[19] Von Rad, *op. cit.*, vol. I, p. 70.

rary life. It is true that in one way or another the conviction connected with the major components of the ancient heritage—the ancestors and Yahweh's promises to them, Yahweh's mighty deliverance in the Exodus events and during the conquest of Canaan, the covenant made at Mount Sinai, the divine instructions which included the demand for exclusive loyalty to Yahweh—kept reasserting themselves and nurturing the vision of a "true Israel," which each generation was supposed to try to become. But there were serious disagreements about the picture of the "true Israel" and also about the path to the goal. According to the view outlined in the preceding section, Yahweh's promises had been fulfilled in the David-Zion complex of persons, events, symbols, and monarchical institutions.[20]

The Northern Kingdom did not agree, and it actually never worked out a practical combination of the premonarchy Yahwist traditions and the political policy making necessary for a stable monarchy with anything approaching the success of the David-Zion construction. Thus, in the north the issue of the "true Israel" could turn toward political revolution against a dynasty charged with having taken a wrong path, or it could claim that, since monarchy had not been an original part of the heritage anyway, the crux of the call to be Yahweh's people was cultic, namely, correct worship and correct performance of the ethical duties prescribed by Yahweh.

The following examples are only two of many possible illustrations of the struggle that went on throughout the period of the two kingdoms (930-587 B.C.) over the character and implications of sacred history. The first is drawn from the history of the Northern Kingdom, and it shows how explosive the ancient claim of Yahweh to exclusive loyalty became when a powerful champion interpreted it radically and proceeded to translate

[20] Psalm 78:56-72 gives particularly interesting evidence. Here the kingdom of Judah interprets the fall of the north to the Assyrians in 721 B.C. as divine punishment, claims that Yahweh has transferred the Israelite heritage to the Southern Kingdom, and identifies the David-Zion establishment as the "true Israel." One of the most obscure and yet most important periods in the history of the literary process by which the comprehensive reconstruction of the age of the ancestors and the age of the Exodus and conquest was accomplished is the period following 721 B.C., when somehow Judah managed to transfer to Jerusalem the results of the extensive literary work that had been going on in the north.

his convictions into actions. The second is drawn from the later period of the history of the Southern Kingdom less than fifty years before Jerusalem was destroyed by the Babylonians and the Davidic dynasty was terminated. It shows how strong the trend had become to think of the core of sacred history in terms of Yahweh's words (his divine instructions) rather than his acts.

Elijah and Yahweh's claim to exclusive loyalty

The first section of this chapter emphasized not only the openness of Yahwism to ideas and practices not originally included in it but also the cultic intolerance that was implied by the demand that Israel must give exclusive loyalty to Yahweh. The second mentioned that the relationship of Yahweh to foreign gods entered a new phase when David incorporated large areas of Canaanite territory into his empire. This increase in the Canaanite element, which brought the fertility-oriented agricultural rites and practices into prominence at the expense of the old ideas about Yahweh, carried a potential explosiveness, but this did not become apparent for a long time. During the century after David's reign, the conviction that Yahweh should be worshiped in a distinctive way and that his will as expressed in the cultic laws called for a destructive kind of loyalty to him gradually deteriorated. Von Rad summarizes the situation succinctly:

> Looked at from the outside, almost everything connected with the cult was still what it had always been. The altars sent up their smoke, the customary prayers were offered, and the religious language and concepts which spoke to men's minds of Jahweh's self-revelation and of his acts may scarcely have changed. But were people still worshipping *Jahweh?* Was it not rather Baal,[21] with his control over the blessings of the world of nature, who was now in their minds? For Baal was nonetheless Baal, even when invoked by the name of Jahweh. Or was the object of worship some indeterminate third party who belonged somewhere between the two? [22]

---

[21] The Canaanite lord of fertility—C.L.

[22] Von Rad, *op. cit.,* vol. II, p. 15.

These questions were not faced seriously in the kingdom of Judah until the middle of the seventh century B.C. But in the Northern Kingdom, the original headquarters of the tribal confederation and thus the heartland of the ancient Yahwist traditions, the peril to Yahwism was brought out into the open and vigorously attacked as early as the reign of King Ahab (875-854 B.C.). A powerful spokesman for Yahweh named Elijah came on the scene and succeeded in forcing the Northern Kingdom to make a decision at the level of basic convictions, even though initially no one else seems to have felt that the issue Elijah pressed was either dangerous or critical. Elijah came from Gilead, a wilderness region east of the Jordan, which had been colonized long before by the Israelite tribes themselves and which had never been developed agriculturally as a part of Canaanite civilization. The Yahwist traditions had survived here and gave Elijah a basis for becoming horrified by what he saw going on in the Northern Kingdom. Specifically, he witnessed the threat to Yahwism created by the policies of King Ahab's father, Omri, and of Ahab himself. Omri and Ahab had embarked successfully on a program of empire building, which in certain respects was a carbon copy of the pattern devised by David. Like David, they deliberately gave their kingdom a new capital city, Samaria, which was an independent city-state with its own political system and its own cult, not in any way connected with Yahweh. But unlike David, Omri and Ahab did not adapt the religious traditions and cult of Samaria to the traditional convictions regarding Yahweh.

There was no covenant of Yahweh with Omri and his house, nor was there an ark of the covenant installed in the city to symbolize Yahweh's occupation of a place formerly alien to him. Baal was the god of Samaria, and he was not displaced in any clear-cut way. In addition, Ahab's Phoenician wife, the famous Jezebel, not only continued to practice her form of worship, a fertility-oriented cult devoted to the Baal of the city-state of Tyre, but was able to support a sizable staff of official functionaries of her cult while at the same time actively trying to eradicate all Yahwist functionaries. In the countryside, the people still worshiped the deity they thought of as Yahweh, but at court and in the city Yahweh was all but disregarded.

Without question Elijah understood the ancient conviction that Israel belonged to Yahweh alone in a much more radical way than it had been understood since the early days of the occupation. At that time and at Joshua's insistence, the tribes had made a covenant with Yahweh at Shechem in which they had promised exclusive loyalty and had actually removed the foreign gods from their midst. Probably most of Elijah's contemporaries, especially the city people, had never been told that a cooperative relationship between Yahweh and Baal was completely unacceptable, that in cult as well as in conviction it was a matter of a stark choice between Yahweh or Baal. Over many generations Israel had settled down in a typical Near Eastern agricultural environment where fertility rites of various kinds were integral to successful farming, and the farmers had accommodated themselves to the indigenous patterns with no clear sense of having betrayed Yahweh. Now Elijah stormed around the countryside issuing the ultimatum that in both city and country there must be a return to the ways of the ancestors who had never "bowed the knee to Baal."

Just how Elijah managed to arouse enough concern to bring about the religious assembly on Mount Carmel reported in the eighteenth chapter of First Kings (verses 20-39) we do not know. Perhaps Elijah's preaching was fanning the flame of resentment that the country folk felt toward the monarchy. Certainly Ahab did not have the advantage of the powerful and widely accepted David-Zion symbolism, which had helped to maintain the stability and continuity of the Davidic dynasty in Jerusalem.

At any rate, a meeting took place that is described as being somewhat like the assembling of the members of the sacral tribal association in the old days and particularly reminiscent of Joshua's Shechem assembly. Mount Carmel had been a holy "high place" from time immemorial, originally a domain of the Baal of Carmel, taken over by Yahweh for a time, then divided between the two cults with a Baal altar and a Yahweh altar standing side by side. When the assembly met, the Baal altar was being used regularly, but the Yahweh altar had fallen into disrepair. How could Elijah convince the people that coalescence, or even coexistence, of the two forms must be repudiated? According to the dramatic account in First Kings, Yahweh alone could convince them and Yahweh did. We do not know what official status the assembly had or how many people were there. We do not know whether King Ahab was actually there. Nor do we know whether the priests of Baal who are said to have entered into contest with

Elijah were anything more than the functionaries connected with the local Mount Carmel cult. We do know that an event occurred then that impressed those who were present in the same way that certain events had impressed previous Israelite generations during the premonarchy period. The people accepted Elijah's interpretation: Yahweh himself had once again intervened miraculously and had answered definitively the question of who really was the Lord of Israel.

The story goes on to report that all the priests of Baal were executed. This was not a matter of vengeance or mere fanaticism. It was a matter of putting into force a law that dated from the days of the tribal association, a law that called for the death penalty on any form of gross disloyalty towards Yahweh. As carried in the tradition it said that "whoever sacrifices to other gods shall be put to death" (Exodus 22:19), precisely the offense of which these men were guilty. Two hundred years later the Deuteronomic reformers emphasized the same law, thereby giving us impressive evidence of the fact that in spite of all tendencies to compromise or even to forget the Yahwist tradition, the continuity was never completely broken.

The original Mount Carmel incident may have been local, but it had national repercussions. As the story in chapter nineteen of First Kings about Jezebel's efforts to kill Elijah indicates, no dramatic revelation by Yahweh brought any wholesale change in the religious situation. Elijah was driven to such depths of despair that he contemplated suicide. But the account shows he became convinced that not only would a faithful minority maintain loyalty to Yahweh but also that a political situation was developing through which Yahweh would punish the house of Omri and the entire kingdom for its disloyalty to Him. In his wilderness hideout Elijah was confronted by Yahweh. A voice came to Elijah and said,

> "What are you doing here, Elijah?"
> And he said,
> "I have been very jealous for the LORD, the God of hosts, because the Israelites have forsaken the covenant with thee, thrown down thine altars, and slain thy prophets with the sword, and I, even I only, am left, and they are seeking to take away my life."
> But the LORD said to him, "Go, return on your way to the desert of Damascus, and when you arrive anoint Hazael to be

> king over Syria. And Jehu, the son of Nimshi, you shall anoint to be king over Israel, and Elisha, the son of Shaphat of Abel-meholah, you shall anoint to be prophet in your place. And it shall be that whoever escapes the sword of Hazael shall Jehu slay; and whoever escapes the sword of Jehu, shall Elisha slay. Yet will I spare seven thousand in Israel—all the knees that have not bowed to the Baal and every mouth which has not kissed him."[23]
>
> I KINGS 19:13-18

The implementation of Yahweh's judgment was the work of Elijah's successor, Elisha. Miracle stories abound in the picture of him given in Second Kings, but the focal point of his work was probably politics. His manipulations led to the anointing of Jehu and the bloody rebellion against the house of Omri. Jehu was a partisan of the kind of uncontaminated Yahwism demanded by Elijah and Elisha, and when Elisha designated him as Yahweh's chosen leader he was following another element in the tradition of the old tribal association, the conviction that leadership was a temporary office bestowed on certain individuals by Yahweh to meet specific crises.

> As they appear in the Old Testament, Elisha and Elijah, and many other key-figures of Jahwism also, were not simply devoted to what we think of as the world of religion and the spirit—faith, instruction, and worship—not even in their role as reformers: they were servants of Israel, and the life of Israel did not have only a religious aspect. She had a political life as well. She was an historical entity, living not only in the realm of the spirit but also in the world of politics: the dangers to which she was exposed were equally great in both of these, and in each she reqiured guidance and protection. Now Elisha regarded himself, and was regarded by others, precisely as the chosen instrument for Israel's defence and preservation—and by "Israel" is meant the true Israel, the Israel to which alone God granted the right to exist.[24]

The dynastic concept of monarchy never established itself securely in the Northern Kingdom. Monarchy remained under the aegis of the ancient charismatic concept of a call to a chosen man endowed with the special gifts required by the historic oc-

---

[23] Translated by Leroy Waterman.
[24] Von Rad, *op. cit.*, vol. II, pp. 28-29.

casion. The program carried through by Elisha harked back to convictions connected with the holy wars, in which the tribes were saved not by chariots and horses but by mighty acts of Yahweh. Jehu was the chosen instrument, but the aftermath of the revolution did not answer the question of how exclusive loyalty to Yahweh and the practical problems of Israel's existence in a world of power politics could be combined. The monarchy remained unstable, and the kings could not meet the Yahwist demand for avoidance of entangling alliances with foreign cults any more than the farmers in the country could refrain from relying on the Baal fertility practices.

The situation continued basically unchanged for another century, and then in 721 B.C. the Assyrians destroyed the kingdom. The expectation of Elijah and his prophetic successors in the north, that complete faithfulness to Yahweh would be achieved, had to be projected beyond this catastrophe. The literary prophets of the eighth century B.C. were quite explicit about the punishment Yahweh would bring through an Assyrian invasion. They were sure that the destruction of the Northern Kingdom was unavoidable, but they were equally convinced that Yahweh would create a new Israel out of a faithful minority who would survive the disaster. Elijah is reported to have shared this hope for a new Israel. In a sense, then, it is not enough to describe his work as an effort to restore an exclusive loyalty conceived in terms of the past. In fact, he was the forerunner of a group of prophetic messengers of Yahweh who waged violent warfare against all ideas deriving from the past and all tendencies toward revision or restoration. These men declared that sacred history was open-ended toward the future, and they found new implications for that future in the ancient demand for exclusive loyalty to Yahweh.

The Deuteronomic reform

For the Southern Kingdom of Judah, still ruled by the Davidic dynasty, the last part of the seventh century B.C. was an age of restoration. The dreaded power of the Assyrian empire was showing signs of decline, and King Josiah drew the logical conclusions from the changes that were occurring as the subjugated peoples began to stir and to hope for freedom. Josiah took the lead, for he saw the first real opportunity in more than two centuries of restoring the rule of the Davidic dynasty over the north, which was now divided among four Assyrian provinces. Gradually he widened his sphere of influence until he even occupied Philistine territory that had not belonged to the kingdom of Solomon and David. He came close to his goal of reviving the old dual monarchy, but in 609 B.C. his life and reign came to a sudden end on the battlefield of Megiddo.

Josiah did more, however, than merely attempt a physical restoration of the Davidic order. He tried to restore its inner character as well, in accordance with the concepts of his own time concerning the essentials of the tradition. It was for this reason that he took so seriously the discovery of a "Book of the Law" during building operations connected with restoring the state sanctuary in Jerusalem, in the eighteenth year of his reign (621 B.C.). The origins of the book are unknown. Presumably it was compiled by a priestly group early in the century and was based on various older collections of laws.[25] A marked feature of the book was the prominence of sermonic material, homiletic elaborations and exhortations designed to communicate the ancient tradition of divine instructions effectively and thus to gain recognition for it in an age when its ordinances were largely flouted. The entire book was cast in the form of a farewell address by Moses to the tribes before they entered Canaan, and it declared that Israel must prove itself loyal to Yahweh by refusing to take over any cult practices indigenous to Canaan. According to the Moses of Deuteronomy, cultic purity could be maintained only by centralizing all Israelite cultic celebrations and ceremo-

---

[25] Both Yehezkel Kaufmann and Gerhard von Rad develop a strong case for a northern origin of the Deuteronomic materials. One important piece of evidence is that no trace of David-Zion symbolism appears in them. Von Rad believes that the original compilers of the legal traditions and the preachers of sermons like those included in the book of Deuteromony belonged to the official priestly group known as the Levites. Kaufmann adds the idea that it was the Judean priesthood that not only took over the work begun in the north but also drew the ultimate inference that Yahweh's will called for the prohibition of all altars except the altar in the Jerusalem temple. See Kaufmann, *The Religion of Israel* (Chicago, 1960), pp. 172-75, 287-90; and Von Rad, *Old Testament Theology,* vol. I, pp. 71-77, 219-31.

nies. Theoretically, this policy could be linked with the original system of one central place of worship for the tribal confederation, but this was the first time in Israelite history that such a demand had actually been made. Local sanctuaries had flourished down through the centuries, and even such champions of exclusive loyalty to Yahweh as Elijah and his successors in the Northern Kingdom, Amos and Hosea, had not specified this type of violent infringment on the traditional religious life of the people as the answer to the crisis of Yahweh versus Baal. Yet this was what the book said, so this is what King Josiah did.

Josiah's concern to restore the Yahwist religious tradition can be seen in the fact that in implementing his decision to accord official recognition to the Book of the Law he did not simply exercise his royal authority and declare it to be a national law. Instead, he reverted to the old Sinai tradition of making a covenant. The report in the twenty-third chapter of Second Kings describes the procedure he followed.

> Then the king sent, and they gathered to him all the elders of Judah and Jerusalem. Thereupon the king went up to the house of the Lord and with him all the men of Judah and all the inhabitants of Jerusalem, including priests and prophets and all the people, both small and great; and he read in their hearing all the words of the book of the covenant which was found in the house of the Lord. Moreover the king stood by the column and made a covenant before the Lord, to walk after the Lord and to keep his commandments and his testimonies and his statutes with all earnestness and zeal, to establish the words of this covenant that are written in this book. And all the people confirmed the covenant.[26]
>
> II Kings 23:1-3

Interestingly enough, the role of Josiah himself in the covenant-making ceremony was parallel to the role of Moses in the original event at Mount Sinai. The partners were Yahweh on the one side and the people, represented by prominent citizens, on the other side, while the king officiated at the ceremony. Under ancient nomadic conditions the implications had been fairly unpolitical, but in the present situation the king's action amounted to a vague amalgamation of the religious order and

---

[26] Translated by Leroy Waterman.

the state. In the period after the destruction of the monarchy the combination of "church and state" actually took place, partly on the basis of Josiah's precedent, with the religious order dominant.

The vigorous steps Josiah took to enforce the Book of the Law are recounted in detail in the section of Second Kings that follows the story of the covenant-making ceremony. We shall quote a representative portion of the report, for it gives a vivid picture of the complex religious practices and conceptions that had to be ruthlessly discarded in order that the simple purity of worship demanded by the Book of the Law could be achieved.

> Then the king commanded Hilkiah, the high priest, and the second priest and the keepers of the threshold to bring out of the temple of the LORD all the vessels that were made for the Baal and the Asherah and for all the host of the heavens; and he burned them without Jerusalem in the limekilns by the Kidron, and carried their ashes to Bethel. He also removed the idolatrous priests, whom the kings of Judah had ordained to offer sacrifice in the high places in the cities of Judah and in the sanctuaries in the cities of Judah and in the sanctuaries around Jerusalem; and those who offered sacrifice to the Baal, to the sun, the moon, and the constellations, and all the host of the heavens. Moreover he brought the Asherah from the house of the LORD without Jerusalem to the Brook Kidron and burned it at the Brook Kidron, and beat it to dust, and cast its dust upon the graves of the common people. Furthermore he tore down the houses of the devotees of the fertility cult which were in the house of the LORD, where the women wove tunics for the Asherah. Then he brought all the priests from the cities of Judah and defiled the high places, where the priests offered sacrifices, from Geba to Beersheba.
>
> II KINGS 23:4-8a

From one point of view the Deuteronomic idea of centralizing all cultic activity can be interpreted as a consistent application of the conviction that the world of nature must not be considered holy in and of itself, that Yahweh must be worshiped as the One who reveals himself in and through human history. The eminent Israeli scholar, Yehezkel Kaufmann, offers such an interpretation.

> The ancient sanctuary of the Aaronic priesthood was the tent, a portable sanctuary unconnected with any sacred site. Although

> later the priesthood adopted the popular idea of the holiness of the land of Israel and, consequently, acquiesced in the worship at rural altars, the tension between the two concepts was dormant rather than dead. The idea that the land in general, and specific sites in particular, were holy savored strongly of the idea of natural sanctity. Popular temple legends sought to overcome this pagan savor by dating the holiness of sacred sites to patriarchal times, explicitly providing a historical-revelational, rather than a natural basis for their sanctity. In time, however, a more extreme idea developed. Cultic sanctity is not to be found anywhere and everywhere, not even in places that were consecrated by an ancient theophany, but only in the place that would be chosen by YHWH in the future. The Deuteronomic temple of the future is diametrically opposed to the pagan temple whose sanctity is "prehistoric," mythological.[27]

From the point of view of sacred history as a dynamic process that takes the past seriously but remains open to new and unexpected mighty acts of Yahweh, however, the fact that the Deuteronomic idea was historical rather than mythological is not decisive. The decisive fact is that the book actually refers to the past, for the so-called "temple of the future" turns out to be the old Mount Zion temple of the Davidic dynasty. Furthermore, the religious addresses that present the instructions of Yahweh for his people not only declare that he has already chosen his temple but also that he has already spoken his definitive word. As Von Rad says:

> There is no longer any question here of adding to the web of the old tradition itself, either by fresh combinations or by some other enriching addition. For these preachers the tradition itself is already fixed, and they understand their duty to it differently; they did not have to develop what had been handed down, but had rather to explain it. [28]

The Deuteronomic reformers saw their people still on the road toward becoming the "true Israel." Yet they believed that because the relationship between Yahweh and Israel had been made perfectly clear through the revelation of his will, no essential problem remained except the not insurmountable one of

---

[27] Kaufmann, *op. cit.*, pp. 289-90.
[28] Von Rad, *op. cit.*, vol. I, p. 72.

obedience. The Deuteronomic Moses encouraged his readers with these comforting words:

> "For this charge which I am enjoining on you today is not beyond your power, nor is it out of reach; it is not in the heavens, that you should say, 'O that someone would ascend to the heavens for us, and get to know it for us, and then communicate it to us, so that we may observe it!' Nor is it beyond the sea, that you should say, 'O that someone would cross the sea for us, and get to know it for us, and then communicate it to us, so that we may observe it!' No, the matter is very near you, on your mouth and in your mind, for you to observe."
>
> DEUTERONOMY 30:11-14

A distinction has to be made between the effect the Book of the Law had on later ages and its own claims about itself. The book was a reform document, and its authors were aware of the fact that their interpretation of Yahweh's will for Israel was one of a long series of attempts to define the contemporary meaning of the Sinai covenant. Later generations forgot the time factor and elevated Deuteronomy, along with the four other books that preceded it in the Old Testament (Genesis, Exodus, Leviticus, and Numbers), to a position of absolute authority. These five books (the Pentateuch) became the heart of the Torah ("teaching"), the most fundamental and most sacred part of the Hebrew scriptures. By 200 B.C. the written Torah was regarded as so sacred that not a sentence or a word could be changed. Israelite religion, which had increasingly become preoccupied with reinterpreting past history, developed into Judaism, which enshrined past history in such a way that it was no longer open to reinterpretation.

4

The Prophetic Attempt to Reopen Sacred History

It is hard for us to understand men like Amos, Hosea, Isaiah, and Jeremiah as they understood themselves because they have influenced our Western heritage so powerfully as pioneers of religious and moral universalism. The distinctiveness of the Israelite life-orientation has often been credited to these great men, especially during the past century when evolutionary theories were applied to Biblical history and the prophets became categorized as "the highest stage in the development of Old Testament religion." It is true that the writings of the prophets give us the most explicit formulations of the experiences and convictions that made the Israelite life-orientation fundamentally different from all other ancient Near Eastern traditions: (1) experiences of ultimacy that led to the conviction that Yahweh was beyond the cosmos and not to be identified with it; (2) experiences of time that led to the conviction that history was a series of events moving toward a goal set by Yahweh and being accomplished by him in and through the movements, crises, and achievements of human affairs; (3) experiences of the cosmos that led to the conviction that the world of nature was the setting rather than the model for the drama of human history. It is also true that the writings of the prophets contain the most eloquent denunciations of social injustice and the most persuasive appeals for social righteousness in the whole of the Old Testament literature, denunciations and appeals to which people in every part of the world have responded in subsequent ages. Thus, the tendency to take the prophets out of their own historical situation and to disregard their own view of their mission is understandable.

Unfortunately, generalizations underestimate the extent to which the experiences and convictions expressed in the sacred history narrative form permeated the core of the Israelite tradition during the many centuries preceding the literary prophets. It will be useful, therefore, to summarize again what might be called the inner logic of sacred history, which differentiated it from myth.

Both myth and sacred history transmitted experiences of authority and ultimacy. But myth located ultimacy in the timeless space of the cyclical order of the cosmos, while sacred history located the holy beyond space and time and yet simultaneously within space and time. The source of all sacredness was Yahweh, conceived to be impenetrable, mysterious, and utterly transcendent. But Yahweh had revealed his will and purpose in the creation events of Exodus and Sinai. This led to the conviction that nothing could be known about Yahweh except his purpose for man revealed in and through the time-space context in which man lives. Therefore, although the *source* of all holiness was utterly beyond the cosmos, the *expression* of holiness occurred in human history, a process conceived to be moving toward a divinely intended goal, a drama whose setting was the no longer divine physical cosmos.[29]

Another reason it is hard to understand men like Amos, Hosea, Isaiah, and Jeremiah is that in the Christian tradition they have simply been pictured as predictors of the coming of Jesus and men whose oracles are the basis for the Christian claim that the church rather than the Jewish people is the "true Israel." However legitimate or illegitimate this claim may be, to cast the prophets primarily in the role of predictors of the events out of which Christianity arose is once again to wrest them out of their

---

[29] In the memorable opening paragraph of his essay on "The Emancipation of Thought from Myth," Henri Frankfort has written:

> When we read in Psalm xix that 'heavens declare the glory of God; and the firmament sheweth his handiwork,' we hear a voice which mocks the beliefs of Egyptians and Babylonians. The heavens, which were to the psalmist but a witness of God's greatness, were to the Mesopotamians the very majesty of godhead, the highest ruler, Anu. To the Egyptians the heavens signified the mystery of the divine mother through whom man was reborn. In Egypt and Mesopotamia the divine was comprehended as immanent; the gods were in nature. . . . The God of the psalmists and the prophets was not in nature. He transcended nature—and transcended, likewise, the realm of mythopoeic thought.

Henri Frankfort (ed.), *Before Philosophy* (Baltimore, Md., 1949), p. 237. The "voice" to which Frankfort refers was most clearly articulated by the prophets, but the convictions it expressed were present long before their time.

original context. In their actual situation the prophets were patriots who sorrowfully, yet resolutely, announced that Yahweh had committed their country to physical destruction. Furthermore, they considered themselves messengers of Yahweh, not as forecasters or predictors. Their predictions of inevitable doom approaching in the form of the Assyrians, or later the Babylonians, had as much to do with the present as they did with the future. Most of their contemporaries looked back at the great events of the past that tradition credited to Yahweh, and believed that these saving events guaranteed perpetual security—even politically and militarily. This was especially true of the southerners, who not only looked upon Jerusalem as invulnerable to military attack but who more and more took it for granted that since Mount Zion was Yahweh's chosen dwelling place he simply would not allow Jerusalem to be conquered. As a result, the prophets used every possible rhetorical device in their preaching to convince their contemporaries that it was an illusion to trust in the past and that the reaction to coming events would be decisive. The message of these lonely, isolated, and often bitterly hated men was judged by some to be irritatingly irrelevant and by others to be dangerously subversive.

Yet these men loved Israel, and in announcing Yahweh's judgment (usually against their strong personal inclinations) they believed that in obeying Yahweh they were serving Israel. Their oracles, filled with capsule summaries of past sacred history, were challenges to their contemporaries, urging them to participate in the dynamic forward movement of sacred history rather than to revert to the cyclical rise and fall of kingdoms and empires. They were confident that disaster would never be Yahweh's last word or his final act. Beyond disciplinary severity lay a new beginning. Amos and Hosea expected a historical resurrection of Israel from its physical death, a new political Israel purged of its rebelliousness and vindicated by Yahweh before all the nations of earth. Isaiah counted on the continued existence of a small religious and moral elite, a "righteous remnant," which would be the nucleus for a new and permanent Covenant People governed by a model king. Jeremiah and the anonymous prophet we call the Second Isaiah seem to have realized that no concrete society in a definite political form will ever completely solve the problem of human order. Nevertheless, they believed that Yahweh would continue working in history and that in some way his covenant people would be a "light to lighten the Gentiles."

Amos and Hosea

Amos and Hosea (ca. 750 B.C.) were the first two prophets who wrote down their messages or whose oracles were recorded by disciples who were contemporary with them. These men saw glaring discrepancies between what they believed were the motivational and behavioral demands of Yahweh's covenant with Israel and the mores of the Northern Kingdom. They criticized both kings and people in the same terms: disloyalty to Yahweh was being expressed not simply in cultic deviations (foreign imports) but especially in moral deviations—various forms of callousness, exploitation, and injustice in social relations. The fact that neither the kings nor the people loved their neighbors as themselves proved that they did not love Yahweh. And if they did not love Yahweh, rituals, liturgies, processions, and support of flourishing religious institutions were expressions of self-assertion rather than of obedience. Amos and Hosea believed that Yahweh was rejecting the cultic tradition. In Amos, Yahweh says:

> "I hate, I spurn your feasts,
> And I take no pleasure in your festal gatherings.
> Even though you bring me your burnt-offerings,
> And your meal-offerings, I will not accept them;
> And the peace-offerings of your fatted beasts I will not look upon.
>
> "Take away from me the noise of your songs,
> And to the melody of your lyres I will not listen.
> But let justice roll down like waters,
> And righteousness like a perennial stream.[30]
>
> AMOS 5:21-24

> [Yahweh says] "They made kings; but it was not of my doing;
> They made princes; but without my knowledge.

---

[30] The passages from Amos, Hosea, and Micah have been translated by J. M. Powis Smith.

> Of their silver and their gold they made
> Idols for themselves, that they might be cut off.
> I loathe your bull, O Samaria.
> My anger blazes against them;
> How long will they be incapable of innocence?
> For from Israel is it;
> A mechanic made it;
> And it is not God.
> Indeed, Samaria's bull
> Shall become splinters."
>
> HOSEA 8:4-6

> [Yahweh says] "What shall I do with you, O Ephraim?
> What shall I do with you, O Judah?
> For your piety is like a morning cloud,
> And like the dew that goes early away.
> Therefore will I hew them by the prophets;
> I will slay them by the words of my mouth.
> And my judgment will go forth like the light.
> For I delight in piety, not sacrifice;
> And in the knowledge of God, rather than burnt-offerings.
>
> HOSEA 6:4-6

The best known of all prophetic exhortations of this type was delivered by the prophet Micah, a near contemporary of Amos and Hosea.

> Wherewith shall I come before the LORD,
> And bow myself before God most high?
> Shall I come before him with burnt-offerings,
> With calves a year old?
> Will the LORD be pleased with thousands of rams,
> With myriads of streams of oil?
> Shall I give my first-born for my transgression,
> The fruit of my body for the sin of my soul?
> You have been told, O man, what is good:
> Yet what does the LORD require of you,
> But to do justice, and to love kindness,
> And to walk humbly with your God?
>
> MICAH 6:6-8

Men who were able to articulate such messages saw that loyal existence under Yahweh meant love, humility, and righteousness of action rather than legality of conduct, whether ritual or moral.

But the real basis for their rejection of the cult was their conviction that the entire past was being rejected by Yahweh. They saw punishing and destructive actions of Yahweh approaching Israel which would demonstrate the inadequacy of the great saving events of the past like the Exodus-Sinai or the David-Zion covenants, but which would also lead to mysterious new acts of preservation.

Passing over the predictions of doom, which were intended to call Israel back to exclusive loyalty to Yahweh, we quote two examples of the positive expectations Amos and Hosea had for the future.

> [Yahweh says] "In that day I will raise up the fallen hut of David,
> And I will wall up its ruins,
> And raise up its breaches,
> And rebuild it as in the days of old;
> In order that they may possess the remnant of Edom and all the nations,
> Over whom my name is called." . . .
>
> "Behold the days are coming . . .
> When the plowman shall overtake the reaper,
> And the treader of grapes him who sows the seed;
> And the mountains shall drip new wine,
> And all the hills shall melt;
> And I will restore the fortune of my people Israel,
> And they shall rebuild the ruined cities,
> And dwell in them and plant vineyards,
> And drink their wine,
> And make gardens, and eat their fruit,
> And I will plant them upon their soil;
> And they shall not again be plucked up
> From upon their soil which I have given them."
>
> AMOS 9:13-15

> [Yahweh says] "In that day, it shall come to pass . . .
> That you will call me, 'My husband,'
> And you will no longer call me, 'My Baal.'
> For I will put away the names of the Baalim from her mouth,
> And they shall no longer be remembered by their name.
> In that day, I will make a league for them
> With the beasts of the field, the fowl of the heavens, and the creeping things of the ground;

And the bow, the sword, and war I will break off from the land;
And I will make them lie down in security."

And I will betroth you to myself forever;
I will betroth you to myself in righteousness, and in justice,
And in kindness and mercy.
And I will betroth you to myself in faithfulness;
And you shall know the LORD.
"It shall come to pass, in that day . . .
That I will answer the heavens,
And they shall answer the earth;
And the earth shall answer the grain, and the wine, and the
oil;
And they shall answer Jezreel;
And I will sow her for myself in the land,
And I will pity 'Her-who-is-unpitied';
And I will say to 'Not-my-people,' 'You are my people';
And he shall say, 'My God.' "

HOSEA 2:16-23

Even though Amos and Hosea believed the past to be dead, they used tradition-hallowed images in their attempts to picture the new Israel Yahweh would create. They used both the David-Zion imagery of a Davidic kingdom and the much more ancient Exodus-Sinai imagery of Yahweh's covenant with Israel. Amos treated the resurrection of Israel in simple terms of restoration, rebuilding, prosperity, and peace. Hosea went further. He introduced a number of terms to describe the reordering of human relationships through true knowledge of Yahweh: righteousness, justice, kindness, mercy, faithfulness, love. These qualities translated the thou-shalt-nots of the Ten Commandments into positive character traits that would guarantee obedience to the spirit of the covenant law. Externalization of relationships between Yahweh and his people in cultic and social mores would be reversed. The meaning of sacred history would first be radically internalized so that then it could be adequately externalized on the plane of historical existence by the "true Israel." In other words, the will of Yahweh would be formed in the "inner man" as a personal order of Yahweh, and this personal order would function effectively as the foundation of the new kingdom of Israel.

References by both Amos and Hosea to the world of nature indicate that their hopes included a cosmic dimension involving every aspect of earthly reality. Curiously enough, the confidence of Amos and Hosea that a new Israel would be created after disciplinary action was parallel in some ways to Egyptian expectations during the First Intermediate Period, as they were expressed in the "Prophecy of Nefer-Rohu," written somewhere around 2050 B.C.

> [I show thee the land topsy-turvy.] The weak of arm is [now] the possessor of an arm. Men salute [respectfully] him who [formerly] saluted. I show thee the undermost on top, turned about [in proportion to] the turning about [of my belly]. Men live in the necropolis. The poor man will make wealth. . . . It is the paupers who eat the offering-bread, while the servants [jubilate]. The Heliopolitan nome, the birthplace of every god, will no [[longer] be on earth].
>
> [[Then] it is that a king will come, belonging to the South,] Ameni the triumphant, his name. He is the son of a woman of the land of Nubia; he is one born in Upper Egypt. He will take the [White] Crown; he will wear the Red Crown; he will unite the Two Mighty Ones; he will satisfy the Two Lords [Horus and Seth] [31] with what they desire.[32]

Since it is integral to the cosmic structure of reality, the institution of divine kingship will be restored. But Nefer-Rohu expressed confidence that continuity with the institutions and the life-orientation of the Old Kingdom would be reestablished because he believed that the divine kingship was integral to the very structure of the cosmos. The pattern of ritual renewal of the cosmos hovered in the background.

The references of Amos and Hosea to the world of nature did not rest on this pattern but on the conviction that Yahweh was Lord of all reality. Therefore, instead of referring to myths about the gods and expecting a repetition of the heavenly archetypal events through which the gods had shaped the cosmos and society, they referred to history whose inner dynamics were oriented toward the future. They were not sympathetic to the restoration of an order already known. Their oracles expressed the conviction that Yahweh was urging his people forward to a new historical order, which they pictured as somehow free from

---

[31] C.L.

[32] Pritchard (ed.), *Ancient Near Eastern Texts,* pp. 445-46.

the evils of the present that were leading Israel to inevitable destruction.

But neither prophet dealt directly with the ambiguities and tensions generated by the fact that for more than two centuries the life of Israel had been built on conflicting experiences. The relationship between Yahweh's demand for exclusive loyalty and the political structure of monarchy had created tensions in the Northern Kingdom because the David-Zion solution of the problem had not been accepted. Neither Amos nor Hosea seems to have realized that if the permanent new order they expected after a tragic interlude was to survive in a world of power politics these conflicting experiences must be reconciled.

Isaiah

The southern prophet Isaiah, who began his work in Jerusalem about 742 B.C., explored this issue with remarkable persistence and profundity. He recognized that unless new ways of talking about the ordering of human affairs could be developed—specifically, symbols connected with kingship—Yahweh's purpose for his people and his way of "making history" though his people would not be understood. The evolution of Isaiah's preoccupation with royal symbolism can be traced in chapters six to twelve of the Book of Isaiah. It begins with a significant detail: the prophet's call to be a messenger of Yahweh occurred in the year that King Uzziah died. The passing of the old king and the transfer of royal power, always critical events, crystallized his concerns. An overwhelming experience of Yahweh's transcendent kingship, described in the first thirteen verses of chapter six, convinced Isaiah that the key to the transformation of the world into the kingdom of Yahweh was a responsive change of heart. He himself responded to Yahweh's challenge in spite of a sense of inadequacy and a nagging awareness that he might not awaken a similar response in his king or in his people. He was gripped so powerfully by the experience of Yahweh's "glory" (ultimacy) that he could not doubt Yahweh's intention to establish his kingly rule here and now. The Yahweh of Exodus, of the holy wars, of David's unbroken record of victories, was a Yahweh who could be counted on to purify his undeserving people, just as he had purified Isaiah, and to bring them to their destined perfection.

The story of the Exodus was the basis for the cult legends including an expectation that Yahweh would vindicate his people in extraordinary ways while they simply trusted him and watched him throw their enemies into flight, leaving them only the mopping-up operations. The Gideon story pointed out that this blind faith might even require Israel to be "weak" in order that no man or group could boast of winning the victory. Since the pivotal point of contact between Yahweh's kingship and the organized institutional life of Yahweh's people had become the king, Isaiah's effort to foster absolute trust in Yahweh was focused first on the king. The practical (or impractical) implications of Isaiah's convictions led him to intervene in a dangerous military situation that developed several years after he had begun his career as a phophet. Israel and Syria combined against Judah in an attempt to replace King Ahaz (r. 735-715 B.C.) with a puppet king who would cooperate with them in an anti-Assyrian coalition. Ahaz was so terrified that he burned his son as an offering in the hope that this sacrifice would satisfy what he took to be divine anger and that it would buy security. Not long afterward, when Ahaz was inspecting the Jerusalem water supply, undoubtedly trying to calculate how long the city could hold out if it was beseiged, the Lord directed Isaiah to meet Ahaz and deliver the following message:

> "Take care, and keep calm! Do not be afraid nor downhearted because of these two tails of smoking firebrands . . ." thus says the Lord GOD: "It shall not stand, and it shall not be! . . . If you do not believe, surely you shall not be established."[33]
>
> ISAIAH 7:4, 7, 9

Isaiah believed that if the king would trust Yahweh completely the military crisis would be dissipated. By not presuming to take any calculated action himself, the king would clear the way for Yahweh to intervene with a mighty act of deliverance. Isaiah also seems to have believed that if Ahaz responded correctly he

---

[33] Translated by Alexander R. Gordon.

would become the agent through whom Yahweh's "glory" could flow into the world and completely transfigure society.

King Ahaz did not respond. In fact, he did not even speak. When Isaiah offered him a "sign" to confirm the truth of his oracle, Ahaz declined. This refusal forced Isaiah to give up any hope he had for a decisive leap toward the transformation of human history into the "kingdom of God" in his generation. He turned toward the future, pressing upon Ahaz the "sign" he did not want. It took the form of an oracle concerning Ahaz's successor.

> "Hear now, O House of David! Is it too slight a thing for you to weary men, that you must weary my God [34] also? Therefore the Lord himself will give you a sign: Behold! a young woman is with child, and is about to bear a son; and she will call him 'God is with us.' Curds and honey will be his food when he knows how to refuse the bad and choose the good. For before the child knows how to refuse the bad and choose the good, the land before whose two kings you stand in dread will be forsaken. The LORD will bring upon you, and upon your people, and upon your father's house, such days as have not come since the day that Ephraim parted from Judah, even the king of Assyria."
>
> ISAIAH 7:13-17

We do not know how much publicity Isaiah and his disciples gave this oracle who announced that they were looking forward to Ahaz's successor. There may have been some trouble; if not, certainly there was frustration. Isaiah decided not to divulge his later prophecies concerning the new ruler to anyone except his immediate disciples, to whom he assigned the role of the "remnant" foreseen by Amos:

> [Yahweh says] "Behold, the eyes of the Lord GOD are upon the sinful kingdom;
> And I will destroy it upon the surface of the ground,
> Except that I will not wholly destroy the house of Jacob."
>
> AMOS 9:8

---

[34] The Gordon translation uses the Lord God or my God rather than the name Yahweh in these passages from Isaiah—C.L.

This group was something more than Amos's remnant, however. It was what we would call a creative minority, and it perpetuated itself for many generations after Isaiah's life work ended. The disciples kept Isaiah's secret and waited for the promised king. The secret message they preserved has been no secret for the past nineteen hundred years:

> The people that walked in darkness
> Have seen a great light;
> Those who dwelt in a land of deep darkness—
> On them has light shone.
> Thou hast multiplied the nation, thou hast increased its joy:
> They rejoice before thee as with the joy in harvest,
> As men exult when they divide the spoil.
> For the yoke that was their burden,
> And the bars upon their shoulder,
> The rod of their master,
> Thou has broken in pieces as on the day of Midian.
> For every boot worn by booted warrior in the fray,
> And war cloak stained with blood,
> Will be for burning—food for the fire.
> For a child is born to us, a son is given to us;
> And the government will be upon his shoulder;
> And his name will be
> "Wonderful counselor, Godlike hero,
> Father forever, Prince of peace."
> Of the increase of his government, and of peace,
> There will be no end,
> Upon the throne of David, and over his kingdom,
> To establish it, and to uphold it,
> In justice and in righteousness,
> From henceforth, even forever.
> The zeal of the LORD of hosts will do this.
>
> ISAIAH 9:2-7

Why did Isaiah make this message "the testimony bound up, and the instruction sealed"? Martin Buber suggests that the last line, "The zeal of the LORD of hosts will do this," is the clue. The oracle not only paints a picture of perfection but also announces that the coming of the never-ending era of prosperity and peace will in no sense be a human achievement. It will be an entirely new creation designed and delivered by Yahweh alone. Such a vision was important only to the circle Isaiah gathered around him, whom he looked upon as the nucleus of the new Israel, and whose very existence seemed to him to be evidence of Yahweh's intentions. Ahaz's successor was not the expected perfect king, which meant that undoubtedly Yahweh was waiting until a national disaster had destroyed the old order before he would establish the new order under the promised king.

Isaiah's preoccupation with symbols of kingship and his conviction that the Davidic dynasty had been designated by Yahweh to be the bearer of kingship forever is nowhere better illustrated than in another oracle much emphasized in the Christian tradition because the early Christians applied it to Jesus:

> A shoot will spring from the stem of Jesse,
> And a sprout from his roots will bear fruit.
> And the spirit of the Lord will rest upon him—
> The spirit of wisdom and understanding,
> The spirit of counsel and might,
> The spirit of knowledge and the fear of the Lord—
> And his delight will be in the fear of the Lord.
> He will not judge by that which his eyes shall see,
> Nor decide by that which his ears shall hear;
> But with justice will he judge the needy,
> And with fairness decide for the poor of the land;
> He will smite the ruthless with the rod of his mouth,
> And with the breath of his lips will he slay the wicked.
> Righteousness will be the girdle round his loins,
> And faithfulness the girdle round his waist.
> Then the wolf will lodge with the lamb,
> And the leopard will lie down with the kid;
> The calf and the young lion will graze together,
> And a little child will lead them.
> The cow and the bear will be friends,
> Their young ones will lie down together;
> And the lion will eat straw like the ox.
> The suckling child will play on the hole of the asp,
> And the weaned child will put his hand on the viper's den.
> They will do no harm nor destruction
> On all my holy mountain;
> For the land will have become full of the knowledge of the Lord,
> As the waters cover the sea.
>
> Isaiah 11:1-9

As the first two lines suggest, here is a second remnant, a representative of the Davidic kingship sprouting from the left-over stem and roots of the house of Jesse (David's father); he will build his kingdom with those who remain of the Covenant People (Isaiah's "remnant" of disciples). The king described in this visionary oracle combines power with goodness and goodness with power. His perfection also has cosmic dimensions; it radiates into the world of nature and transfigures it into a realm of harmony in which all forms of life affirm one another instead of preying upon one another.

Before describing the king and the world of nature, Isaiah forecast the central realm from which knowledge of Yahweh and of his instructions would spread through the whole world of nations and peoples.

> Now in the end of the days,
> The mountain of the LORD's house will be
> Established on the top of the mountains,
> And lifted above the hills.
> And all the nations will stream to it,
> Many peoples will go and say:
> "Come! let us go up to the mountain of the LORD,
> To the house of the God of Jacob;
> That he may instruct us in his ways,
> And that we may walk in his paths;
> For out of Zion goes forth instruction,
> The word of the LORD out of Jerusalem."
> Then will he judge between the nations,
> And will arbitrate for many peoples;
> And they will beat their swords into plowshares,
> And their spears into pruning-hooks;
> Nation will not lift up sword against nation,
> And they will learn no more the art of war.
>
> ISAIAH 2:2-4

Jerusalem, the holy city, located at the top of Mount Zion, the holy mountain, is a direct application of the Mesopotamian ziggurat symbolism in a setting where no artificial mountain needs to be built because a suitable hill is already there. The imperial cosmological symbolism is clear: just as Babylon is the center of empire, a "gate of the gods" (Babi-lani) with the ziggurat as the connecting link between earth and heaven, so Mount Zion shall be exalted above every mountain, above every ziggurat, and Jerusalem will be the point of meeting between Yahweh and the whole of mankind. But it is also clear that we are no longer in human history as we normally experience it. We have reached the *eschaton,* the "end of days," when all tensions between divine purpose and human society have been resolved, when Yahweh himself will be the judge among the nations, and when political institutions now essential for maintaining existence in a precarious world will fade away.

Thus the prophecies of Isaiah move from an appeal to the real king, Ahaz, to the "sign" of a more responsive successor, Emmanuel; then they move on from Emmanuel to the Prince of Peace who will build his kingdom with the remnant Isaiah is forming around himself, his disciples; the next step is a shift from the Prince of Peace to a single remnant of the Davidic dynasty on whom the spirit of Yahweh has descended; and finally even the monarchy in any realistic political sense disappears because the spirit of Yahweh has transformed human nature and a universal order of harmony and peace emanates from Yahweh's house on Mount Zion.

Jeremiah

Isaiah instructed his disciples to wait for a future that would be created by Yahweh alone. Apparently they followed his instructions, and the sheer waiting may have led to a certain sterility. At any rate, a century passed before Jeremiah, another prophet comparable to Isaiah, appeared on the scene. When he did appear he seems to have been more influenced by the writings of Hosea than by the prophecies and symbols treasured by Isaiah's disciples. Jeremiah reverted to the Amos-Hosea type of expectation: a remnant would survive political catastrophe, and it would be ruled by a Davidic-model king. Like Amos and Hosea also, Jeremiah concentrated on the untransfigured present rather than on futuristic, super-historical dreams that tended to abandon the present to its disorder.

But Jeremiah, like Isaiah, was forced to give up hope for a decisive leap forward in his own generation. Isaiah had been disappointed by King Ahaz, who refused to put complete trust in Yahweh ahead of political and military calculations. Jeremiah was disappointed by the Deuteronomic program of reform described earlier in this chapter (see pp. 139-44). Jeremiah's personal struggle concerning the will of Yahweh and his certainty that a stormy future lay ahead for the kingdom of Judah convinced him that Yahweh had neither spoken his last word to his people nor performed his last mighty act of creation in human history. The crisis confronting Jeremiah's people had its counterpart in his career, and in leaving a record of his struggle in the form of a spiritual autobiography he created a new type of religious expression. This record shows that he broke through the density of Israel's collective tradition and emerged on a new level of human individuality. Specifically, he became convinced that, at least temporarily, the Chosen People of Yahweh had been replaced by a chosen man—Jeremiah himself. This appears to be megalomania, but as translated into more general concepts by Voegelin, Jeremiah's insight seems remarkably sane: "the order of society in history is reconstituted in fact through the men who challenge the disorder of the surrounding society with the order they experience as living in themselves." [35]

Four oracles reported in the first chapter of the Book of Jeremiah are a remarkable demonstration of the prophet's ability to find symbols for expressing the experiences which convinced him that Yahweh was making a complete change in his strategy.

> The word of the LORD came to me, saying,
> "Before I formed you in the womb I knew you,
> And before you were born I set you apart for my service—
> I appointed you a prophet to the nations."
> Then said I,
> "Ah, Lord GOD! I cannot speak;
> For I am only a boy."
>
> But the LORD said to me,
> "Do not say, 'I am only a boy;'
> For to all to whom I send you shall you go,
> And all that I command you shall you speak.
> Do not be afraid of them;
> For I am with you to deliver you,"
> Is the oracle of the LORD.

---

[35] Voegelin, *op. cit.*, vol. I, p. 483.

Then the LORD stretched forth his hand, and touched my mouth.
And the LORD said to me,
"See! I put my words in your mouth;
This moment I give you authority over the nations and kingdoms,
To root up and to pull down, to wreck and to ruin,
To build and to plant."

The word of the LORD came to me, saying,
"What do you see, Jeremiah?"
I answered,
"I see a twig of an almond tree."
Then the LORD said to me,
"You have seen well; for I am watching over my word to carry it into effect."
A second time the word of the LORD came to me, saying,
"What do you see?"
I answered,
"I see a boiling pot, facing from the north."

Then the LORD said to me, "Out of the north shall trouble boil over all the inhabitants of the land. For behold! I am summoning all the kingdoms of the north," is the oracle of the LORD; "and they shall come and set up their several thrones at the entrances of the gates of Jerusalem, and against all her walls round about, and against all the cities of Judah. And I will pronounce my judgments against them for all the wickedness they have done in forsaking me, and offering sacrifice to other gods, and worshiping the works of their own hands. You, then, gird up your loins, and arise, and speak to them all that I command you. Do not be dismayed before them, lest I dismay you before them. For behold! I make you this moment a fortified city, an iron pillar, and a bronze wall, against the whole land—the kings of Judah, its princes and priests, and its common people. They shall fight against you, but they shall not overcome you; for I am with you to deliver you," is the oracle of the LORD.[36]

JEREMIAH 1:4-19

The first oracle announces that the prophet is the son of God. Long ago the son of God symbol had been used to refer to the

[36] Translated by Alexander R. Gordon.

Covenant People. Later on, David and his dynasty had claimed it: the Davidic king was the son of God. (Isaiah, incidentally, used the symbol in both ways.) Now the sonship has been transferred to Jeremiah.[37] The royal dimension is somewhat obscured by the fact that he is appointed "a prophet to the nations" rather than a king, but the third oracle adds this dimension. Not only is the prophetic message intended for the nations rather than for Israel alone, but Jeremiah is given kingly authority over the nations. He is in charge of them. It is true that the conviction that Yahweh is the universal Lord of history already appears in Amos:

> "Are you not like the Ethiopians in my sight,
> O Israelites"; it is an oracle of the LORD.
> "Did I not bring up Israel from the land of Egypt,
> Also the Philistines from Caphtor, and the Syrians from Kir?"
>
> AMOS 9:7

But that Yahweh's messenger is a "prophet to the nations" does not become fully intelligible until Jeremiah makes explicit the implication that as the messenger of the universal Lord of history he brings a message for all men.

Even so, the kingly authority of the prophet to the nations is highly unusual, for it is not visible. The third oracle contains a paradox. Yahweh says, "See! I put my words in your mouth. This day I give you authority over the nations and kingdoms. . . ." Jeremiah's authority will be audible rather than visible.

The second oracle projects Jeremiah into a situation of protest. Like Moses, who was reported to have resisted Yahweh's command to lead the tribes out of Egypt, Jeremiah protests that

---

[37] Archeologists have found an inscription of Assurbanipal, the Assyrian ruler who controlled the Kingdom of Judah when Jeremiah was a boy, which uses the same type of language:

> "I am Assurbanipal, offspring of Assur and Belit . . . whose name Assur and Sin, the lord of the tiara, have named for the kingship from distant days, whom they formed in his mother's womb, for the rulership of Assyria; whom Shamash, Adad, and Ishtar, by their unalterable decree, have ordered to exercise sovereignty."

D. D. Luckenbill, *Ancient Records of Assyria and Babylonia* (Chicago, 1926), vol. I, section 765.

he is a poor choice for the role of messenger. And like Moses, he is overruled. Furthermore, Yahweh says, "Be not afraid of them; for I am with you to deliver you." Traditionally the phrases "I am with you" and "I will help you" had been associated with the name Yahweh. The same phrase occurs also at the end of the fourth oracle, which suggests that Jeremiah plumbed the depths of the Exodus-Sinai tradition. Finally, we should mention the symbolism of the dramatic battle that Yahweh foresees between the "old Chosen People" and the new "Chosen One," between the Kingdom of Judah and Jeremiah. Jeremiah becomes a "Jerusalem" himself: "For behold, I make you this day a fortified city, an iron pillar, and a bronze wall . . . ." Jeremiah must take upon himself the crisis confronting his people: What does it mean *now* that Yahweh is the God of Israel and that Israel is the Covenant People of Yahweh?

We have described the most fundamental dimension of Jeremiah's prophetic experience. Two more dimensions should be added, one public and the other personal. As a result of his effort to speak Yahweh's words Jeremiah became a marked man, a public enemy suspected of treason and treachery. At one point certain men from his home town of Anathoth, apparently ashamed of Jeremiah's bad reputation and resentful of aspersions being directed toward him, decided to take matters into their own hands:

> The LORD informed me, and I knew—
> I saw what they were doing.
> But I had been like an innocent lamb
> That is led to the slaughter;
> I knew not that they had plotted against me, saying,
> "Let us destroy the tree with its sap,
> Let us cut him off from the land of the living,
> That his name may be remembered no more!"
> O LORD of hosts, thou who judgest righteously,
> Who testest the heart and the conscience,
> Let me see thy vengeance upon them,
> For to thee have I confided my cause!
>
> Therefore thus says the LORD regarding the men of Anathoth who seek your life, saying, "You shall not prophesy in the name of the LORD, lest you die by our hands!"— thus says the LORD of hosts:

"Behold! I will punish them;
Their young warriors shall die by the sword,
And their sons and their daughters shall die by famine.
No remnant shall be left to them,
For I will bring trouble upon the men of Anathoth,
Even their year of reckoning."

JEREMIAH 11:18-23

Another plot against Jeremiah's life is noted in chapter eighteen:

"Come and let us hatch a plot against Jeremiah,
For instruction shall not pass from the priest,
Nor counsel from the wise, nor the word from the prophet;
Come and let us smite him for his speech,
And let us pay no more heed to any of his words!"

Pay thou heed to me, O LORD;
And listen to my plea!
Shall evil be repaid for good,
That they have dug a pit for my life?
Remember how I stood before thee
To intercede in their favor,
To avert thy wrath from them!

JEREMIAH 18:18-21

Finally, during the last days before Jerusalem was conquered by the Babylonian army, Jeremiah was arrested as a deserter when he tried to leave Jerusalem on business during a temporary raising of the siege at the time when Egyptian forces had moved up from the south and the Babylonians had to deal with this threat.

Now when the Chaldean army had raised the siege of Jerusalem because of the advance of Pharaoh's army, Jeremiah set out from Jerusalem on a journey to the land of Benjamin, to take possession of the property that belonged to him among the people there. But just as he reached the Benjamin Gate, a sentry who was posted there . . . arrested Jeremiah the prophet, saying, "You are deserting to the Chaldeans."

Jeremiah replied, "It is false; I am not deserting to the Chaldeans."

But he would not listen to him. So Irijah arrested Jeremiah, and brought him to the princes. And the princes were so angry with Jeremiah that they beat him and put him in prison in

> the house of Jonathan the secretary, which had been turned into a prison. Having thus come to the dungeon-cells, Jeremiah remained there for a number of days.
>
> Then King Zedekiah sent for him, and received him; and the king asked him secretly in his palace, "Is there any word from the Lord?"
>
> And Jeremiah said, "There is. You shall be given into the hand of the king of Babylon."
>
> . . .
>
> King Zedekiah then gave orders, and Jeremiah was committed to the guard-court, and given a loaf of bread daily from the bakers' street, until all the bread in the city was consumed. So Jeremiah remained in the guard-court.
>
> Jeremiah 37:11-18, 21

If it had not been for a friend, Ebedmelech, Jeremiah would have been killed. Certain princes actually threw him into an old cistern and left him there to die. He sank in the mud, but there was not enough water to drown him, and Ebedmelech succeeded in persuading the king to have him pulled out before he starved. Jeremiah was still in jail when the Babylonians took over the city, and they, rather than his own countrymen, released him. We have reviewed this series of narrow escapes as one way of indicating the tragic proportions of Jeremiah's love for his people and of their hatred toward him.

The private, personal dimension of Jeremiah's career—his inner struggle during his public rejection and disgrace—is revealed in a great number of autobiographical reports. We shall limit ourselves to five examples. The first begins with a clear piece of evidence that Jeremiah broke away from the compact experience of collective guilt and collective punishment that thwarted the discovery of geniune individuality up to this point in Biblical history.

> The heart is treacherous above all things, and desperately sick—
> Who can understand it?
> "I the Lord am a searcher of the heart,
> A tester of the conscience;
> That I may give to every man according to his ways,
> According to the fruit of his doings."
>
> Jeremiah 17:9-10

In the same passage Jeremiah goes on to draw out the implications, and then he protests vehemently against Yahweh's failure to reward him for his obedience by punishing those who oppose him:

O LORD, thou hope of Israel,
All who forsake thee shall be put to shame,
Those who prove faithless to thee in the land shall be brought to confusion,
Because they have forsaken the LORD,
The fountain of living water.
Heal me, O LORD, that I may be healed;
Save me, that I may be saved;
For thou art my praise.
Lo! they continue saying to me,
"Where is the word of the LORD?
Pray, let it come!"
Yet I never urged thee to bring trouble upon them,
Nor longed for the fatal day—
Thou knowest!
That which came out of my lips was open before thee.
Be not a terror to me,
Thou who art my refuge on the day of trouble!
Let them be put to shame that persecute me,
But let me not be put to shame;
Let them be confounded,
But let me not be confounded;
Bring upon them the day of trouble,
With double destruction destroy them!

JEREMIAH 17:13-18

The next two examples show Jeremiah in open contention with Yahweh, raising questions and demanding answers.

Ah me, my mother! that you bore me
As a man of strife and a man of contention to all the earth!
I have neither lent nor borrowed,
Yet all of them curse me.
So be it, O LORD, if I have failed to entreat thee,
Or to plead with thee for the good of my enemies,
In their time of trouble and trial!
Have I an arm of iron,
Or a brow of bronze?

JEREMIAH 15:10-12

Jeremiah is defensive about his vengeful wishes, but he refuses to repress them or to give them up: "So be it." Incidentally, the answer to the question is "yes." In the oracles of chapter one of the Book of Jeremiah we heard Yahweh say that he would make Jeremiah "an iron pillar and a wall of bronze." The passage continues:

> Thou knowest, O Lord!
> Think of me, and visit me;
> Avenge me on my persecutors,
> Through thy forbearance put me not off.
> Know that for thy sake I have borne reproach
> From those who despise thy words.
> As for me, thy word is my joy and delight;
> For I bear thy name, O Lord, God of hosts!
> I sat not in the company of the sportive,
> Nor made merry with them;
> Under thy mighty power I sat alone,
> For thou didst fill me with indignation.
> Why is my pain unceasing, my wound incurable,
> Refusing to be healed?
> Wilt thou really be to me like a treacherous brook,
> Like waters that are not sure?
>
> Jeremiah 15:15-18

This time there is no answer. Yahweh charges Jeremiah with disloyalty and challenges him to renewed obedience, repeating again the "Yahweh formula":

> Therefore thus says the Lord:
> "If you turn, I will restore you,
> And you shall stand in my presence;
> And if you bring forth what is precious, without anything base,
> You shall be my mouthpiece.
> They may turn to you,
> But you shall not turn to them.
> And I will make you toward this people
> A fortified wall of bronze;
> They may fight against you,
> But they shall not overcome you;
> For I am with you to help you,
> And to deliver you," is the oracle of the Lord.
>
> Jeremiah 15:19-20

Jeremiah finds no peace. The questions keep coming back. In the next example we find him presenting them as a legal case, as though he were in court, and asking for a decision.

> Thou must be in the right, O Lord,
> If I take issue with thee;
> Yet would I lay my case before thee:
> Why does the way of the wicked prosper?
> Why do all the faithless live in comfort?
> Thou plantest them, and they take root;
> They grow, and they bring forth fruit;
> Near art thou in their mouths,
> But far from their thoughts.
>
> Jeremiah 12:1-2

Once again Jeremiah assumes that individuals should be dealt with as individuals. He also insists that the guilty must be punished and the virtuous (like himself!) rewarded. Why, when misery comes, is it inflicted on the faithful as well as on the wicked?

> Yet thou, O Lord, knowest me,
> Thou seest me, and testest my mind toward thee.
> Pull them out like sheep for the shambles,
> And devote them to the day of slaughter!
> How long must the land mourn,
> And all the herbs of the field wither?
> Through the wickedness of those who dwell in it
> Beast and bird are swept away;
> For they say, "God is blind to our ways."
>
> Jeremiah 12:3-4

Again there is no answer; only a counterquestion:

> [Yahweh says] "If you have raced with men on foot, and they have beaten you,
> How will you compete with horses?
> And if you take to flight in a safe land,
> How will you do in the jungle of Jordan?"
>
> Jeremiah 12:5

The final two autobiographical excerpts are even more personal than the first three, in that they reveal Jeremiah's longing to be free of the burden of being Yahweh's messenger, his discovery that Yahweh had grasped him so firmly that he cannot escape from doing his duty as he sees it, and his temptation to give in to resentful despair.

> Thou hast duped me, O LORD, and I let myself be duped;
> Thou hast been too strong for me, and hast prevailed.
> I have become a laughing-stock all day long,
> Everyone mocks me.
> As often as I speak, I must cry out,
> I must call, "Violence and spoil!"
> For the word of the LORD has become to me
> A reproach and derision all day long.
> If I say, "I will not think of it,
> Nor speak any more in his name,"
> It is in my heart like a burning fire,
> Shut up in my bones;
> I am worn out with holding it in—
> I cannot endure it.
> For I hear the whispering of many,
> Terror all around.
>
> JEREMIAH 20:7-10

> Cursed be the day on which I was born,
> The day on which my mother bore me—
> Let it not be blessed!
> Cursed be the man who brought the good news to my father,
> "A son is born to you"—
> Wishing him much joy!
> Let that man be like the cities
> Which the LORD overthrew without mercy;
> Let him hear a cry in the morning,
> And an alarm at noon;
> Because he let me not die in the womb,
> That my mother might have been my grave,
> And her womb have remained pregnant forever!
> Why came I out of the womb,
> To see trouble and sorrow,
> That my days might be spent in shame?
>
> JEREMIAH 20:14-18

Jeremiah lived through the destruction of the Kingdom of Judah. Who would be the vessel of sacred history in the future? Jeremiah did not form a remnant like Isaiah. He used the symbolism of Amos and Hosea, in which the image of a remnant simply meant whatever people would be restored to organized existence under a truly just and righteous Davidic king. The first eight verses of the twenty-third chapter of Jeremiah constitute a classic prophecy of this type. Even though Jeremiah realized much more fully than Amos that Yahweh was the God of the nations as much as the God of the Covenant People, he still believed that the new Israel would be the center of a new world order. The element he added to this hope for the future was his reinterpretation of the covenant symbol:

> "Behold, days are coming," is the oracle of the LORD, "when I will sow the household of Israel and the household of Judah with the seed of men and with the seed of cattle; and as once I watched over them to root up and to pull down, to wreck, to ruin, and to harm, so will I watch over them to build and to plant," is the oracle of the LORD. "In those days shall they say no more, 'The fathers have eaten sour grapes, and the children's teeth are set on edge'; but everyone shall die for his own guilt—everyone who eats the sour grapes shall have his own teeth set on edge.
>
> "Behold, days are coming," is the oracle of the LORD, "when I will make a new covenant with the household of Israel and with the household of Judah, not like the covenant which I made with their fathers on the day that I took them by the hand to lead them out of the land of Egypt—that covenant of mine which they broke, so that I had to reject them—but this is the covenant which I will make with the household of Israel after those days," is the oracle of the LORD: "I will put my law within them, and will write it on their hearts; and I will be their God and they shall be my people. And they shall teach no more every one his neighbor, and every one his brother, saying, 'Know the LORD;' for all of them shall know me, from the least of them to the greatest of them," is the oracle of the LORD; "for I will pardon their guilt, and their sin will I remember no more."
>
> JEREMIAH 31:27-34

Voegelin suggests that in this vision Jeremiah had at least a glimpse of the insight that "the existence of a concrete society in a definite form will not resolve the problem of order in history, that no Chosen People in any form will be the ultimate omphalos of the true order of mankind."[38] In other words, Jeremiah may have come close to articulating a profound view of the secular meaning of sacred history: two basic experiences of order—order necessary for meaningful living and order necessary for survival—are always at odds with one another in human history, and the tension between them will never be resolved completely or permanently, although the attempt to achieve resolution is the very stuff of the dynamics of human society.

In an ironic reversal of the ancient Exodus from Egypt, the last defenders of Jerusalem forced Jeremiah to go to Egypt with them, where he is said to have been murdered because he insisted on announcing again and again that Yahweh would destroy the remnant that had escaped to Egypt just as he had destroyed Jerusalem.

Second Isaiah

Half a century later, one more attempt was made to interpret the meaning of "Yahweh, the God of Israel, Israel, the People of Yahweh" in line with the prophetic tradition. The unknown prophet, whom we call the Second Isaiah because he wrote chapters forty to fifty-five of the Book of Isaiah, made use of the entire range of symbols that had been developed from Amos through Jeremiah. He developed most profoundly a symbol that had never been explored fully, the symbol of the Servant of Yahweh. The term had been traditionally applied to Moses, Joshua, David, and Solomon; it had also been applied to the bands of ninth-century prophets, and finally to a particular prophet—Isaiah. Jeremiah used it as a general designation of the prophets and also in connection with nonprophetic servants of Yahweh's will in history—even the King of Babylon! (Jeremiah 25:9)—but he never applied it to himself. Second Isaiah made it central, especially in four poems that have come to be known as the "Servant Songs."

The scholarly literature on these songs alone, quite apart from

---

[38] Voegelin, *op. cit.*, vol. I, p. 491.

other aspects of chapters forty to fifty-five of the Book of Isaiah, is so extensive that we hesitate to discuss the songs without dealing with a whole series of much-debated questions.[39] Nevertheless, we shall assume that the Servant of Yahweh at least means the people of Israel, whatever more it might mean, and simply confine ourselves to a tentative answer to the question: What influence did the Servant image developed by Second Isaiah have on the prophetic vision of a new chapter in sacred history?

Second Isaiah's message concerning Yahweh—Creator, Judge, and Savior—was expressed most profoundly in oracles such as those we encounter in chapter forty pointing to an utterly transcendent ultimacy:

> Who has directed the mind of the LORD,
> And instructed him as his counsellor?
> With whom took he counsel for his enlightenment,
> And who taught him the right path?
> Who taught him true knowledge,
> And showed him the way of intelligence?
> Lo! the nations are like a drop from a bucket,
> Like fine dust in the scales are they counted.
> Lo! the coast-lands weigh no more than a grain;
> And Lebanon is not enough as fuel for sacrifice,
> Nor are its beasts enough for burnt-offering.
> All the nations are as nothing before him,
> Blank ciphers he counts them.
>
> ISAIAH 40:13-17

Second Isaiah's message concerning the Servant is clearest in the second and the fourth Servant Songs. The opening lines of the second song remind us of the first Jeremiah oracle, except that the key phrase is "You are my servant, Israel" rather than "I appointed you a prophet to the nations," but it is plain that the Servant, also, has a mission to all nations.

> Listen, you coast lands, to me;
> Hearken, you peoples afar!
> The LORD called me from birth,
> From my mother's womb he gave me my name.

---

[39] See Otto Eissfeldt's essay, "The Prophetic Literature," in H. H. Rowley (ed.), *The Old Testament and Modern Study* (New York, 1951).

> He made my mouth like a sharp sword,
> In the shadow of his hand he hid me;
> He made me a polished arrow,
> In his quiver he concealed me.
> He said to me, "You are my servant,
> Israel, through whom I will show forth my glory."
> But I said, "In vain have I labored,
> Idly and for nought have I spent my strength;
> Nevertheless, my right is with the Lord,
> And my reward with my God."
> And now the Lord,
> Who formed me from the womb to be his servant,
> Says that he will bring back Jacob to himself,
> And that Israel shall be gathered to him—
> For I am honored in the eyes of the Lord,
> And my God has become my strength—
> He says, "It is too slight a thing for your being my servant
> That I should but raise up the tribes of Jacob,
> And restore the survivors of Israel;
> So I will make you a light of the nations,
> That my salvation may reach to the end of the earth."
>
> Isaiah 49:1-6

The final song begins with the Servant pictured as the exalted ruler over mankind:

> [Yahweh says] Lo! my servant shall prosper,
> He shall be exalted, and lifted up, and shall be very high.
>
> Isaiah 52:13

This announcement is answered by a chorus of kings and nations who introduce an entirely new element. Not only is the royal rule of the Servant hidden—as was Jeremiah's—but it is hidden under the direct opposite of royal power, namely, suffering.

> "Who could have believed what we have heard?
> And the arm of the Lord—to whom has it been revealed?
> For he grew up like a sapling before us,
> Like a root out of dry ground;
> He had no form nor charm, that we should look upon him,
> No appearance, that we should desire him.
> He was despised, and avoided by men,
> A man afflicted by pains, and familiar with sickness;

And like one from whom men hide their faces,
He was despised, and we took no account of him.

"Yet it was our sicknesses that he bore,
Our pains that he carried;
While we accounted him stricken,
Smitten by God, and humbled.
He was pierced for our transgressions,
He was crushed for our iniquities;
The chastisement of our welfare was upon him,
And through his stripes we were healed.
All we like sheep had gone astray,
We had turned everyone to his own way;
And the LORD made to light upon him
The guilt of us all.

"When he was oppressed, he humbled himself,
And opened not his mouth—
Like a sheep that is led to the slaughter,
Or like a ewe that is dumb before her shearers,
He opened not his mouth.
Through violence in judgment was he taken away,
And who gave thought to his fate—
How he was cut off from the land of the living,
For our transgressions he was stricken to death?
They made his grave with the wicked,
His tomb with evil-doers;
Although he had done no violence,
Nor was any deceit in his mouth."

ISAIAH 53:1-9

The unbelievable message that the reconciliation of Yahweh's "ultimacy" and mankind's "order" is hidden in the mystery of representative suffering has been accepted. Now heavenly voices announce:

Yet the LORD was pleased to crush him by sickness,
That when he had made himself a guilt-offering,
He might see posterity, might prolong his life,
And the pleasure of the LORD might prosper in his hand.

ISAIAH 53:10

Finally, Yahweh himself takes over the theme of salvation and brings the song to a triumphant conclusion:

> Now through his suffering shall he see it, and be satisfied;
> Through his affliction shall my servant, the Righteous One, bring righteousness to many,
> And shall carry the burden of their guilt.
> Therefore will I divide him a portion with the great,
> And with the strong shall he share the spoil;
> Because he poured out his lifeblood,
> And was numbered with transgressors,
> While he bore the sin of many,
> And for transgressors he interposed.
>
> ISAIAH 53:11-12

The symbol of the Suffering Servant has played such a conspicuous role in the Christian tradition that it is difficult for us to see it in its post-exilic Judaic setting. The simplest way of doing that is to take the first words of Second Isaiah quite literally:

> "Comfort, O comfort my people," says your God:
> "Speak to the heart of Jerusalem, and call to her—
> That her time of service is ended,
> That her guilt is paid in full,
> That she has received of the LORD's hand double for all her sins."
>
> ISAIAH 40:1-2

Add to this oracle the call of Cyrus, the Persian emperor, who without knowing it has obeyed the will of Yahweh by making it possible for Judahite exiles to return to Jerusalem in order to rebuild it, and the picture is complete (Isaiah 44:24-45:13). Israel is the Servant, and the Servant has been given disciplinary punishment by Assyria and Babylonia; now these arrogant and cruel empires have been crushed by Cyrus, and the Servant is brought home by Yahweh to make a new beginning.

> "Ashamed and confounded are all who have risen up against him,
> The makers of idols are driven to confusion;
> But Israel is saved by the LORD with an everlasting salvation;
> You shall not be ashamed nor confounded forever and ever."
>
> ISAIAH 45:16-17

The scene of this new beginning is ordinary, untransfigured history, and the future role of the Servant is a permanent missionary role in which the old conflict between two basic experiences of order—order necessary for survival and order necessary for meaningful living—has been resolved by the disappearance of the first and by a reinterpretation of the second. No provision is made for survival, no political or social structures are envisioned. Israel is simply a witness, a messenger, and this is the message:

For thus says the Lord who created the heavens—
He is the true God—
Who formed the earth and made it—
He established it—
He created it not a chaos,
He formed it for a dwelling-place:
"I am the Lord,
And there is no other.
I spoke not in secret,
In a land of darkness;
I said not to Jacob's offspring,
'Seek me in chaos!'
I the Lord speak what is right,
Tell what is true.
Assemble and come, draw near together,
You survivors of the nations!
No knowledge have those who carry about
Their carved images of wood,
And offer their prayers to a god
That cannot save.
Let them take counsel together, then let them show us,
And bring forward proof of it!
Who announced this of old,
Foretold it long ago?
Was it not I the Lord—
No other God than I—
A victorious and a saving God—
None apart from me?
Turn to me, and be saved,
All ends of the earth!
For I am God, and there is no other—
By myself have I sworn—
Truth has gone out of my mouth,
A word that shall not return,
That to me every knee shall bow,
Every tongue shall swear,

Saying, 'Only in the LORD
Is victory and strength.' "
ISAIAH 45:18-24

But what about the symbol of the Servant as representative sufferer? Some modern Jews, looking back over the past twenty-five hundred years, believe that this is precisely the role the Jewish people have played consistently down through the centuries because they have insisted on continuing to witness to the one true God. Rabbi Leo Trepp interprets the message of Second Isaiah in the following way:

> Why does Israel suffer so much? The second Isaiah speaks out, addressing himself to the problem. Suffering need not be regarded as the wages of sin; it may be a test of strength, a test of faith, a sign of being chosen. The suffering servant of God makes it clear to a skeptical world that nothing can make him waver in his dedication. Were he always blessed, he would not be servant but man of privilege. It would be easy for him to love God. Were he to know that reward and punishment are always linked to man's actions as effect follows the cause, he might serve God for selfish reasons, to escape suffering or find happiness. The true servant of God must be willing to be tested, and maintain his faith in adversity. By his steadfastness he becomes a witness, and by his dedication he becomes an inspiration to the world. . . .
>
> Isaiah's words, like those of Job dealing with the same problem, have been a source of inspiration to the Jew. In his encounter with the world he was told again and again that his suffering was surely evidence of sinfulness. Actually he bore the disease in behalf of his tormentors, who lived in peace, hoping they might change their ways. He bore it for the sake of his children, that they—as Jews—might carry on the task. He did not falter, though the door of escape was open if he but renounced his faith. He did all this to justify the Righteous God, knowing that some day his suffering would be justified and made worthwhile, having ennobled mankind to recognize God and to serve His purpose.
>
> Such heroism in suffering is not easy. Isaiah knew he had to strengthen those who became weary and despondent at the endlessness of the trial. His words have brought new determination to the generations after him:
>
> "Why sayest thou, O Jacob, and speakest O Israel, 'My way is hidden from the Lord and my right passes over from my God'? Hast

> thou not known, hast thou not heard, that the everlasting God, the Creator of the ends of the earth, fainteth not, neither is weary? His discernment is past searching out. He giveth power to the faint; and to him that has no might He increaseth strength. Even youth may faint and be weary, and young men may utterly fall; but they that wait for the Lord shall renew their strength; they shall mount up with wings as eagles; they shall run and not be weary; they shall walk and not faint."
>
> ISAIAH 40:27-31
>
> Justification lies not in the reward, but in the eternal renewal of strength. Waiting should weaken; helplessness will ordinarily sap one's strength, just as failure to know God's ways should lead to doubt. The very opposite has happened in history. Nations and individuals rose in youthful strength and arrogance, cruel, ruthless, and destructive. They became weary and faint, and so they fell. But Jews have renewed their strength with every fall, with every enforced march from country to country. Walking through history they have found in their faith an everlasting source of energy. Suffering is both test and glory. Guided by this knowledge Israel has endured and will endure to the day when God will say the words: "Comfort ye, comfort ye My people." [40]

The Christian interpretation has been quite different, of course. The early church identified the Servant as Jesus. Later on the church has often thought of itself as bearing this role for the sake of mankind. From the standpoint of the present study, however, the real issue between Jews and Christians is not just the matter of identifying the Suffering Servant. It is the question whether the open-ended view of sacred history proposed by the prophets was the core of their message, and more than that, whether it was a reaffirmation of the core of the Israelite tradition. So far as the Jews are concerned, the facts of history are that the prophetic attempt to reopen sacred history was repudiated not only by those who were contemporaries of the prophets but, even more important, by the Judaism that developed in the Jerusalem community whose imminent resurrection was greeted

---

[40] *Eternal Faith, Eternal People* (Englewood Cliffs, N. J., 1962), pp. 28-29. This work is an especially valuable introduction to Judaism because it gives most of its attention to the much-neglected history of the Jewish people and their traditions during the Christian era.

so joyfully by Second Isaiah in the oracle that begins with the proclamation: "Comfort ye, comfort ye my people!" (Isaiah 40:1) This rejection of the prophetic claim must not be taken to mean that the Jewish community did not appreciate other aspects of the work of the literary prophets. After all, the prophetic literature became a part of the sacred scriptures! This community was different from the pre-exilic kingdoms in that it was not really a political state. It was a protectorate in the Persian and then the Hellenistic empires, managed by priestly officials rather than governed by kings. It was also different in that it bound itself to a written body of instructions it accepted as unconditionally valid in any time or historical situation. Formerly the commandments had been flexible; they had served the people of Israel as guideposts through the confusion caused by intimate contact with Canaanite and other Near Eastern traditions. Now Israel had to serve the commandments as they had been "frozen" at certain stages of interpretation under past conditions.

Sacred history, therefore, could not move on to anything new; but the most striking phenomenon was that apparently the post-exilic Jerusalem community did not experience the historical character of its existence. This group wrote no history of any kind about itself for three centuries, even though it spent much of its time energetically collecting and editing all the written materials handed down from the past. The gap was from about 450 B.C. to 170 B.C. After 170 B.C. a detailed historical record became available once more in the two books of the Maccabees, which told the story of how the Jews threw off foreign rule briefly before succumbing to the Romans in 63 B.C. Thus, early Judaism, which entered history when the Torah ("teaching") of Yahweh came to be regarded as an absolute entity, lived and served Yahweh in an enigmatic "beyond history." During most of the Christian era Judaism has lived in a similar unhistorical dimension. Modern Zionism and the establishment of the state of Israel have raised the question whether a new chapter of sacred history is being written, and among the Jews themselves—and particularly within Israel—there is violent disagreement.

The traditional Christian answer to the questions whether the open-ended view of sacred history proposed by the prophets was the core of their message and whether it was the core of the entire Israelite tradition has been "yes" in both cases. All Christians agree that the coming of Jesus and the founding of the church opened sacred history at least one more time after its many centuries of resting on past events. But many Christians and official church bodies have tended to look on the New Testament period very much as the Jews look on the Exodus-Sinai-Canaan period, as immutable foundations whose meaning continues to be renewed as successive generations accept it as their life-orientation. Today there is serious disagreement among Christians as to whether sacred history is still open, and if so in what sense.

Curiously enough, while it may be pointed out that Judaism rejected the radical type of historical dynamism advocated by the prophets, and that Christianity was especially hospitable toward it once the church became the dominant religious institution in Western culture, the fact remains that the narrative form of sacred history has remained the characteristic Western mode for communicating comprehensive orientations to life. The Renaissance, the Enlightenment, and more recently the modern democratic and communistic political movements, as well as philosophies of human progress based on the success of modern science, have expressed their basic convictions by constructing their own secularized versions of a sacred history that culminates in the victorious emergence of their special life-orientation. Thus it would seem that the breakthrough of the ancient Israelites into historical existence under Yahweh has permanently affected the core convictions of Western culture.

Recommended Paperbacks

Albright, William F. *The Biblical Period from Abraham to Ezra: A Historical Survey.*
New York: Harper Torchbooks, Harper & Row, 1963.

A remarkably succinct survey, very useful as a background for Biblical study.

Buber, Martin. *Moses: The Revelation and the Covenant.* New York: Harper Torchbooks, Harper & Row, 1958.

One of the greatest and most influential modern Jewish interpretations of the case of the Israelite religious tradition.

Eliade, Mircea. *Cosmos and History,* translated by Willard Trask. New York: Harper Torchbooks, Harper & Row, 1959.

A fascinating examination of the nostalgia of archaic societies for "archetypes" and "models" in relation to the Biblical experience of sacred history.

Rowley, H. H. (ed.) *The Old Testament and Modern Study.* New York: Oxford University Press, 1951.

The best survey available in paperback. The essays are directly related to the materials and the issues discussed in this chapter.

four

PHILOSOPHY AND HELLENIC CULTURE

THE great Hellenic culture that we associate especially with the city-state of Athens did not begin in Greece. Although its traditions went back to the early Achaean culture (ca. 1600 B.C.) and to the impressive Mycenaean civilization that dominated the Greek mainland from around 1400 B.C. to 1200 B.C., Hellenic culture actually began along the west coast of Asia Minor among the descendants of Achaean and Mycenaean refugees who had been driven out of Greece by invasions. A barbarian onslaught around 1200 B.C. shattered the Achaean-Mycenaean civilizations, forcing great numbers of people to emigrate to Asia Minor and leaving a cultural vacuum in mainland Greece except for an enclave in Attica, the region around Athens. A century later the Dorians moved in, and when they extended their control to include Attica a second emigration to Asia Minor took place. During the next several centuries Hellenic culture emerged out of the successful preservation of Achaean and Mycenaean traditions by the descendants of these refugees, and it reached its highest level of achievement in the old Greek homeland, with Athens as its most famous center.

I

Archaic Traditions

Homer's "Iliad" and "Odyssey"

The most powerful vehicle for establishing a new Hellenic life-orientation was the epic poetry associated with the name of Homer. The greatness of the Homeric epics, the *Iliad* and the *Odyssey,* can be seen in the fact that they not only established a continuity between the defunct Mycenaean society and their own times for descendants of that society, but they also induced numerous other groups to accept this particular "past" as their own and to join in creating Hellenic culture. This achievement is similar to the power of the Exodus-Sinai traditions to draw various tribes into the confederation that became the Israelite people. The images of the cosmos and the society of gods and men in the *Iliad* and the *Odyssey* communicated a common body of convictions first to groups in Asia Minor and later to a number of widely dispersed city-states stretching as far west as Italy, as far south as North Africa, and as far north as Macedonia.

Modern study of the *Iliad* and the *Odyssey* has gone through the same stages of inquiry and analysis as modern study of the Hebrew scriptural documents. The final composition shows evidences of saga cycles going back to 1500 B.C., reworkings, interpolations, and a welding of older materials into a new literary work. Probably the *Iliad* in its present form was written about 750 B.C. and the *Odyssey* by 700 B.C. We shall not, however, discuss questions of authorship.[1] Our primary interest is the convictions and images that unified the epics as we read them today. We still know nothing about "Homer," but we know at least three things: (1) The Hellenes themselves knew that the divine society of the gods on Mount Olympus was of late origin. They did not trace the Olympian account of the cosmos back further than the epics, and in the epics themselves the creation was hardly mentioned. (2) They knew that the mythical tradition, as well as legends about their ancestors, had been given their present narrative form by definite persons, the poets. (3) They identified Homer as the first man who transfigured the myths and legends of their past into song.

Thus the element of a free manipulation of traditions seems to have been generally recognized. The epics remind us of the Memphite Theology and of the Deuteronomic Moses, in which we saw a deliberate and conscious manipulation of traditions by priestly groups in order to communicate certain interpretations of traditional materials to people whose contemporary situation was different from the situation in which the materials originated. But the Olympian gods did not derive directly from religious cult or from priestly speculations. The poets were laymen.

---

[1] For an excellent introduction to the problem of authorship, as well as a survey of many other aspects of documentary analysis, see Werner Jaeger, *Paideia* (2nd ed., New York, 1945), vol. I.

A striking example of selectivity is the fact that the Homeric epics consistently suppress the earth-bound components of Mycenaean religious convictions and cultic practices that connect death with fertility and that connect both with a ritual renewal of the cosmic order similar to those characteristics of the Mesopotamian and Egyptian traditions. Furthermore, in raising the sky-god Zeus to lordship over gods and men the epics do not project a Hellenic version of cosmological myths like those that were organized into the Mesopotamian Enuma Elish creation epic. As Bruno Snell has said:

> Although in the Homeric poems the control and the meaning of the plot rest with the gods, the writer is not primarily interested in what happens on the upper stage . . . . The human action does not serve a higher, a divine cause, but quite the reverse: the story of the gods contains only so much as is needed to make the happenings on earth intelligible.[2]

In other words, the epics already foreshadow a break with myth because they do not focus on the establishment of the cosmic order by the gods. They draw on memories of an actual historical past, and they picture the Olympian society of the gods in terms of the same memories of the rich feudal world of Mycenaean Greece as they use to portray the world of King Agamemnon and the heroes Achilles and Odysseus. The kings and princes of Mycenae had been separated from serfs and peasants by rank, prestige, and power; the gods are separated from mortals in the same way. The surest method for arousing resentment and retaliation in kings and nobles is to infringe on their sense of status; the same thing happens when men forget that they are mortals and infringe on the sense of status of the gods. Like many powerful human aristocrats, the gods indulge in jealousy and favoritism, and sometimes they resort to dubious strategies in order to secure the success or the safety of their protégés. This does not make them "bad." The gods are simply given the prerogatives of a Mycenaean king. The will of a powerful aristocrat is his law. He does not do things because they are right; they are right because he does them.

---

[2] *The Discovery of the Mind,* translated by T. G. Rosenmeyer (New York, 1960), p. 37.

Some gods are crude or immoral, some are chivalrous or self-sacrificing. It has been argued that this curious mixture of irresponsible power and crude moral ideas with qualities appropriate to sensitive, morally responsible persons, which is evident in the Homeric picture of the gods, should be explained in evolutionary terms. Some scholars assign the crude and immoral aspects to an early primitive period in the growth of archaic Hellenic traditions concerning the gods and the more sensitive, moral actions to a later period. The present author agrees with W. K. C. Guthrie, who concludes his discussion of the character of the gods by saying: "The mixture was there all the time, and only serves to strengthen their resemblance to the Homeric *basileus* [king], for in him alone is that peculiar combination repeated." [3]

Almost without exception, the epics present Zeus as the king of gods and men, the bestower of destinies and the final judge. A typical example is a passage in the sixth book of the *Odyssey* where Odysseus tells a woman about his misfortunes and asks her aid. He expresses the hope that if she helps him the gods will reward her with a happy marriage, but she replies:

> "Stranger, you do not seem like a bad or a foolish man; but happiness is something which Olympian Zeus above allots to men, whether good or bad, to each according to his will. Your fortune is what he has given you, and you must endure it in any case." [4]

The section of the *Iliad* that speaks most directly about the origins of the world order, however, reveals a long-standing rivalry between Zeus and his brother gods Poseidon and Hades, and it suggests that the present structure of divine society of the Olympian gods may not be permanent, even though they themselves are believed to be immortal. The fifteenth book of the *Iliad* begins with Zeus waking one morning to discover that with the help of the god Poseidon the Achaeans are about to conquer the Trojans. Zeus suspects that his wife, Hera, has put Poseidon

---

[3] *The Greeks and Their Gods* (Boston, 1955), p. 126.

[4] Homer, *The Odyssey*, translated by W. H. D. Rouse (New York, 1949), p. 77. All quotations in this chapter will follow Rouse unless another translator is named.

up to this, and that they timed the battle carefully so that the Achaean victory would be complete by the time he awakened. Zeus sends Iris to tell Poseidon that he must stop meddling in the war and go home. Poseidon replies angrily:

> "Confound it, that is a tyrant's word, though he may be strong! I am his equal in rank and he will constrain me by force! We are three brothers, the sons of Cronos and Rheia—Zeus, and I, and Hadês who rules the lower world. All was divided among us in three parts, and each has his prerogative. We cast lots, and I got the sea, Hadês the gloomy darkness, Zeus the broad heavens high amid the clouds: earth and Olympos were left common to all. Therefore I will not live at the beck and call of Zeus; let him enjoy his own share in peace, even if he is a strong one. But let him not think to scare me with his strong hands as if I were something contemptible. He would do better to try scolding and scaring his own sons and daughters, who must obey whether they like it or not." [5]

Iris reminds him that the Avenging Spirits (the Eumenides) always support the older brother, and suggests that he should stop being so stubborn and unbending. He replies:

> "Iris, my dear goddess, you are quite right. A messenger with news to bring should understand the proper thing. But I tell you it hurts me through and through, when I am his partner, and I have an equal share, and yet he wants to scold me with angry words. Look here, I will give way, though it makes me indignant. But let me say something more—here is a threat which I mean to carry out. If he goes against me and Athena and Hera and Hermês and Hephaistos, and spares Ilios, if he will not destroy the city and give victory to the Achaians, between us two there will be hatred which nothing can heal." [6]

Poseidon's threat does not materialize, for in the end Agamemnon and his Achaean heroes conquer Troy. The most interesting feature of the episode, however, is the division of the cosmos

---

[5] Homer, *The Iliad,* translated by W. H. D. Rouse (New York, 1950), p. 177. Unless otherwise indicated, all quotations from the *Iliad* will follow this translation. It is easy to read, lively, and just as useful for our study as translations that attempt to retain the poetic form of the original work.

[6] *The Iliad,* p. 178.

into allotted portions with its implication that Zeus is not the one who does the allotting. The Greek word for "allotted portions" is *moira,* which also came to mean destiny, fate, and even chance or luck. Who is the ultimate power behind Zeus, Poseidon, and Hades? Homer suggests that it is their father Cronus. The later poet Pindar says it is *moira* itself, which he personifies as the Lady of the Lots. In his version of the division of the cosmos among the gods he pictures Lady Luck presiding over the casting of lots. She throws the dice and Zeus can do no more than confirm the decision, although polite deference is shown him as first among the gods. In a word, destiny or fate is more ultimate than the gods.

The original meaning of *moira* can be transferred quite easily from a physical context to a social context. In the social context it becomes a moral territory. Transgression of the boundaries set by the mores of society and by the inherent limitations that go along with being one individual among many, one group among many, brings inevitable punishment. The word most often used to define transgression is *hubris,* pride in the sense of self-elevation above one's proper station. *Moira* is not moral in a personal sense, however; it is moral in the sense of being completely impartial. Foresight, purpose, and design belong to gods and to men alike. But the moment either gods or men cross the boundaries of their legitimate position in the cosmic or social scheme of things, they set in motion a sort of compensatory backlash or recoil that sooner or later will exact retribution. This notion of *moira* remains hazy and undeveloped in the Homeric epics, but as we shall see, it becomes a central theme in the Hellenic attempt to explore compelling experiences of a mysterious dimension of reality beyond the Olympian gods, a power to which gods as well as men are subject.

Early in the preceding chapter, we compared the way of remembering that was characteristic of the mythically oriented civilizations with the way of remembering that was characteristic of the Israelite people—cult legend resting on a core of historical fact, developing into the sacred history narrative. In this chapter we have said that the heroes of the Homeric epics are legendary personages belonging originally to a historic society, and that in creating a historical past the epics foreshadow a break with myth. Yet they do not supply the base for a dynamic historical orientation. The realm of the gods is full of vitality and tension, but it is not going anywhere. The realm of men is full of activity also; the Achaeans conquer the Trojans, and Odysseus finally reaches home again after many adventures, but the life-orientation depicted in the epics is not going anywhere either.

In the first chapter of his *Mimesis: The Representation of Reality in Western Literature,* Erich Auerbach compares the genius of the Homeric style with that of the Israelite historiographers of the ninth century B.C. who reconstructed the pre-Exodus past on the basis of legendary memories of the patriarchal ancestors (Abraham, Isaac, and Jacob). For his purpose Auerbach chooses one example from the Odyssey and one from the book of Genesis. The Homeric episode is taken from Book Nineteen: Odysseus has at last come home, but not even his wife Penelope recognizes him. Then his old nurse Eurycles touches an old familiar scar just above his knee as she is about to wash his feet as an act of hospitality toward a tired traveler. She almost cries out at her joyful discovery, but Odysseus restrains her, and his identity remains a secret to everyone else. Auerbach observes:

> All this is scrupulously externalized and narrated in leisurely fashion. The two women express their feelings in copious direct discourse. Feelings though they are, with only a slight admixture of the most general considerations upon human destiny, the syntactical connection between part and part is perfectly clear, no contour is blurred. There is also room and time for orderly, perfectly well-articulated, uniformly illuminated descriptions of implements, ministrations and gestures; even in the dramatic moment of recognition, Homer does not omit to tell the reader that it is with his right hand that Odysseus takes the old woman by the throat to keep her from speaking, at the same time that he draws her closer to him with his left. Clearly outlined, brightly and uniformly illuminated, men and things stand out in a realm where everything is visible; and not less clear—wholly expressed, orderly even in their ardor—are the feelings and thoughts of the persons involved.[7]

Then Auerbach points out that a long digression is introduced between preparations for the foot washing and the actual event of recognition and the dropping of the foot into the basin. The reader is given a lengthy and detailed account of the boar hunt

[7] Translated by Willard Trask (New York, 1957), pp. 1-2.

in which the boy Odysseus received the wound that left the scar. The literary question is whether the story of the boar hunt is a device to increase suspense. Auerbach answers "no" because the story is actually so well told that as long as he is hearing it the reader forgets all about the foot washing that has been interrupted. The real reason for the digression is a fundamental characteristic of the Homeric style. Nothing that is mentioned can be allowed to be left half in darkness and unexternalized.

The example from the book of Genesis is the account in chapter twenty of Yahweh's testing of Abraham through the command that he sacrifice his only son, Isaac. One-tenth as long as the incident of Odysseus' scar, this narrative leaves almost everything unexpressed. Only as much information is given as is necessary to highlight the decisive points of the story. Everything else is left in obscurity. Time and place are undefined. Thoughts and feelings are suggested by the silence and the fragmentary speeches. There are no digressions. The whole story, permeated with unresolved suspense and directed toward a single goal, remains mysterious and "fraught with background." Abraham, though, torn between desperate rebellion and hopeful expectation, remembers Yahweh's promise and renders him a silent obedience whose multilayered complexity defies the capabilities of the Homeric style of psychological description.

> . . . the tendency to a smoothing down and harmonizing of events, to a simplification of motives, to a static definition of characters which avoids conflict, vacillation, and development, such as are natural to legendary structure, does not predominate in the Old Testament world of legend. Abraham, Jacob, or even Moses produces a more concrete, direct, and historical impression than the figures of the Homeric world—not because they are better described in terms of sense (the contrary is the case) but because the confused, contradictory multiplicity of events, the psychological and factual cross-purpose, which true history reveals, have not disappeared in the representation but still remain clearly perceptible.[8]

Auerbach emphasizes especially the fact that although heroes like Odysseus, Achilles, and Agamemnon are splendidly described, and although their emotions are constantly displayed in their

[8] *Ibid.,* p. 17.

words and actions, they undergo no significant development of personality. They appear to be of an age fixed from the very first, and their life histories are clearly set forth once for all. Even Odysseus, whose many years of wandering would seem to give ample opportunity for biographical development, is the same when he returns home as when he left twenty years earlier. Time can only touch the Homeric heroes outwardly, and even these changes of appearance are not often brought to our attention.

According to the Israelite perspective men are differentiated into full individuality only during the course of an eventful life. The Biblical stories present the historical process of formation undergone by persons whom Yahweh has chosen to be examples. Time grasps the great figures of Israelite tradition in the depths of their inner life. They are fallible, subject to misfortune and humiliation, often rebellious, always beset by inner conflict. Yet they become magnificent persons, expressing an inner quality and stature that their youth gave no grounds for anticipating. The clue, of course, lies in

> . . . the claim of the Old Testament stories to represent universal history, their insistent relation—a relation constantly redefined by conflicts—to a single and hidden God, who yet shows himself and who guides universal history by promise and expectation . . . .[9]

The contrast between the detailed horizontal breadth of the Homeric descriptions of man and the vertical depth of the Biblical description rests finally in the difference between the Olympian gods and Yahweh. Unfortunately, Auerbach fails to tell us that direct comparison between the Olympians and Yahweh is at least partially inaccurate. These "ultimates" are not strictly commensurate with one another. Yahweh is the real ultimate for Israel. The Olympian gods are the "practical ultimate" for archaic Hellas. Behind them lies a mysterious, incomprehensible background. The real ultimate, acknowledged by Homer but never explored, is destiny (*moira*)—the cosmos viewed as the context for the life both of gods and of men and thus more ultimate than either of them. Yet this is a static background, even when viewed from the standpoint of the Greek belief that the

---

[9] *Ibid.*, p. 14.

transgression of one's proper limits (*hubris*) causes a kind of compensatory recoil of the cosmos against the transgressor. Eventually tragic drama and philosophy expressed the Greek experiences of historical growth and of the multilayeredness of human existence with a profundity that rivaled the Biblical view of man and with an array of analytical concepts that went far beyond the Biblical style of presentation. One of the early preparatory steps was the restoration of certain parts of the pre-Homeric tradition of myth and cult that had been left out of the *Iliad* and the *Odyssey:* fertility motifs involving blood and soil and the annual rites of passage from the death of winter to the rebirth of spring, and motifs that expressed the centrality of the female principle, which had complemented the male-centered orientation of the Achaean aristocrats during the Mycenaean period but which had apparently become irrelevant for the refugees who fled to Asia Minor when the Mycenaean civilization was shattered.

Hesiod's "Theogony" and "Works and Days"

The restoration of these motifs in literary form was mainly the work of the poet Hesiod, who lived around 700 B.C. Born and reared on the mainland of Greece in Boetia, Hesiod knew and accepted the Olympian society of gods with Zeus as its king, but he was also familiar with a host of other indigenous traditions concerning the gods. Significantly enough, one of his two major works was a *Theogony,* that is, a story of the birth of the gods.

Hesiod's *Theogony* begins with three primordial realities: Chaos, Earth, and Eros. Chaos and Earth become productive when they are influenced by the erotic attraction of desire awakened in them by Eros. Out of Chaos arise Darkness and Night, and from them are born Fire and Daylight. Mother Earth gives birth to her male partner, the starry Heaven ("That he might enfold her all around"), and she also gives birth to the Sea. Having prepared a heavenly realm for the gods, she brings forth the high mountains to provide a solid foundation for the heavenly city of the gods. The primacy of the female principle tells us that Hesiod is drawing on traditions that do not appear in the Homeric epics, which reached their final form about the same time.

The stage is set. Eros brings Father Sky and Mother Earth together through the attraction of desire, and of this marriage the oldest gods are born. The separation of the cosmos into its major elements is a process in time, and the establishment of order is not an immediate event but a prolonged dramatic struggle between older and younger generations of the gods. We are back in the world of the Enuma Elish. Moreover, Hesiod's consciously contrived myth insists that the victorious younger generation of gods is morally superior to its forebears because it acknowledges justice (*dike*) rather than brute strength as its ultimate norm. Dynamic Dike, a new goddess created by Hesiod, replaces the static Homeric *moira*. According to Hesiod, Zeus is the father of Order, Justice, and Peace. Therefore the victory of Zeus and his Olympians over Cronus and his Titans means victory of the forces of true order over the dreary cycle of atrocities begetting revenge and revenge begetting new atrocities, which was apparently the main characteristic of the life of the Titans. Zeus puts an end to the war of all against all, for while he wins victory by force, he stabilizes the cosmos by distributing to each of the immortals an honorable share in the new order. We cannot go into the details of who is who and of who does what under the rule of Zeus, but obviously Hesiod tries to overcome the complex and confusing array of local and regional myths by creating a hierarchy of typical gods. His *Theogony* must be ranked with the works of Homer as indispensable foundations of the unity of Hellenic civilization. Voegelin says:

> The mythopoetic work of the two poets was a spiritual and intellectual revolution; for inasmuch as it established the types of cosmic and ethical forces, as well as the types of their relations and tensions, it created, in the form of the myth, a highly theorized body of knowledge concerning the position of man in his world that could be used by the philosophers as the starting point for metaphysical analysis and differentiation.[10]

The other major work of Hesiod, *Works and Days,* is important because it expresses his convictions about the relation of the will of the gods to human affairs along lines that foreshadowed the fundamental ethical outlook achieved by classical Greek

---

[10] *Order and History* (Baton Rouge, Louisiana, 1957), vol. II, pp. 136-37.

culture. At the same time, it illustrates again—although in a manner quite different from the style of the *Theogony*—that Hesiod is working within the symbolic framework of the mythical tradition.

The *Works and Days* is a huge admonitory speech addressed to Hesiod's lazy, greedy brother Perses, who long before had bribed the village magistrates in order to get the larger portion of their father's inheritance, and who is now involving Hesiod in another lawsuit to rob him still further, with the help of conniving judges. As he does in the *Theogony,* Hesiod identifies himself as the author; he is the first Hellenic poet who steps out of anonymity. In the *Theogony* he announces that the Muses have visited him and have appointed him to speak the truth—a prophetic call. In the *Works and Days* it is evident that his personal distress has led him to become concerned about the health of a social order that aids and abets injustices such as those he is suffering. Like the Israelite prophets, he is impelled to speak out critically against the accepted mores. Hesiod is a pioneer in another sense also. He is the first Hellene to set himself up as a leader without basing his claim to leadership on noble birth or exercising his leadership in another way than through holding public office. His claim is that he will tell his hearers the truth. His aim is to induce them to seek the truth and to accept it, even if they do not like what the truth reveals.

The parallels between Hesiod and the Hebrew prophets is more than casual, as we can demonstrate by means of two brief quotations from *Works and Days.* The first is a vision of doom; the second is a vision of hope.

> Neither will the father be of one mind with his children, nor the children with their father; neither guest with host, nor friend with friend; neither will brother be dear to brother as aforetime. Men will dishonor their quickly aging parents, finding fault with them and abusing them with bitter words, monstrously overbearing, not knowing the vengeance of the gods; nor will they make return to their aged parents of the cost of their upbringing. . . . Neither will be in favor the man who keeps his oath, or the law-abiding, or the man of excellence; men will rather praise the evil-doer and the works of hybris [hubris].[11] Right will lie with brute strength, and shame will

[11] C.L.

> be no more; the worse will damage the better man, speaking crooked words against him and swearing an oath upon them. Envy, discord-talking, rejoicing in mischief, will be the companion of all men to their sorrow.[12]
>
> But when they give straight judgment to strangers and to the men of the land, and go not aside from what is just, their city flourishes and the people prosper in it. Peace, the nurse of children, is abroad in their land, and all-seeing Zeus never decrees cruel war against them. Neither famine nor disaster ever haunt men who do true justice; but light-heartedly they tend the fields which are all their care. The earth bears them victual in plenty, and on the mountains the oak bears acorns upon the top and bees in the midst. Their woolly sheep are laden with fleeces; their women bear children like their parents. They flourish continually with good things, and do not travel on ships, for the grain-giving earth bears them fruit.[13]

These passages sound so much like certain messages of Isaiah, Micah, and Hosea that we may well ask who borrowed from whom. Actually, no question of literary influences needs to be raised. We are studying experiences and their symbolization, and Hesiod's experiences are fully intelligible in the context of Hellenic history. He says to his brother:

> "Lay up all this in your heart: give ear to justice, and wholly forget violence. This is the way that Zeus has ordained for mankind. Fish and wild beasts and the winged birds shall eat one another, for there is no justice among them. But to man he has given justice, the highest good of all." [14]

The centrality of justice for Hesiod is indicated also by his choice of images. Justice is the goddess Dike, the daughter of Zeus, who sits beside him to complain when men do wicked things so that Zeus will be sure to punish them. She is the guarantee that Zeus will not allow an unjust cause to triumph. For Hesiod, she is therefore integral to the "real ultimate," for Hesiod's Zeus is not merely a Homeric "practical ultimate." The

[12] *Ibid.,* lines 182 ff., vol. II, p. 159.

[13] *Ibid.,* lines 225 ff., p. 161.

[14] *Works and Days,* Verse 274, translated and quoted by Werner Jaeger in *Paideia,* vol. I, p. 68.

justice of Zeus is destiny; *moira* is given no independent status superior to Zeus. Obedience to Zeus brings peace and order. Injustice brings strife (the goddess Eris) and destruction.

But the Eris of strife is not the only Eris. Hesiod makes a significant innovation by claiming that strife is not necessarily bad. Tense and strenuous competition is good. In fact, men must be stirred to peaceful rivalry or they will not face the hard necessity of daily toil cheerfully. Instead, they will give in to jealousy, greed, laziness, and the sort of shady shenanigans in which brother Perses has been indulging. So Hesiod adds a "good Eris" to the "bad Eris," and he says that Zeus has given the good Eris a dwelling among the roots of the earth (Mother Earth again!). She inspires the idle man and also the "poor but willing" man to apply themselves when they see and envy the prosperity of their hard-working neighbors. Righteousness and work are inseparable.

> "Let me tell you this from my true knowledge, Perses, you silly child. . . . It is easy to reach misery even in crowds—the way is smooth, and lies not far away. But the immortal gods have placed sweat before success. Long and steep is the path for it, and rough at first. Yet when you have reached the top, then it is easy despite its hardness." [15]

Man's goal is excellence (*arete*). The specific excellence that Hesiod recommends is neither the excellence of the warrior aristocrat nor the excellence of the wealthy landowner. It is the excellence appropriate to the common man, the working man, and even more specifically, the peasant. In trying to make something of himself this man engages in the quiet, strong rivalry of work. He shall eat bread in the sweat of his brow, but that is a blessing and not a curse, for through work he can achieve his excellence. Hesiod is obviously setting up this "education" against the aristocratic training of Homer's heroes. But can the excellence Hesiod values be taught and learned? Werner Jaeger, who has devoted three excellent volumes to a study of the Greek ideal of *paideia*—training, education, culture—answers the question in this way:

> . . . Hesiod's poetry shows us a social class, hitherto debarred from culture and education, actually realizing its own poten-

[15] *Ibid.,* p. 70.

> tialities. In the process, it uses the culture of the upper class and the stylistic medium of courtly poetry; but it derives its real content and its ethos from the depths of its own life. It is because the Homeric epic is not simply the poetry of one class, but has grown from the root of an aristocratic ideal to overshadow all humanity, that it can help the men of an entirely different class to create their own culture, discover their own purpose in life, and work out its inherent law. That is a great achievement. But this is something even greater—the peasant, by thus realizing his own powers, leaves his isolation and takes his place among the other elements in Greek society. Just as the culture of the nobility affects every class of society when its spiritual energy is intensified by Homer, so the ideals of the peasant, interpreted by Hesiod, reach far beyond the narrow frontiers of peasant life. Granted that much of the *Work and Days* is real and useful only for farmers and peasants, still the poem gives universal meaning to the fundamental ideals of peasant life. That is not to say that the pattern of Greek life was to be defined by agrarian civilization. Actually, Greek ideals did not receive their final and characteristic form until the rise of the city-state, and were relatively little influenced by the native culture of the peasant. But it is therefore all the more important that throughout Greek history Hesiod should have remained the prophet of that ideal of work and justice which was formed among the peasantry and kept its force and meaning within a widely different social framework.[16]

Let us return to Hesiod himself. As a poet-prophet he preached the good news of hard work and of justice. Obeying the Muses who impelled him to speak the truth of which he was convinced, he stood publicly against many attitudes and mores of his society. In doing so he not only reflected on the excellence appropriate to the man of the soil, but he also reflected on the excellence of man as man:

> Best of all is the man who considers everything himself and sees what is going to be right in the end. Good, too, is he who obeys another man who says what is good. But the man who neither understands for himself nor takes another's advice to heart, he is a useless fellow.[17]

---

[16] Jaeger, *op. cit.*, vol. I, pp. 73-74.
[17] *Ibid.*, p. 71.

These words were used by Aristotle centuries later as the first postulate of his ethical and educational system. He quoted them in full in the *Nicomachean Ethics* in his preliminary discussion of the correct basis of ethical instruction, where he concluded that the science of ethics can be cultivated only by men whose characters are mature enough to serve as instruments for the kind of "knowing" upon which moral excellence depends. Hesiod was such a man.

The Homeric epics and the works of Hesiod indicate that even in the archaic period of Hellenic culture there was opportunity for a remarkable degree of freedom in the handling of traditions and in the exploration of their implications for changing social needs. It should be noted again that both Homer and Hesiod were laymen engaging in religious speculations and constructions that in every other ancient culture were reserved primarily for priestly bureaucrats. Even in Israel the role of the priests in formulating, collecting, and editing the written tradition was central. In contrast, the Hellenic religious tradition was not only given a nonpriestly foundation by these works written around 700 B.C. but also continued to be nonpriestly into the classical period and beyond. As Voegelin has pointed out:

> The style of Hellenic civilization is indelibly characterized by the absence of temporal and ecclesiastic bureaucracies. Through a miracle of history the geographic area of Hellenic civilization remained undisturbed by foreign invasions from the Doric migration to the Persians Wars, that is, roughly from 1100-500 B.C. During six hundred years, while in the Near and Far East the imperial civilizations with their inevitable bureaucracies were founded, overthrown, and re-established, the geopolitical paradise around the Aegean could develop the "free" civilizations, first, of local clans and aristocracies, and later, of poleis that were so small that no bureaucratic administration of formidable size was needed. Under these historically unique circumstances the transition from archaic to classic Hellas could assume the form of intellectual adventures by individuals, unhampered by the pressure of hierarchies which tend to preserve traditions.[18]

---

[18] Voegelin, *op. cit.,* vol. II, p. 166.

2

The Hellenic City-State

Since the life-orientation of Hellenic culture was shaped most decisively by the fact that the search for the divine ultimate and the human ideal became related integrally to the search for the true order of society in the city-state (the polis), a brief historical survey will precede our study of the intellectual adventures that led to the creation of tragic drama and to philosophy.

By 700 B.C., when the earliest Greek literature available to us was written, an early phase of kingship had passed, and a phase of rule by the landed aristocracy was in an unsettled state. The pressure of increasing population and the rise of a mercantile economy had already led to the initiation of the vigorous movement of colonization that planted city-states throughout mainland Greece, southern Italy, and even on the Mediterranean coast of Africa during the two centuries from 800 to 600 B.C. The polis was the autonomous, nontribal unit of political order. It embraced the numerous tribes, aristocratic clans, and extended families (three generations under one roof). Blood relationships were so important that the cities preserved the fiction of "families" for their subdivisions even though the blood lines gradually became obsolete when citizenship was extended to the lower classes. For example, in 508 B.C., when Cleisthenes set out to break the domination of Attica by aristocratic families, he divided the territory into ten regions and each region into ten districts (*demes*). Citizenship was determined by residence in one of the hundred districts. This fact gave citizenship to a large number of persons at the same time that it confined the old tribes to their religious functions—cult places, a priesthood, burial rites.

The net effect was a democratization of the constitution, but the old patterns persisted in the new district communities. Every citizen bore the name of the *demos* of 508 B.C. in which his family lived, a fact that created new artificial "family trees" in addition to the old aristocratic genealogies which persisted in private.

Even though a person no longer lived in the district where his ancestor had lived in 508, he still carried the name of that district. Together with all the other citizens who traced their relationship to the district in the same manner, he revered its cult heroes just as the nobility revered its biological ancestors. Thus the style of existence originally created by the aristocratic families spread throughout Hellenic political culture, while the education of the peasants along the lines prepared by Hesiod produced eligible candidates for citizenship in the polis. This family style of group identification was a major reason why the polis never really developed into a community of individual citizens and also why it was never able to achieve large-scale political organization.

The pattern of development in the various Hellenic city-states was by no means uniform. At one end of the spectrum was Sparta, where after the Messenian revolt the situation of conquest became fossilized in the form of an aristocratic constitution. At the other end was Athens, where the dominant pattern eventually became that of an urbanized democracy. By and large, the dynamics of history were on the side of the "common people," because they learned to participate to an amazing degree in the culture that had originated in the old aristocratic society. The aristocracy did not become vociferous until its position was endangered by the impact of democracy. Then, too late, it became a political party. In Athens the polis was an effective political institution for barely two centuries, from Solon to the demagogues who presided over its dissolution.

Although there were great obstacles to a development of the polis toward a national territorial state, on a small scale, the device of extending citizenship to regions surrounding the cities worked fairly well. Athens integrated Attica by granting Athenian citizenship to the villages. In about 432 B.C. a more ambitious attempt was made. A number of Chalcidian cities created a Greater Olynthus, using the device of dual citizenship. Everyone retained his citizenship in his own community; citizenship in Olynthus was added to it. Federation was the only other practical alternative. Some federations rested on military alliances; these tended to dissolve when danger decreased, or they were held together by sheer force. Other federations rested on the acknowledgment of a common religious center. But these amphictyonic leagues did little to prevent the death struggle that was going on continually between federations. Even among themselves, taking the Delphian Amphictyony as an example, about the best the member cities could do was to swear that they would not kill more than half the population of a member polis when they fought among themselves, that they would not cut off the water supply of a member polis either in war or in peace, and that they would submit boundary disputes to arbitration. This last oath failed to preserve peace because the losing party often resorted to war anyway.

The only power centers that shaped the history of Greece in world politics were the Spartan League and the Athenian Empire. For some time after 549 B.C. Sparta dominated the Peloponnesus, and at the beginning of the Persian Wars Sparta was given military command of all the cities that united in defense of Greece. After the battles of Plataea and Mycale in 479 B.C., however, when the danger to the mainland had been averted temporarily, the Spartan League did not give positive leadership, and internal conflicts broke out again, especially between Sparta and Athens. In 478 B.C. Athens took over the military hegemony because of her vital interests in the Aegean islands and in the Greek communities of Asia Minor. This was a voluntary Hellenic confederacy at first, but the war against Persia did not go well, and both Sparta and Boetia resisted the expansion of the Athenian maritime league. So by 454 Athens not only had to give up ambitions for expansion but was compelled to consolidate the existing situation by transforming the voluntary confederacy into an Athenian Empire. In 445 B.C. the coexistence of an Athenian and a Spartan sphere of influence was recognized by everyone; all hopes of pan-Hellenic unification died.

The following century—that of the Sophists, Socrates, Plato, and Aristotle—was the century of struggle to the death between the federations. Sparta took over Athens in 404 B.C. In 386 B.C. the war between Sparta and Persia led to an unprecedented arrangement in which for the first time the status of Greek cities was guaranteed by a non-Hellenic power, Macedonia. By 362 B.C. the Macedonians were intervening actively in Hellenic affairs, and in 331 B.C. even Sparta had to submit to Macedonian hegemony in Greece in order to help Alexander the Great wage a final war against the Persians. Political initiative had passed out of the hands of the polis, never to return.

3

The Break with Myth

Tyrtaeus (c. 650 B.C.)

The first poet who celebrated the emergence of the polis was Tyrtaeus of Sparta, who proclaimed that the only legitimate ultimate concern for man is the common good of his polis. Whatever helps the community is good; whatever injures it is bad. The polis being ultimate, the true excellence of man is the human quality that will help the polis most. First the poet lists virtues that do not qualify:

> I would not mention or take account of a man for the prowess of his feet or for his wrestling, even if he had the stature and strength of the Cyclopes and outran the Thracian Boreas. And were he more beautiful in face and body than Tithonus, and richer than Midas and Cinyras, and more kingly than Tantalus' son Pelops, and sweeter of tongue than Adrastus, I would not honour him for these things, even if he had every glory except warlike valour.[19]

Tyrtaeus opens his attack by dismissing the athletic prowess that was highly prized among the Hellenes and displayed most impressively in the Olympic games. By the time of Tyrtaeus, records of the games had already been kept for a hundred and thirty years (since 776 B.C.). In the second part of his attack Tyrtaeus denotes the Homeric excellences of the early aristocratic society: comeliness, wealth, royalty, and persuasiveness. The one heroic virtue he does not demote is courage, for the new excellence he places ahead of all others is a new "savage valor"—the courage of the Homeric heroes transformed into the courage of the citizen-soldier inspired by patriotic devotion to his polis.

---

[19] Tyrtaeus, fragment 12, translated and quoted by Werner Jaeger in *Paideia*, vol. I, p. 91. In the following sections all numbers of fragments from pre-Socratic thinkers are those assigned in the standard Diels-Kranz collection, *Fragmente der Vorsokratiker* (7th ed., Berlin, 1954).

> For no one is a good man in war, unless he can bear to see bloody slaughter and can press hard on the enemy, standing face to face. That is areté! That is the best and fairest prize which a young man can win among men. That is a good which is common to all—to the city and the whole people—when a man takes his stand and holds his ground relentlessly among the foremost fighters and casts away all thought of shameful flight.[20]

Tyrtaeus borrows directly from Homer; he models several of his poems on battle scenes in the *Iliad* in which a leader addresses his men at a moment of danger in order to rally them. In his hands Homer becomes a teacher of the present rather than a narrator of the past. The new note is the nationalistic exaltation of the polis. The polis transcends every individual citizen; every citizen is expected to live and to die for it. Death is beautiful, if it is a hero's death; to die for one's polis *is* a hero's death. Though the individual dies, the polis lives on to glorify him by remembering his name. Tyrtaeus rhapsodizes:

> But he who falls among the foremost fighters and loses his dear life in winning glory for his city and his fellow citizens and his father—his breast and his bossed shield and his breastplate pierced with many wounds in front—he is lamented by young and old together, and the whole city mourns for him in sad grief; and his tomb and his children are honoured among men, and his children's children likewise and his whole race after him; never is his name and fair fame destroyed, but though he lies beneath the earth he becomes immortal.[21]

Another dimension must be added. The polis is ultimate not only because it inspires the life of its citizens but also because it has power to compel, to threaten, and to impose sanctions. Tyrateus contrasts a glorious death on the battlefield with the doom of expulsion from the polis that falls on the man who tries to avoid his civic obligation to become a citizen-soldier-hero. This man will be ostracized. He will suffer the pitiless fate of exile, a wanderer who will be a stranger wherever he goes—a man without a country.

---

[20] *Ibid.*, pp. 91-92.
[21] *Ibid.*, p. 92.

This image of the citizen-hero, resting on the conviction that the polis is ultimate in life and in death, swept through Hellas and remained dominant until the city-state was submerged in the Hellenistic empires. Even the most highly differentiated and sophisticated individuals in the history of Hellenic culture, men like Plato and Aristotle, were still oriented toward the polis. But "savage valor" was replaced by other qualities of excellence that came to be valued more highly. Eventually Plato ranked courage fourth in his priority list behind wisdom, justice, and temperance. "Savage valor" could save a polis in times of military crisis, but it could not handle the problems of conflicts of interest within the polis.

Solon (c. 600 B.C.)

Half a century after Tyrtaeus did his writing, Solon presided over a constitutional reform in Athens that took up again Hesiod's theme of justice and righteousness and applied it to the comprehensive ordering of the domestic life of the polis. Constitutional historians praise Solon for his role in molding the Athenian constitution. Without question this was a notable achievement, for the constitution established the principle of the equality of all citizens under the law. It was the first time the equalitarian implications of the notion of justice were given concrete and practical expression. But Solon was a statesman who did more than enumerate principles. The distinterested way in which he exercised leadership was decisive in demonstrating what equality under the law really means. He stood between two factions: the landed aristocrats, who did not want to give up their traditional privileges, and the poor people, who were greedy for more than they could handle sensibly. He was not above these factions; he shared the passions and interests of both. Yet he would not allow either party to "gain unrighteously" over the other. As Jaeger says:

> All his acts and words indicate that the leading aim of his reforms was to find a just medium between excess and deficiency, between excessive power and helplessness, between privi-

> lege and serfdom. Therefore he could wholeheartedly support neither party in the state: yet both parties, rich and poor, really owed to him the strength they had won or retained. He constantly illustrates, by impressive images, his dangerous position not so much above as between the two opponents. He recognizes that his strength lies chiefly in the impalpable moral authority of his severely disinterested character.[22]

What is especially impressive about Solon's public career is that he successfuly resisted the temptation to use his enormous power for his own advantage. With no trouble at all he could have imposed himself as a tyrant on Athens. Instead, he warned that tyranny—the domination of one noble family and its head, supported by the common people, over all the rest of the aristocracy—was the most dreadful danger that faced his city. The justice he created in the polis was the justice he incarnated in his person.

Solon was convinced that justice is an inseparable part of the divine world order. Over and over again he proclaims in his poetic writings that it is impossible to ignore *Dike* because sooner or later injustice will be punished. *Hubris* will inevitably cause a backlash, a ruinous fall. He writes:

> Driven by avarice, the leaders of the people enrich themselves unrighteously: they spare neither the goods of the state nor the temple treasures, and they do not preserve the venerable foundations of Diké—who in her silence knows all the past and all the present, but does not fail to come in time to punish.[23]

In another fragment of his writings that has been preserved, Solon says the same thing even more pointedly.

> This city of ours will never be destroyed by the planning
> of Zeus, nor according to the wish of the immortal gods;
> such is she who, great hearted, mightily fathered, protects us,
> Pallas Athene, whose hands are stretched out over our heads.
> But the citizens themselves in their wildness are bent on destruction of their great city, and money is the compulsive cause.

---

[22] Jaeger, *op. cit.*, vol. I, p. 146.

[23] Solon, fragment 6, translated and quoted by Werner Jaeger in *Paideia*, vol. I, p. 141.

> The leaders of the people are evil-minded. The next stage
> will be great suffering, recompense for their violent acts,
> for they do not know enough to restrain their greed and
> apportion orderly shares for all as if at a decorous feast.[24]

These lines were written early in Solon's career. He lived to see the day when his warning was verified, and one man, Pisistratus, seized absolute power for himself and his family. Then Solon wrote:

> If you have suffered for your weakness, do not blame the gods! You yourselves allowed these men to grow great by giving them power, and therefore you have fallen into shameful servitude.[25]

So far as we know, Solon is the first man who interpreted the total process of social existence as a more or less autonomous realm in which men are directly, genuinely responsible for order or disorder, and in which what happens can be analyzed as a chain of cause and effect. He thinks of historical causality in much the same way as the Ionian "physiologists" of his generation—Thales, Anaximander, and others—thought about the causality of nature. He still uses the Olympian imagery, however, especially the image of the divine retribution of Zeus, which falls upon evildoers like a spring storm:

> Suddenly it scatters the clouds, stirs the depths of the sea, rushes down on the fields and ruins the fair work of men's hands; and then it rises up again to heaven, the sun's rays shine out on the rich earth, and no cloud is seen. Such is the retribution of Zeus, which lets none escape. One man makes amends soon, another late; and if the guilty man escapes punishment, his innocent children and his descendants suffer in his stead.[26]

Solon goes on to underline the relentless inevitability of destiny by introducing another image.

---

[24] Solon, fragment 3, translated by Richard Lattimore in *Greek Lyrics* (Chicago, 1960), p. 20.

[25] Fragment 8, translated and quoted by Werner Jaeger in *Paideia,* vol. I, pp. 142-43.

[26] *Ibid.,* fragment 1, p. 144.

> We mortals, good and bad alike, think that we shall get whatever we hope for, until misfortune comes, and then we complain. The sick man hopes to become well, the poor man to become rich. Everyone strives for gold and profit, each in a different way, as a merchant-sailor, farmer, or craftsman, bard or seer. But the seer himself cannot avert misfortune even if he sees it impending.[27]

Once men set a chain of events in motion, the consequences are predictable, yet unavoidable. But there is more here than "whatever a man sows, that shall he also reap." Solon uses the word *doxa,* illusion or delusion: "All of us suffer from the *doxa* that we will get whatever we hope for." Having crossed the boundary of hard-headed realism about life into the territory of inordinate desires and delusionary pursuits, we are not prepared to face squarely the fact that there is risk in all human action, that destiny actually brings good and ill to us in proportions that do not correspond logically to our expectations. Realistic expectations must take into account that honest effort fails and wicked men prosper; that the innocent suffer while the guilty escape the consequences of their deeds. Solon is convinced that the unpredictable dimension in destiny does not reduce human striving to senselessness. He believes that ultimately the will of the gods is just, even though the divine order is beyond human understanding. Therefore he concludes that destiny seems senseless to us only if we refuse to give up our inordinate desires and our delusionary pursuits.

> Many bad men are rich, many good men poor; but we, we will not exchange virtue [arete] for these men's wealth; for the one endureth whereas the other belongeth now to this man and now to that.[28]

"The fault, dear Brutus, is . . . in our stars"—not that we are underlings but that we make something the object of all our striving which has neither measure nor end in itself. Solon concentrates his analysis on wealth, the very thing he has done so much

---

[27] *Ibid.,* p. 145.
[28] Fragment 15, translated by J. M. Edmonds and included in his *Elegy and Iambus* (Cambridge, 1961), vol. I, p. 133.

to bring to Athens through his economic as well as political leadership. He might just as convincingly analyze power, the particular temptation to illusion that he has faced and overcome, or he might analyze our modern notion of success. He chooses to discuss wealth, and what he says about it is highly interesting. The pursuit of wealth is not an expression of true excellence precisely because it contains no defense against excess, no boundaries. The more we get the more we want. Note the ancient spatial image of destiny as a system of provinces. Solon is saying that destiny is cosmic *order* because boundaries guarantee each province its place in the total configuration. But he does not give in to the static implications of the spatial image. To be alive is to be on the move, and Solon passionately loves the exuberance of life. So his question is this: How can we deal constructively with the tension between the normal human desire for the goods of exuberant existence and the powerful drive toward a limitless, pathological striving for more and more and more of these goods that inevitably leads to social as well as to individual disintegration?

Solon's answer is that true excellence rests on an act of faith in the utterly reliable, yet never fully known, order of the gods, a faith that the gods will see to it that the man who renounces his illusions will act justly (in accordance with *dike*) and thus will achieve right order—no easy achievement. As he himself says:

> 'Tis very hard to tell the unseen measure of sound judgment, which yet alone hath the ends of all things.[29]

The true measure is unseen. It is not a yardstick that can be applied directly to the complexities of every concrete situation. No conceptual model is available that can capture the quality of sound judgment that Solon recommends; conceptually he describes judgment in conventional terms like the maintenance of order, or reasonable and skillful adjustment of conflicting claims. Solon himself, the person who judges, is the model. He demonstrates that even though the pattern that gives judgment its balance is grasped by faith and not by sight, balanced judgment can actually be achieved. It is a judgment that overcomes the obsession of inordinate desires and combines realistic insight with the will to put it into action.

---

[29] Fragment 16, *ibid.*

Solon became an archetypal personage, far more inuflential in later history that his poetry would ever lead one to suppose he could be. Bruno Snell gives a good summary:

> The fact that once upon a time in ancient Attica a man did not make use of the power which fell to his lot, but renounced it for the sake of justice, was to be of immeasurable consequence for the laws and politics of Greece and Europe as a whole. For Solon himself the immediate results were disappointing enough. He lived to see the tyranny which Pisistratus received from the willing hands of a fickle populace. But the sentiment which inspired him to put the internal affairs of Athens in order, and which he broadcast in his poetry for all to hear, has since become an integral part of politics, in spite of numerous attempts to abuse it, or to stamp it out: the idea, i.e., that justice is a permanent entity which stands above men, and that justice, not violence, is the norm of public affairs. In the Attic state of the fifth century this concept won a new lease of life, and found itself raised to a higher power; when the axiom of justice for all came to be underpinned with the fact of individual accountability, the final stage of the evolution had been reached.[30]

Xenophanes (c. 530 B.C.)

Tyrtaeus preached the ultimacy of the polis and the human excellence that defends it, "savage valor." Solon's ultimate was the eternal law of justice, and he proclaimed that the human excellence that will maintain the polis is mature judgment guided by the "unseen measure" of this law. Xenophanes of Colophon (Asia Minor), who emigrated to the Hellenic communities located in southern Italy, called for a third excellence:

> But if anyone were to win a victory with fleetness of foot, or fighting in the Pentathlon, where the precinct of Zeus lies between the springs of Pisa at Olympia, or in wrestling, or in virtue of the painful science of boxing, or in a dread kind of contest called Pancration: to the citizens he would be more glorious to look upon, and he would acquire a conspicuous seat of honour at competitions, and his maintenance would be pro-

[30] Rosenmeyer, *op. cit.*, p. 176.

> vided out of the public stores by the City-State, as well as a gift for him to lay aside as treasure.
>
> So too if he won a prize with his horses, he would obtain all these rewards, though not deserving of them as *I* am; for my craft (wisdom) is better than the strength of men or of horses. Yet opinion is altogether confused in this matter, and it is not right to prefer physical strength to noble Wisdom. For it is not the presence of a good boxer in the community, nor of one good at the Pentathlon or at wrestling, nor even of one who excels in fleetness of foot—which is highest in honour of all the feats of strength seen in men's athletic contests—it is not these that will give a City-State a better constitution. Small would be the enjoyment that a City-State would reap over the athletic victory of a citizen beside the banks of Pisa! These things do not enrich the treasure-chambers of the State.[31]

Like Tyrtaeus, Xenophanes opposes the popular culture of the polis in which the Olympic champion has become the successor to the Homeric hero. "It is not right to judge strength higher than holy wisdom." But what is this new excellence that will presumably fatten the storerooms of the polis? It is not honesty, initiative, thrift, hard work, and other economic virtues similar to those praised by Hesiod. It is excellence of a theological-intellectual nature, an improved understanding of the gods. Xenophanes is convinced that the mythical symbolic form, given pan-Hellenic authority through Homer and Hesiod, is inadequate, "unseemly." Furthermore, he is convinced that if the traditional myths about the gods are allowed to continue to represent "the ultimate," the religious tradition will endanger the common good of the polis. As in the case of most Greek authors who wrote before the fifth century B.C., we have available for analysis only fragments rather than complete works. The poem quoted above seems to be complete, but it is an exception. Voegelin has arranged the pertinent fragments of Xenophanes' poems in three groups:

1. The attack itself was directed against the improper representation of the gods. "Homer and Hesiod have ascribed to the

---

[31] Fragment 2, translated by Kathleen Freeman and included in her *Ancilla to the Pre-Socratic Philosophers* (Cambridge, 1962), p. 21.

gods all things that are a shame and disgrace among men, such as stealing, adultery, and cheating each other" [Fragment 11]. The reason for such misrepresentation Xenophanes apparently sought and found in the naiveté of the early poets. "Mortals suppose that gods are born, and have clothes, voices and bodily forms like theirs." [14] Men create gods in their image, down to racial differences: "Ethiopians make their gods flat-nosed and black, the Thracians let theirs have blue eyes and red hair." [16] And if horses and oxen and lions could make works of art like men "they would form their gods horse-like and oxen-like, each after its own kind." [15]

2. To such fancies Xenophanes opposed his own conception of God: "One God is greatest among gods and men, not like mortals in body or thought." [23] The divine is a living being though not of articulated form, for "all through it sees, all through it thinks, all through it hears." [24] Without effort it sways all things through its thought. [25] "It ever abides in the self-same place and never moves; nor is it seemly for it to go now hither now thither." [26]

3. Concerning source and certainty of his knowledge Xenophanes raised no specific claims: "The gods did not grant knowledge of all things to mortals from the beginning, but by seeking they find in time what is better" [18]; and "there never was nor will be a man who knows about the gods and all the things I speak of. Even if by chance he should say the full truth, yet he would not know that he does so; there is fancy in all things." [34] [32]

To his claim that "it is not right" to rank strength above wisdom Xenophanes adds the claim that "it is not seemly" (appropriate) to speak of the gods as though they were men. He offers a list of qualities that he believes *are* appropriate: oneness, universality, unchangeableness, and cosmos-ordering intellectual power, but he can give no criterion for deciding how these qualities are to be symbolized adequately. The most he can say is that although there seems to be a historical development

[32] Translated and quoted by Eric Voegelin, *Order and History,* vol. II, p. 172.

from less adequate to more adequate images, still "there is fancy" (imagination) in all symbolic forms through which men express their experiences of ultimacy. Xenophanes may be aware that in their day Homer and Hesiod moved toward a more universal conception of ultimacy by simplifying and unifying the Olympian pantheon. But two centuries have passed, and now many people are embarrassed by the fact that the myths portray gods who do not live up to accepted human standards. The trouble is that a kind of literalism has developed that blocks the functioning of the gods as symbols that point to the dimension of mystery in reality, to experiences of beyondness and ultimacy. Xenophanes, however, simply diagnoses the situation in terms of a "cultural lag." His analysis is that his contemporaries are still hanging on to inappropriate images and figures of speech inherited from their ancestors, even though they ought to know better by now.

Xenophanes' diagnosis has had far-reaching historical consequences, not least in the eighteenth and nineteenth centuries. In the nineteenth century, for instance, Auguste Comte constructed a grandiose schematic model of the standard stages through which human thought must pass before it reaches maturity. According to Comte, human thinking begins with anthropomorphic theology, moves to metaphysical philosophy (in which concepts function the way the gods used to), and finally rises to positive science and to genuine knowledge. This schematic model still exerts great power in our own century, especially in combination with various components of the modern myth of progress.

Xenophanes' repudiation of the Olympian gods is too easy. In fact, it is based on a fallacy. He assumes that the complex of images expressed in myths was intended to be a rational construction. To put it concretely, he assumes that the experience of Homer and Hesiod was as differentiated as his own, and then he beats them over the head because they did not make the same distinctions he makes. He does the same sort of thing that many modern scholars do when the study of myths becomes a necessary part of their job of understanding the past. They assume that primitive and archaic civilized men intended to give a scientific account of, say, the creation of the world; therefore creation myths must be dismissed as childish, crude, or irrational, because obviously they are far from being scientific. Xenophanes says that "there is fancy in all things," but he seems to be unable to appreciate the type of fancy that created the imagery surrounding the Olympian gods.

Nevertheless, Xenophanes deserves great honor as the pioneer of Hellenic preoccupation with the problem of the appropriate symbolization of the divine. In our survey of the speculative development in Egyptian priestly circles during the period of the ascendancy of the god Amon, we said that these thinkers came amazingly close to a theoretical recognition of the fact that they could talk most effectively about the utter hiddenness of Amon by saying what he was not, and about the dynamic presence of Amon in the cosmos by using analogies to objects and qualities of human experience, being aware all the time that no image or symbol derived from human experience is literally applicable to ultimate reality. Although Xenophanes can offer no final criterion for determining appropriateness or inappropriateness, his descriptions of the "One" that grasps him and elicits devotion and loyalty from him suggest that for him also the seemliness of images rests as much on what they deny as on what they affirm. The One is not mortal, but neither is it immortal like the gods. They came into being; the One always was and always will be. The One does not see or think or hear as men do: it sees, thinks, and hears "all through," comprehensively, exhaustively. It does not achieve its order as men do: through thought it sways all things, and it does so without effort. The negatives are interesting, and we see also that Xenophanes himself skirts the edge of anthropomorphism in his positive use of "sees, thinks, and hears," even though he insists that these powers are superpersonal.

Thales (c. 585 B.C.) and Anaximander (c. 560 B.C.)

A generation later Heraclitus criticized Xenophanes for not having drawn a direct parallel between the thinking of the One and human thinking instead of having given the impression that the "thought that sways all things" must somehow be quite different from human thought. "Much learning does not teach one to have intelligence; for it would have taught Hesiod and Pythagoras, and again Xenophanes and Hecataeus." [40] "You could not in your going find the ends of the soul, though you travelled the whole way: so deep is its Law" [*Logos*—thought, power of reason]. [45] [33] Man possesses a depth dimension that is universal (at least potentially) and "deep-knowing" like the One. We shall consider this deeper *logos* very soon in our discussion of Parmenides and Heraclitus; but first it is important to relate the work of Xenophanes to the speculations about the physical cosmos which were being carried on by some of his contemporaries, notably Thales and Anaximander. All three men lived in the Asia Minor region of Hellas, the region in which Homer's epics probably were written. Thales and Anaximander came from the city of Miletus, while Xenophanes came from Colophon. Even during the classical period of Greek culture the work of these men was known only in fragmentary form, but certain features of their approach to reality and certain major concepts they used were remembered.

Unlike Xenophanes, who attacked the religious tradition, Thales and Anaximander quietly disregarded the Olympian god symbols and concentrated their attention on the natural world rather than on man and society. Thales speculated on the origin and organization of the cosmos in the manner of Hesiod, except that when Thales explained what he meant by his statement, "All things are full of gods," he simply said that water—the element water, not Oceanus, or Poseidon—is the primal reality that permeates all entities and all phenomena, uniting them into a cosmos. There are three major modes of being in nature: solids, liquids, and gases. Water manifests itself in all three modes. Therefore water is a meaningful image of the hidden unifying power at work throughout the cosmos. Anaximander went a step further. He became convinced that no particular "thing" in the cosmos (like water) can be the clue to the unity of all "things." Therefore he spoke about the "Non-Limited."

These thinkers and their colleagues achieved one of the great differentiating insights in human history. They discovered that

---

[33] Fragments 40 and 45, Freeman, *op. cit.*, p. 27.

nature, as given in man's sense experience, is an autonomous realm. The experience that they could transcend themselves outward into the seemingly endless variety of fascinating phenomena of the world, rather than upward into the Heaven or down into the Hades of the gods, led them to develop not only a method of speculation but also a new form of expression. They explicated their experience of nature's order by means of concepts rather than by means of mythical symbols of gods.

The most obvious correlation between the work of the "physiologists" and the work of Xenophanes is that between the Non-Limited and the One. Aristotle writes of the speculation that lies behind both images:

> Everything is either a source or derived from a source. But there cannot be a source of the infinite or limitless, for that would be a limit of it. Further, as it is a beginning, it is both uncreatable and indestructible. For there must be a point at which what has come to be reaches completion, and also a termination of all passing away. That is why, as we say, there is no principle of *this,* but it is this which is held to be the principle of other things, and to encompass all and to steer all, as those assert who do not recognize, alongside the infinite, other causes, such as Mind or Friendship. Further, they identify it with the Divine, for it is "deathless and imperishable" as Anaximander says, with the majority of the physicists.[34]

But Aristotle's summary is much more characteristic of Anaximander than of Xenophanes. Anaximander thinks his way to a new conception of the Divine; Xenophanes is grasped by an immediate experience of awe and of the sublimity of the One. Xenophanes' passionate attack on the inadequacy of traditional pictures of the Divine derives its power from reverence and its cutting edge from conviction. Xenophanes is profoundly impressed by the disturbing implications for traditional religious imagery of the rational speculation being developed by men like Thales and Anaximander, and he is impressed also by the compatibility of concepts such as boundlessness, immovability, a first

---

[34] Aristotle, *Physics,* Book III, ch. IV, translated by Hardie and Gaye (New York, 1941), p. 259.

principle which itself had no beginning, and so on, with his experience of ultimacy.[35]

We do not have space to go into the question of the dependence of Anaximander and the "physicists" on the religious tradition for their fundamental presuppositions. One of the most interesting treatments of this relationship is that of F. M. Cornford, who describes the Milesian philosophy as "the elucidation and clarifying of religious, or even pre-religious, material. It does not create its new conceptual tools; it rather discovers them by ever subtler analysis and closer definition of the elements confused it its original datum." [36] This statement still does not tell us anything about the quality or depth of Anaximander's religious concerns. Here we can do no more than make an educated guess. Was the tremendous effort to penetrate the ancient ultimate, *moira,* by means of thought a detached, theoretical enterprise and nothing more? Or was it perhaps rooted in a profound and passionate urge to deprive destiny of its frightful mystery by subjecting it to rational analysis? In one of the rare fragments that has been preserved Anaximander says:

> The Non-Limited is the original material of existing things; further, the source from which existing things derive their ex-

---

[35] The concept of appropriateness ("seemliness") introduced by Xenophanes became very significant for Greek culture generally, and Werner Jaeger has traced its wider historical influence on the problem of what descriptions befit the divine nature and what descriptions do not, as he does in the following description of Xenophanes' influence:

> His own formulations are so striking that nothing is left for posterity but to quote his celebrated words and ring the changes upon them. We need only mention a few main stages in the history of his influence. Euripides' treatment of the gods in his tragedies is largely determined by Xenophanes' criticism of the inappropriateness of the way in which they were represented in the traditional myths; so are Plato's recommendations for the use of myth as an educational device in the *Republic.* Xenophanes' doctrine provides the basis for the discourse of the Stoic in Cicero's dialogue, *De natura deorum.* The Stoic distinction between mythical and philosophical theology, which reached St. Augustine by way of Varro, eventually goes back to Xenophanes . . . . Late Greek invents a special term to designate the theological category of 'that which befits the divine nature'. . . . Probably this word was coined by the Stoics; at any rate, through them it came down to the Church Fathers, who made it one of the cornerstones of Christian theology.

Theology of the Early Greek Philosophers, translated by Edward S. Robinson (London, 1947), p. 50.

[36] *From Religion to Philosophy* (New York, 1957), p. 126.

> istence is also that to which they return at their destruction, according to necessity [moira]; for they give justice and make reparation to one another for their injustice, according to the arrangement of Time.[37]

This passage suggests that Anaximander's concern with the Non-Limited was not unrelated to the melancholy experience of the transience of all finite things—for many men the existential matrix of passionate search for participation in an eternal ultimate.

Anaximander's choice of imagery in the fragment just quoted merits comment, for it both gives us a preview of the later development of speculation about the cosmos and human existence and carries with it an echo of the past. He uses legal terms, and implicit in his picture of the coming-to-be and the passing-away of all things in nature in terms of a lawsuit before the tribunal of time is the concept of universal natural law. This picture is a projection into the cosmos of the experience of law in maintaining order in human society. In certain respects it closely parallels the imagery of the Mesopotamian view, "as on earth, so in heaven." Moreover, when we study Heraclitus, we shall find that he adds the other direction characteristic of the Mesopotamian cosmological myth, "as in heaven, so on earth."

In any case, Anaximander and Xenophanes represent two distinct types of experience. The "physiologist-physicist" transcends himself outward into the boundlessness of nature while the "theologian" transcends himself inward into the boundlessness of the One, whose all-encompassing thought he dimly recognizes to be the essence of his own humanity. Aristotle is the mature representative of the first type, Plato of the second.

We have said that Xenophanes attacks the Olympian imagery of Homer and Hesiod because it attributes to the gods "all things that are a disgrace among men," providing citizens with a convenient excuse for selfish, immoral, antisocial behavior. Does he actually make any practical contribution to strengthening the moral fiber of the polis? If he were asked this question he might ask in return, "What do you mean by 'practical'?" Upon being reminded that he himself has claimed that his brand of wisdom "fattens the storerooms of the polis" and contributes more to a lawfully ordered life than the athletic skill that many citizens call a "divine excellence," he would probably say: "Selfish urges,

[37] Fragment 1, Freeman, *op. cit.*, p. 19.

which harm the good of the polis economically and socially, can be overcome successfully *if* men know that there is a true, lasting good. I have removed the 'if.' Now men can know the One, which is truly good and absolutely permanent. This knowledge is what I mean by wisdom. Tyrtaeus stressed courage, Solon stressed just and prudent judgment, but wisdom is the most important excellence of all."

4

The Emergence of Philosophy as a Deliberate Form of Thought and Expression

Xenophanes leaves us puzzled about the connection between knowledge of the One and the economic prosperity of the polis. Already we can feel the beginning of tension between the concrete vitalities and interests of the polis and the universalistic implications of speculation. Like Israel, the Hellenic polis must struggle to remain alive in the hazardous world of power politics, while the prophets and philosopher-theologians call for acknowledgment of the true ultimate: Yahweh the Lord of the universe in Israel, the universal divine in Hellas. Unfortunately, in both instances, the burden of the message consists not of information that can be handed over to the citizens but rather of convictions based on new differentiations of experience. Just as the prophets are patriots, so are the philosophers. Yet both groups become increasingly isolated because they reject convictions, attitudes, and mores prevalent in their societies and because their fellow-citizens do not participate in the process of differentiation.

Parmenides (c. 475 B.C.)

Parmenides of Elea (southern Italy), with his radical reinterpretation of the concept of *doxa* (illusion or delusion), is the pioneer in declaring the independence of philosophy. Solon's identification of illusion with the blindness caused by an inordinate desire for wealth or power is easy to understand; it ties in with familiar experiences shared by everyone. But Parmenides in his major work, a poetic epic written about 485 B.C., calls the entire realm of sense experience a realm of delusion. He claims that the commonly accepted knowledge gained through the five senses and habitually transmitted by tradition and custom must be rejected if truth is to be known. He announces that the nameless goddess of light has revealed to him the only ways of inquiry thinkable, and that she has directed him to "*the* way."

> And the goddess received me kindly, and took my right hand in hers, and thus she spoke and addressed me:
>
> "Young man, companion of immortal charioteers, who comest by the help of the steeds which bring thee to our dwelling: welcome!—since no evil fate has despatched thee on thy journey by this road (for truly it is far from the path trodden by mankind); no, it is divine command and Right. Thou shalt inquire into everything: both the motionless heart of well-rounded Truth, and also the opinions of mortals, in which there is no true reliability. But nevertheless thou shalt learn these things [opinions] also—how one should go through all the things-that-seem, without exception, and test them.
>
> "Come, I will tell you—and you must accept my word when you have heard it—the ways of inquiry which alone are to be thought: the one that IT IS, and it is not possible for IT NOT TO BE, is the way of credibility, for it follows Truth; the other, that IT IS NOT, and that IT is bound NOT TO BE: this I tell you is a path that cannot be explored; for you could neither recognise that which is NOT, nor express it.
>
> "For it is the same thing to think and to be.
>
> "Observe nevertheless how things absent are securely present to the mind; for it will not sever Being from its connection with Being, whether it is scattered everywhere utterly throughout the universe, or whether it is collected together.
>
> "It is all the same to me from what point I begin, for I shall return again to this same point.
>
> "One should both say and think that Being Is; for To Be is possible, and Nothingness is not possible. This I command you to consider; for from the latter way of search first of all I debar you. But next I debar you from that way along which wander mortals knowing nothing, two-headed, for perplexity in their bosoms steers their intelligence astray, and they are carried along as deaf as they are blind, amazed, uncritical

> hordes, by whom To Be and Not To Be are regarded as the same and not the same, and [for whom] in everything there is a way of opposing stress.
>
> "For this [view] can never predominate, that That Which Is Not exists. You must debar your thought from this way of search, not let ordinary experience in its variety force you along this way, [namely, that of allowing] the eye, sightless as it is, and the ear, full of sound, and the tongue, to rule; but [you must] judge by means of the Reason [Logos] the much-contested proof which is expounded by me.
>
> "There is only one other description of the way remaining, [namely], that [What Is] Is. To this way there are very many sign-posts: that Being has no coming-into-being and no destruction, for it is whole of limb, without motion, and without end. And it never Was, nor Will Be, because it Is now, a Whole all together, One, continuous; for what creation of it will you look for? How, whence [could it have] sprung? Nor shall I allow you to speak or think of it as springing from Not-Being; for it is neither expressible nor thinkable that What-Is-Not Is. Also, what necessity impelled it, if it did spring from Nothing, to be produced later or earlier? Thus it must Be absolutely, or not at all. Nor will the force of credibility ever admit that anything should come into being, beside Being itself, out of Not-Being. So far as that is concerned, Justice has never released [Being] in its fetters and set it free either to come into being or to perish, but holds it fast. The decision on these matters depends on the following: IT IS or IT IS NOT. It is therefore decided —as is inevitable—[that one must] ignore the one way as unthinkable and inexpressible [for it is no true way] and take the other as the way of Being and Reality. How could Being perish? How could it come into being? If it came into being, it Is Not; and so too if it is about-to-be at some future time. Thus Coming-into-Being is quenched, and Destruction also into the unseen." [38]

This piece of methodical philosophizing is the first of which we have a record. It rests on a mystical experience of "being" that further differentiates Xenophanes' experience of the universal One. Parmenides claims that there is a specific faculty in man's reason (*nous*) that can bring nonsensual, intelligible reality into man's grasp provided he systematically ignores the realm of sense perception and refuses to speculate on the plu-

---

[38] Fragments 1, 2, 4, 6, 7, *ibid.*, pp. 42-44.

ality of things that the senses perceive. *Nous* can perceive being, nd logical argumentation (*logos*) can articulate the content of nis type of perceiving.

Sense experience leads to opinion; logical analysis of sense xperience leads to logical contradictions that cannot be resolved. Only systematic logical construction based on the experience of nmovable, eternal, unified, interconnected, indivisible, homo-eneous, impenetrable being is able to grasp ultimate truth. With elentless logic Parmenides deduces each of these characteristics f being. In repeating over and over again, "That which is can-ot not be: that which is not cannot be," Parmenides expresses his xultant realization that a logical contradiction cannot be re-olved. In insisting that logical reasoning can give knowledge of he absolute necessity (*ananke, dike, moira*) that is the innermost uality of being, he speaks with the logician's triumphant belief n the necessary sequence of his thoughts. Parmenides' great dis-overy is the compulsion of pure thought, freed from the inter-erence of sense experience. His conviction is that what we today vould call logical "law," or "the rules of the game" in a particu-ar logical system, is the one and only objective table of organi-ation (law) of reality itself.

But what can the man on the street, who trusts his eyes and ars, make of Parmenides? Someone introduces him to the great nan, and Parmenides begins explaining that his speculation is n incarnation of the truth of being achieved through logical operations on the experience of "being is; not being is not." The irst reaction of the man in the street will be, "What's that?" Ten minutes later, utterly mystified and probably bored by the lemand that in order to find out he must first regard every-hing his eyes and ears tell him as illusion, he goes on his way nuttering, "So what?" One answer is that Parmenides does not belong so much to the polis and its destiny as he belongs to the uture. His clear-cut distinction between perception and thought, he way of the senses and the way of logic, still persists today in he tension between empiricist and rationalist modes of philoso-phizing. But there is another answer to the man in the street. Parmenides invites him to become aware of the fact that the di-vine *nous*, the "organ" that can grasp ultimate being, is a part of his native equipment as a man. He will not really under-stand himself unless he pays attention to dimensions of his ex-perience that point to the presence in him of this superior power.

Perhaps this invitation, which Parmenides and his fellow philosophers issued again and again to their contemporaries, will be refused. But we should never forget that most of the Hellenic philosophers believed that even their most abstract and sometimes abstruse speculations were relevant to the life of the polis. They believed that their search for true reality was a search for the "ultimate" to which the citizens of the polis must be attuned if they wanted to order human affairs properly.

The most impressive characteristic of Parmenides is the relentlessness with which he pursues the course of logical argumentation. But his classic articulation of a single component (*logos*) in the life of the human spirit is one-sided. He pays little attention to aspects of human activity that cannot be conquered by pure logic—emotion and suffering, decision making and creativeness—aspects that deserve equally careful speculative articulation. This judgment may not be fair; if the last major section of Parmenides' intellectual epic had been preserved we might find that he gave a more adequate treatment to other aspects of human experience than we have supposed. The section is named *Doxa,* and he tells us that in it he will recount what the goddess of light tells him about the common world of daily experience. She promises to give him a "likely account" of the arrangement of the world. Perhaps Parmenides recognizes that our experience of that which comes into existence and passes out of existence can be described fairly accurately, completely, and consistently. Perhaps he makes it clear that the conflict between truth and delusion is not a conflict between true and false propositions, but rather a conflict between two types of experience in the same human. The notion of a likely account reminds us of Xenophanes' statement that "all things are full of fancy." As we shall see, this conception of the role of imagination is continued and elaborated by Plato in his philosophy of myth. In his *Timaeus* Plato defines myth as a "likely story" and defends its importance. The dominating experience of Parmenides seems to have been an absolute certainty that his *nous* perceives Being, a certainty supported and illustrated by the conclusive demonstration of Being's ultimacy which he can supply through logic (*logos*).[39]

---

[39] Eric Voegelin is particularly impressed by the symbol of the ways and "*the* way," which Parmenides introduced into the Hellenic tradition, especially

Heraclitus (c. 500 B.C.)

Heraclitus of Ephesus (Asia Minor), a contemporary of Parmenides, also passionately desires certainty. But in his search for it he includes a much more serious exploration of the "realm of delusion," where Parmenides says that "likelihood" is the most one can hope to achieve. Heraclitus considers emotion and suffering, creativeness and decision making—all of which are related intimately to sense experience—just as important as the transcendent realm of Xenophanes' universal One and Parmenides' pure Being. He claims that a new world of knowledge can be opened if men will turn their attention inward and contemplate the dynamics of *all* dimensions of their experience. Werner Jaeger calls him the first philosophical anthropologist, meaning that Heraclitus makes explicit the break with the ancient conviction that immortality and divinity are inseparable. Heraclitus realizes that the archaic symbolization of gods in human shape is actually a symbolization of areas and forces of the human soul. He absorbs the Olympian gods into the soul, and then he places this vastly deepened and more complicated human individual under the "Alone Wise," which is his name for the truly ultimate.

---

in relation to the fact that in the Biblical tradition the ways of the righteous and the unrighteous appear (see Psalm 1) but not the "way of truth." He writes of *Parmenides:*

> In his didactic poem (*c.* 485), the Eleatic philosopher created the symbol of the 'Way of Truth' that leads man beyond the deafness and blindness of Doxa toward his fulfillment. The Way of Truth was a 'type' in the Platonic sense. This way, from the immortalizing pathos of the polis to the truth for the individual soul, runs parallel in time to the way, in Israelite history, from the Chosen People to the Suffering Servant of Deutero-Isaiah. The process in which the soul disengages itself from collective existence and achieves its attunement with transcendent-divine reality, was in both instances on principle the same—with the important difference, however, that in no period of Jewish history before the appearance of Christ had the articulation of the life of the soul, as well as of the way of truth, reached an intenseness and a precision of symbolism comparable with the Hellenic of the fifth and fourth centuries B.C. Only with Jesus does the symbol of the Way of Truth appear in the Jewish orbit.

Order and History, vol. II, p. 203.

> Travel over every road, you cannot discover the frontiers of the soul—it has so deep a *logos*.[40]

And equally significant:

> The soul has a *logos* that augments itself.[41]

For Heraclitus, the human *logos* is not the conceptual thinking and the logical argumentation of Parmenides, whose logic depends on the assumption that conceptualization and the systematic, consistent interrelation of concepts is precisely a process of delimitation, of drawing clear-cut boundaries. The way Heraclitus expresses himself makes this difference obvious. The fragments available to us contain no lengthy passages of logical argumentation. We are confronted by oracles, brief and often tantalizingly opaque single sentences:

> I explored myself. [101]
>
> Eyes and ears are bad witnesses for men whose souls are barbarous. [107]
>
> If you do not hope, you will not find the unhoped-for, since it is hard to be found and the way is all but impassable. [18]
>
> Nature loves to hide. [123]
>
> What comes within the range of eye, ear, and learning, that I prize most highly. [55]
>
> The invisible harmony is better than the visible. [54]
>
> From all is One, and from One is all. [10]
>
> The most beautiful cosmos is like a garbage-heap strewn at random. [124]
>
> Immortals—mortals, mortals—immortals, they live each other's death and die each other's life. [62] [42]

Fortunately we have a paragraph that seems to set the theme of Heraclitus' teaching concerning the divine *logos* and which includes motifs that appear in other fragments.

---

[40] Fragment 45, translated by Werner Jaeger, *Paideia,* vol. I, p. 180.

[41] Fragment 115, translated by Eric Voegelin, *Order and History,* vol. II, p. 228.

[42] All fragments translated by Eric Voegelin and quoted in *Order and History,* vol. II, pp. 228, 233, 235.

> Although this Logos is eternally valid, yet men are unable to understand it—not only before hearing it, but even after they have heard it for the first time. That is to say, although all things come to pass in accordance with this Logos, men seem to be quite without any experience of it—at least if they are judged in the light of such words and deeds as I am here setting forth. My own method is to distinguish each thing according to its nature, and to specify how it behaves; other men, on the contrary, are as forgetful and heedless in their waking moments of what is going on around and within them as they are during sleep.[43]

Logos refers both to a sense or meaning existing from eternity and to Heraclitus' discourse (*logos*). Since all things come to pass in accordance with the eternal *logos,* it must be a law or order of the cosmos. Heraclitus' own *logos,* his exposition revealing the true meaning of experience, will be strange to those who try to grasp it because, unfortunately, the mass of men are sleepwalkers who experience reality without becoming aware of the full dimensions of their selves, especially of the dimensions of meaning provided by the divine *logos*. Heraclitus says such things as these:

> But though the Logos is common, the many live as if they had a wisdom of their own. [2]
>
> Those who are awake have a world one and common, but those who are asleep each turn aside into their own private worlds. [89]
>
> It is not meet to act and speak like men asleep. [73]
>
> Those who speak with the mind must strengthen themselves with that which is common to all, as the polis does with the law and more strongly so. For all human laws nourish themselves from the one divine—which prevails as it will, and suffices for all things and more than suffices. [114] [44]

These are striking sentences. Omit the notion of a divine law and Heraclitus sounds very modern; he seems to say that the one

---

[43] Fragment 1, translated by Philip Wheelwright in his *Heraclitus* (Princeton, 1959), p. 19.

[44] Translated by Eric Voegelin and quoted in *Order and History,* vol. II, pp. 231-32.

common world, which is the corrective for our tendencies to be sleepwalkers in our private worlds, is that with which science deals. The oracles become a call for empirical objectivity over and against emotional subjectivity. But this is not what Heraclitus is saying. The social universality of the human *logos* is not the universality of scientific language and method, although if Heraclitus were living today he would in no way belittle the impressive and productive results achieved by scientists because their "logos" makes possible dependable worldwide communication within the scientific community. Heraclitus had in mind the community of the polis, its daily life, and its need to be attuned to the one divine *logos* by which all human laws are nourished. There is a law in the universe, as in the city, and the human must correspond to the divine. There is a way up and a way down, and what goes up must come down. The human *logos* awakens to the divine *logos* and ascends toward knowledge of it; then it comes back down, joins other awakened souls in sharing the universal (common) insight, and this elite community of awakened souls devotes itself to waking the sleepwalkers so that the order of the polis can be attuned to the truth of nature and its divine law.

Heraclitus combines the way up (the Xenophanes and Parmenides dimension of the human soul) and the way down (the dynamic depth dimension of the soul), and to this vertical dimension he adds Anaximander's horizontal "scientific" dimension—the power of the human mind to range throughout the entire natural cosmos. His special discovery, however, is the picture of human selfhood implied by man's ability to transcend any given set of circumstances and any given level of experience through imagination and reflection. His *logos* is mysteriously deep and limitless; it seems akin to the divine *logos* while at the same time it participates in the ceaseless changing processes of nature. "From all is One, and from One is all." [10] The cosmos is nature, the nature we can see and touch and hear and smell; and at the very same time and in the very same phenomena the cosmos is the manifestation of the invisible, universal divinity. To the man who is asleep—in Heraclitus' meaning of being asleep—its surface resemblance to "a garbage-heap strewn at random" hides its true structure, which is orderly, a "cosmos" and not a "chaos." In other words, the Greek cosmos is not something found through observation of the external world. Earlier we quoted the fragment that sketches Anaximander's picture of the cosmos:

> The Non-Limited is the original material of existing things; further, the source from which existing things derive their existence is also that to which they return at their destruction, according to necessity; for they give justice and make reparation to one another for their injustice, according to the arrangement of Time.[45]

This is human experience of law, human social order, projected into the cosmos. When Heraclitus says that things "live each other's death and die each other's life," he seems to be saying the same thing. And when he goes on to picture the "Alone Wise" as alive with psychic power and as actively steering all things through all things (external and internal) by its thought, he is saying that the doorway to understanding reality is the depth dimension of the human soul rather than the world outside man. "I sought for myself," he says, and he finds in the depths of the self not only the cosmos but also the "Alone Wise," in which all things cohere.

Nevertheless, "That which alone is wise is one; it is willing and unwilling to be called by the name of Zeus." [32] [46] Man can know about the divine wisdom, but he cannot possess it. The term "philosopher" is introduced into the stream of Hellenic speculation by Heraclitus in this context. The man who is awake, who enters into the process of seeking understanding, should not be called wise (*sophos*) but rather a lover of wisdom (*philosophos*). He is on the right road. This, and not the Q.E.D. (*quod erat demonstrandum*) of logical demonstration, is his certainty. It is far more than the tentativeness we are likely to associate with "being on the right road." It is an unwavering confidence, born of mystical experience and intuitive insight. Like the medieval Christian thinker Anselm, Heraclitus might say of his way of philosophizing: "I believe in order to understand." And like Anselm, he is drawing on a tradition that provides him with

---

[45] Fragment 1, translated by Kathleen Freeman in her *Ancilla to the Pre-Socratic Philosophers,* p. 19.

[46] Fragment 32, *ibid.,* p. 27.

convictions and experiences for his analysis and speculation. We cannot proceed before we take a look at this tradition.

There is a passage in Plato's *Timaeus* that formulates a conception of the soul presupposed not only by Heraclitus but also by Xenophanes and Parmenides. Plato says:

> With regard to the kind of soul which is dominant in us we should consider that God has given it to each of us as a *daimon,* dwelling as we said at the top of the body; and because of its affinity with Heaven it draws us away from Earth, for most truly we are a heavenly growth, not an earthly one. The Divine, indeed, has placed our head in the direction from where the soul had its first origin, as it were as its root, thus making the body upright. Now, when a man abandons himself to his desires and ambitions, indulging them incontinently, all his thoughts of necessity become mortal, and as a consequence he must become mortal every bit, as far as that is possible, because he has nourished his mortal part. When on the contrary he has earnestly cultivated his love of knowledge and of true wisdom, when he has primarily exercised his faculty to think immortal and divine things, he will—since in that manner he is touching the truth—become immortal of necessity, as far as it is possible for human nature to participate in immortality. For incessantly he is engaged in the cult of the Divine; and since he keeps in good order the *daimon* that lives in him he will himself become thoroughly *eudaimon* [blessed].[47]

This passage rejects the archaic Greek conviction concerning the virtual identity between divinity and immortality. As the experience of immortality advances from vague intimations to full consciousness of the fact that the divine can be experienced as immortal only because the experiencing soul somehow shares in the divine, two things happen. On the one hand, the divine takes on a new quality of ultimacy. It is not immortal; it is eternal. On the other hand, the human soul, conscious of the experience of transcendence that gives it intimations of immortality, recognizes that this quality is a precarious something that can be gained or lost. Immortality is not an item of information about oneself. As Plato says, "We are a heavenly

---

[47] (90 a-b), translated and quoted by Voegelin, *Order and History,* vol. II, pp. 205-06.

growth," meaning that we have both a divine origin and a responsibility to develop immortal qualities. They do not grow automatically, and they can be lost unless they are cultivated. A meaningful life, therefore, is best described as the cult of the divine within the soul.

This view of man contrasts sharply with the Homeric view. In Homer and Hesiod gods are gods and mortals are mortals; even the heroes born of a union between an immortal and a mortal are mortal. The view we have now introduced stems from traditions of mainland Greece that survived the pre-Homeric invasions, plus certain elements that may be traced to foreign shamanistic influences.[48] The movements known as Orphism and Pythagoreanism had much to do with the powerful expression and far-reaching spread of these traditions during the sixth century B.C. Their major influence was the propagation of the conviction that the soul is essentially immortal and therefore in some sense closely related to the divine.

Our discussion of Xenophanes, Parmenides, and Heraclitus should make clear that the belief in the possibility of significant participation in the ultimate and concern with the nurturing of immortal qualities in the human soul opened a new chapter in the Hellenic search for the meaning of human existence. These concerns and convictions helped make possible the transition from belief that the gods are outside man to the understanding that they symbolize movements within human selfhood. In Heraclitus the true range of humanity comes into view in correlation with the "Alone Wise," which is radically beyond any human capabilities, mortal or immortal. This is the curious paradox we mentioned earlier in connection with Xenophanes' attack on anthropomorphism. When a really profound view of man is attained, one that can be used appropriately as an analogy with which to talk about the divine or the sacred, the ultimate dimension of reality has become so mysterious and unfathomable that it cannot be described. In this situation, then, perhaps the mystery of the human person emerges as a more appropriate symbol of the divine mystery than Xenophanes would have thought possible. As we have seen, the Biblical tradition never

---

[48] See E. R. Dodds' chapter, "The Greek Shamans and the Origin of Puritanism," in his book, *The Greeks and the Irrational* (Boston, 1957).

uses impersonal or nonpersonal symbols for Yahweh, although sensitive members of the people of Israel knew very well that they could not describe Yahweh literally.[49]

From materials related to the mystery cults whose initiates were assured of the immortality of their souls, we mention two items that bear significantly on later philosophy. The first is the so-called Orphic myth of man's origin; the second is the doctrine of transmigration.

"Whence came mankind and whence became so evil?" The answer is a myth: it all began with the wicked Titans, the generation of gods vanquished by Zeus. They trapped the infant Dionysus, tore him apart, boiled him, roasted him, and then ate him. This propensity of the Titans to cannibalism, especially their habit of swallowing their young in order to prevent them from growing up and displacing their parents, is a point Hesiod emphasizes in his picture of the superiority of the Olympians over the savage and brutal Titans. Apparently, the Dionysus episode took place after Zeus had established his supremacy, for as soon as he found out about it he hurled a thunderbolt at the Titans and burned them up. From the smoke of the remains sprang the human race. Men thus inherited the wicked tendencies of the Titans, tempered by a tiny portion of the divine Dionysian soul that was mixed with the smoke. Since the Titans were born of Mother Earth and Dionysus was born of Heaven, human nature is a compound of earthly and heavenly elements. Man's duty is to develop the Dionysian element (usually identified with the soul) and to suppress the Titanic element (usually identified with the body and its desires and passions). The heart of Dionysus was saved by Athena. She brought it to Zeus, and from it Zeus caused Dionysus to be reborn. Thus the pattern has been established. The initiate participants in the living reality of the divine Dionysus, whose nature he already shares partially, and in the cult ritual he experiences full participation in the

[49] Paul Tillich's volume, *Biblical Faith and the Search for Ultimate Reality* (Chicago, 1964), is focused directly on the tension between the Biblical and the philosophical attempts to create adequate, appropriate symbols; it seeks to defend the continuing legitimacy of Biblical dramatic and philosophical conceptual modes of symbolization, even though the two modes cannot be fully harmonized with one another.

god. He is also "reborn." E. R. Dodds comments on the psychological power of the myth and ritual:

> The Titan myth neatly explained to the Greek puritan why he felt himself to be at once a god and a criminal; the "Apolline" sentiment of remoteness from the divine and the "Dionysiac" sentiment of identity with it were both of them accounted for and both of them justified. That was something that went deeper than any logic.[50]

But what about the destiny of the soul? Is "rebirth" in the cult the last word? What happens to the occult soul or self when the body dies? Apparently doctrines of transmigration (reincarnation, metempsychosis) were widespread and influential in sixth century Hellas. The poet Pindar, in a poem praising the manly virtue and wealth and power with which a certain Theron is blessed, also includes the assurance of reward in the hereafter as a blessing. He goes on to describe the afterworld, whose gates are unbolted only at the moment of death. The souls undergo a judgment that leads to torments for the wicked and, for the truly noble, to a life free from tears and toil and need. But both groups will be reborn again on earth. Only the person who has managed to live three earthly and three post-earthly lives without polluting his soul will be allowed to enter Cronus' lofty hall on the Islands of the Blest. Numerous other descriptions of the soul's repeated migrations from one earthly body to another might be cited. The most famous are the myths that Plato includes in the *Gorgias* and in the *Republic.* The latter pictures the life of the soul in terms of thousand-year cycles, at the end of which it brings to a close one connected series of births and deaths and begins another. There is individual choice of a destiny at the beginning of each cycle. The previous thousand years of recurring lifetimes should have educated the soul to make a wiser choice. Within the thousand-year series, however, each rebirth carries with it the excellence or lack of excellence that the soul has accumulated during the previous life.

Dodds believes that the widespread popularity of various notions concerning transmigration indicate that the Hellenes

---

[50] *The Greeks and the Irrational,* p. 156.

were deeply troubled about problems of human suffering, especially innocent suffering, or suffering beyond all rational bounds of a logic of punishment.

> Morally, reincarnation offered a more satisfactory solution of the Late Archaic problem of divine justice than did inherited guilt or post-mortem punishment in another world. With the growing emancipation of the individual from the old family solidarity, his increasing rights as a judicial "person," the notion of a vicarious payment for another's fault began to be unacceptable. When once human law had recognized that a man is responsible for his own acts only, divine law must sooner or later do likewise. As for post-mortem punishment, that explained well enough why the gods appeared to tolerate the worldly success of the wicked, and the new teaching in fact exploited it to the full, using the device of the "underworld journey" to make the horrors of Hell real and vivid to the imagination. But the post-mortem punishment did not explain why the gods tolerated so much human suffering, and in particular the unmerited suffering of the innocent. Reincarnation did. On that view, no human soul was innocent: all were paying, in various degrees, for crimes of varying atrocity committed in former lives. And all that squalid mass of suffering, whether in this world or in another, was but a part of the soul's long education—an education that would culminate at last in its release from the cycle of birth and return to its divine origin. Only in this way, and on this cosmic time-scale, could justice in its full archaic sense—the justice of the law that "the Doer shall suffer"—be completely realised for every soul.[51]

To this explanation of the appeal of reincarnation, we shall add a comment by Werner Jaeger, who emphasizes the importance of the doctrine in paving the way for increased awareness of the individual psyche as a combination of "life-soul" and "consciousness-soul," and for greater precision in analyzing new differentiations in the experience of selfhood.

> Leaving aside the problem of how and where the doctrine of metempsychosis arose (insoluble because nearly all the relevant traditional material has been lost), it is plain that what was really fruitful in this doctrine and pregnant with future in-

---

[51] *Ibid.*, pp. 150-51.

> fluence was not the mythical conception of transmigration, but the impetus the theory was to give to the development of the idea of the soul as the unity of life and spirit, and the vigour with which it conceived this psyche as a spiritual being in its own right, quite independent of the corporeal.[52]

The responsibility of the individual for his own destiny becomes an increasingly important concern, as noted in our discussion of Xenophanes, Parmenides, and Heraclitus. It goes far beyond the type of responsibility emphasized by Solon, for whom responsibility meant the social responsibility of the individual to the community. In Heraclitus, the order of the soul is pictured as branching out into the order of society, and both the individual and society participate in the dynamic cosmic order. In spite of this theoretical unity, Heraclitus himself seems more at home in the cosmos than in Ephesus, the polis of which he is a citizen.

> The Ephesians would do well to hang themselves, every grown man, and leave their polis to the beardless boys, for they have banned Hermodorus, the best man among them, saying: "None of us will be the best, and if he is, he will have to be it elsewhere and among others." [121]
>
> "One man is to me ten-thousand if he be the best." [49]
>
> "The people must fight for its law as for its walls." [114] [53]

The last aphorism implies that the Ephesians are not at all enthusiastic about searching for the law that nourishes itself from the divine law, or about struggling to live according to it once it is found. The conventional order of the polis cannot remain an unquestioned ultimate once the mystic-philosophers have discovered unsuspected depths and heights in man's imaginative, emotional, and intellectual capacities. Now, to be fully human means combining the common *logos* and the divine *logos,* which is something more than being a citizen in a Hellenic city-state, although it includes this citizenship.

The full potentials of the spiritual adventure of poets and philosophers in Hellas were realized in the generation of

---

[52] *Theology of the Early Greek Philosophers,* p. 84.

[53] All fragments translated and quoted by Voegelin in his *Order and History,* vol. II, pp. 238-39.

Parmenides and Heraclitus. On the one hand, the ultimate dimension of reality was experienced as "ultimately" as is conceivable in Parmenides' Being and in Heraclitus' Alone Wise, both of which were acknowledged to be mysterious, invisible, and universal. On the other hand, the human dimension became mysterious also; these men discovered heights and depths within themselves that gave promise of unprecedented growth, whose indeterminate limits shaded off into the divinity of the ultimate. At this point the widely different histories and experiences of the Hellenic poets and philosophers on the one hand and of the Israelite prophets (especially Jeremiah and Second Isaiah) on the other converge in a most interesting way. In his study *The Transformations of Man,* Lewis Mumford points out that a profound change of a religious and moral nature began during the sixth century B.C. in the Persia of Zoroaster and the India of the Buddha, as well as in Israel and Hellas, and he adopts the term coined by the German philosopher Karl Jaspers to identify the centuries of change: "the axial period." Mumford interprets what happened during the axial period as follows:

> From this time on the human personality can be formally divided into three parts, lately detected and described by Sigmund Freud, but always more or less acknowledged since the time of Aristotle. First: a basic biological self (the Old Adam), connected with man's animal past, stable, durable, requiring tens of thousands of years to produce any fundamental organic changes. This primeval self is the seat of all the vital processes: it holds, in its organs and tissues, the ultimate potentialities of mind and spirit; but it is to the more developed self as the quarry is to the carved statue. Second: a derivative social self, shaped by man's transmitted culture, by nurture, discipline, education, externalized in institutions and structures that create a common recognizable form for all its members. This self shows the beginnings of a differentiated ego; but it is largely a creature of habit and tradition; and in civilized regimes it splits up into an occupational self, a domestic self, a political self, as various situations impose their appropriate roles and dramas. In its most inclusive form it becomes the corporate "national self," on its way to a common human goal, but unable on its own terms to reach it. These civilized fragments are the relatively uniform blocks of stone, far removed from the quarry, but still to be shaped into individualized statues.
>
> Finally, there is an ideal self, the superego, the latest layer

> of the self, though dimly visible from the moment of man's emergence; the most frail, the most unstable, the most easily overthrown part of the human psyche, perhaps also the most subject to debasement. Yet this ideal self seeks a position of dominance, for it represents the path of continued growth and development.
>
> One is born *with* the first self, the biological substratum or id: one is born *into* the second self, the social self, which makes the animal over into a modified human image, and directs its purely animal propensities into useful social channels, carved by a particular group. But one must be reborn if one is to achieve the third self. In that rebirth, the latest part of the self, assuming leadership, projects a destination that neither man's animal nature nor his social achievements have so far more than faintly indicated. In this detachment lies the promise of further growth.[54]

So far the description is limited to what Mumford calls the "axial religions." He goes on to describe the axial philosophies.

> But there is another stream of development, paralleling the movement of the axial religions, that one must not neglect. For a long time it seemed an alternative way, sanctioned by reason and less dependent upon the uncontrollable impulses of the unconscious or the uncertainties of faith. This development is that of the axial philosophies. These philosophies rest on intuitions and proposals similar to those of axial religion: they likewise invoke man's higher nature and set goals that demand a break with the instinctual, the habitual, the conventional. Though axial philosophy does not neglect nonrational forces in the personality—did not Socrates listen to his daimon? did not Plato reserve his highest doctrine for direct oral communication?—it emphasizes the rational and the humanly controllable. These new leaders cling to the method of intellectual criticism and clarification, orderly knowledge, pedagogical discipline: whether they are quickened by mystical illumination or prophetic anxiety or intellectual curiosity, they are above all teachers.[55]

Mumford's statement that for a long time philosophy "seemed an alternative way" to the way of religion indicates that he views

---

[54] *The Transformations of Man* (New York, 1962), pp. 66-67.
[55] *Ibid.*, p. 72.

Hellenic philosophy—and most pre-twentieth-century Western philosophy as well—as best understood in the context of man's life-orienting convictions. The present author agrees. The axial philosophers are above all teachers who are concerned to communicate convictions.

5

The Religious Education of Athens

Up to this point we have met only one Athenian, the poet and statesman Solon. Most of the representative poets and philosophers of the seventh and sixth centuries B.C. lived and worked in the fringe areas of Hellas, notably in Asia Minor and in southern Italy. After the Athenians led the Greeks to victory over the invading Persians at Marathon in 490 B.C., however, Athens surged to the forefront of Hellenic life. Within two generations the Athenians assimilated everything that had been achieved during the two previous centuries. Athens became the permanent intellectual and cultural capital of Hellas, as well as the temporary center of pan-Hellenic political and military affairs.

We are especially interested in the relationship between the polis and the philosophers' image of a true humanity attuned to the ultimate. If the spiritual adventure of the poets and philosophers was to become something more than an irritation of the polis by a scattering of individuals, it would have to generate a Great Awakening among a significant percentage of the citizens of an actual polis. Such a great awakening was the unique achievement of the Athenian people. Their surprising victory over an apparently invincible Persian army at Marathon gave the Athenians an impressive new image of themselves and a superb confidence in their destiny. The glory and agony of Marathon, and the realization that a full-scale major war with Persia would undoubtedly have to be faced sooner or later, also gave them a vivid experience of the precariousness of the polis. They realized that it was an order achieved in the midst of disorder through sacrifices and risks. These experiences prepared the Athenians to respond to tragic drama, a new symbolic form that combined the common convictions underlying the life of the polis with the uncommon insights concerning divine ultimacy and human order that had been achieved by the poet-philosophers.

Tragic drama

Solon not only refused to seize absolute power for himself but also warned the Athenians of his generation that they would succumb to tyranny unless they vigilantly guarded against it. He lived to see Pisistratus, the aristocratic champion of the poor people from the hills, seize power. One measure that Pisistratus took to break the power of the hereditary family priesthoods of the aristocratic clans was to make the worship of the god Dionysus a state cult. Not long afterward, around 535 B.C., Thespis appeared at the annual Dionysian festival with his chorus of *tragodoi* (goat-singers). Like other choruses, they sang epic songs extolling the greatness of gods and heroes. But apparently Thespis took it upon himself to speak the words attributed to the god or hero in the narrative that was being sung, and this innovation opened the way to drama.[56]

From its beginning, tragedy was established as a cult institution of the people, but it did not remain a cultic performance tied specifically to the god Dionysus. The festival acquired the even more explicit function of unifying the polis after Cleisthenes effected the democratic reform in 508 B.C., which included the reorganization of Athens on a territorial basis. This measure effectively stifled the power of the noble clans and extended citizenship to a great number of people who formerly had not had a direct stake in the inner life of the polis. The battle of Marathon was won by citizen-soldiers. The period of prosperity and reconstruction that followed the victory brought with

[56] See Peter D. Arnott, *An Introduction to the Greek Theatre* (Bloomington, Indiana, 1963).

it an intensive cultivation of the arts, and the annual six-day dramatic competition during the Dionysian festival became an important feature of Athenian life. The dramatists who competed with one another in teaching the Athenians "who they were" resurrected the rich tradition of myth that all the people held in common, and through a free manipulation of familiar themes they contributed more than any other group to the Great Awakening.

Some thirty-three tragedies have survived; fortunately they were those written by the tragedians who were acknowledged by the Greeks themselves to be the greatest—Aeschylus, Sophocles, and Euripides. We will here confine ourselves to describing certain themes in Aeschylus' *The Suppliants* (484 B.C.) and his Oresteian trilogy (485 B.C.). Both the single play and the trilogy praise the order of the Athenian polis while at the same time they challenge its citizens to participate in the new depths and heights of personal maturity and responsibility that the philosophers have discovered.

In *The Suppliants,* Danaus has fifty daughters; his brother Aegyptus has fifty sons. When Aegyptus defeats Danaus in a struggle for rule over the Nile valley, his fifty sons demand that the fifty girls be turned over to them. The girls and their father manage to escape to Argos, the Greek polis in which their ancestress Io lived. The Danaids ask Pelasgus, the king of the polis, to give them sanctuary. Aeschylus constructs a very unpleasant dilemma for Pelasgus. The girls are not even Hellenes and have, in addition, broken the law of their own country by running away. If he gives them refuge there will be a costly war, for the Aegyptians are sure to try to get them back. On the other hand, the suppliants can appeal to Zeus because they are related to him distantly by way of Io, who bore to Zeus their ancestor. To make matters worse, they threaten to commit suicide by hanging themselves on the statues of the gods of the polis if Pelasgus refuses them their plea. This will pollute the city and bring retribution. In his perplexity Pelasgus says:

> A deep, saving counsel here there needs—
> An eye that like a diver to the depth
> Of dark perplexity can pass and see,
> Undizzied, unconfused. First must we care
> That to the State and to ourselves this thing

Shall bring no ruin; next, that wrangling hands
Shall grasp you not as prey, nor we ourselves
Betray you thus embracing sacred shrines,
Nor make the avenging all-destroying god,
Who not in hell itself sets dead men free,
A grievous inmate, an abiding bane.
—Spake I not right, of saving counsel's need? [57]

The king stands sunk in thought. He searches his soul, the soul whose depth dimension Heraclitus first described. Bruno Snell writes:

> Nowhere in early poetry does a man go through a similar struggle to arrive at a decision, nowhere does he, as in this scene, reflect "downward into the depth" of his soul in order to make up his mind? . . . The Homeric scenes in which a man deliberates what he ought to do are deficient in one distinctive feature which makes the decision of Pelasgus what it is: a wholly independent and private act. In Aeschylus the hero's choice becomes a problem whose solution is contingent on nothing but his own insight, but which is nevertheless regarded as a matter of compelling necessity.[58]

This is only one half of the decision that must be reached, however. Pelasgus insists that he can give no reply and no promise before he consults with the citizens of the polis in solemn assembly. The suppliant sisters (who are the Chorus in the play) argue that *he* is the "source of sway, the city's self," but Pelasgus will not take unilateral action. He invites the father of the girls, Danaus, to attend the town meeting, and eventually Danaus returns to announce that the citizens of Argos have faced the dilemma squarely and courageously:

With one assent the Argives spake their will,
And, hearing, my old heart took youthful cheer.
The very sky was thrilled when high in air
The concourse raised right hands and swore their oath:—
Free shall the maidens sojourn in this land.
Unharried, undespoiled by mortal wight:

---

[57] Translated by E. D. A. Morshead, in Oates and O'Neill (eds.), *The Complete Greek Drama* (New York, 1938), vol. I, p. 22.
[58] *The Discovery of the Mind,* pp. 102-03.

No native hand, no hand of foreigner
Shall drag them hence; if any man use force—
Whoe'er of all our countrymen shall fail
To come unto their aid, let him go forth,
Beneath the people's curse, to banishment. [59]

The glory of the polis lies in this, that the citizenry has willingly opened its soul to the tragic dilemma and has resolved to act heroically. Pelasgus has not ordered the citizens to acquiesce in the decision he believes to be just. He has persuaded them, and they have freely agreed. The joyful maidens join in a festive prayer, a portion of which goes as follows:

Fly forth, O eager prayer!
May never pestilence efface
        This city's race,
Nor be the land with corpses strewed,
        Nor stained with civic blood!
The stem of youth, unpluckt, to manhood come,
Nor Ares rise from Aphrodite's bower,
The lord of death and bane, to waste our youthful flower.

        Long may the old
Crowd to the altars kindled to consume
        Gifts rich and manifold—
Offered to win from powers divine
A benison on city and on shrine:
        Let all the sacred might adore
        Of Zeus most high, the lord
        Of guestright and the hospitable board,
Whose immemorial law doth rule Fate's scales aright:
        The garners of earth's store
        Be full for evermore . . . .

And let the people's voice, the power
That sways the State, in danger's hour
        Be wary, wise for all;
Nor honour in dishonour hold,
But—ere the voice of war be bold—

[59] *The Suppliants,* translated by E. D. A. Morshead in *The Complete Greek Drama,* p. 29 [translator's italics].

Let them to stranger peoples grant
Fair and unbloody covenant—
Justice and peace withal;[60]

The atmosphere changes quickly, however, when the pursuing Aegyptians arrive on the scene. With the full support of the polis, Pelasgus refuses to give up the girls. The ominous threat of war becomes imminent. The Aegyptians sense the resoluteness of Argos, and they hesitate. The play ends on this note; we do not learn whether or not the issue is contested on the battlefield. But this much is certain: whatever happens, both leader and citizens will acquit themselves nobly.

The three plays known as the Oresteian trilogy are in effect one continued story. Philip Vellacott summarizes the interlocking plots as follows in the introduction to his translation of the trilogy:

> The play *Agamemnon* opens in Argos a few hours after the capture of Troy; and its climax is the murder of Agamemnon, on his return, by Clytemnestra. In *The Choephori* Agamemnon's son Orestes, who had grown up in exile, returns to Argos at Apollo's command to avenge his father; he kills both Clytemnestra and her lover Aegisthus, and departs pursued by the Furies. Finally, in *The Eumenides,* Orestes stands his trial before Athene and the Athenian court of Areopagus. The Furies accuse him, Apollo defends him; the mortal votes are evenly divided; and Athene gives her casting vote for his acquittal. The Furies at first threaten Athens with plagues, but are at last persuaded by Athene to accept a home and a position of honour in her city.[61]

The Oresteian trilogy begins with *Agamemnon.* The Greek commander-in-chief, Agamemnon, returns home after the fall of Troy, only to be murdered by his wife Clytemnestra to avenge his sacrifice of their daughter Iphigenia in order to save his fleet from destruction. In the meantime, Clytemnestra has taken a lover, Aegisthus, and once she has killed her husband (together

---

[60] *Ibid.,* pp. 30-31.

[61] Aeschylus, *The Oresteian Trilogy,* translated by Philip Vellacott (Baltimore, 1956), p. 14.

with his prize of war, the prophetess Cassandra) both she and he look forward to a peaceful and happy life together. Aegisthus has his own reasons for rejoicing. He looks upon the death of Agamemnon as just retribution for the murder of his father Thyestes by Atreus, Agamemnon's father. He says:

> O happy day, when Justice comes into her own!
> Now I believe that gods, who dwell above the earth,
> See what men suffer, and award a recompense:
> Here, tangled in a net the avenging Furies wove,
> He lies, a sight to warm my heart; and pays his blood
> In full atonement for his father's treacherous crime.[62]

So Clytemnestra and Aegisthus consider their separate duties of vengeance discharged, and they are ready to close the case. The Chorus (twelve elders of the polis), however, knows that they are deluding themselves. The drama closes in an atmosphere of foreboding; the Chorus announces:

> Aegisthus, we acquit you of insults to the dead.
> But since you claim that you alone laid the whole plot,
> And thus, though absent, took his blood upon your hands,
> I tell you plainly, your own life is forfeited;
> Justice will curse you, Argive hands will stone you dead.[63]

The name of Orestes, the son of Agamemnon and Clytemnestra who is in exile, is invoked by the Chorus, and the possibility of further bloodletting throws a shadow across the future.

The sense of foreboding is justified. Clytemnestra and Aegisthus have miscalculated. Orestes lives, and he returns to Argos to avenge his father's murder. This is the story of the second drama, *The Libation-Bearers* (*Choephori*). Orestes finally kills his mother and Aegisthus, but his feelings about the execution are far different from his mother's feelings when she killed Agamemnon and Cassandra. Clytemnestra had gloated with fierce exultation as she looked down at her dead husband and his dead mistress:

---

[62] *Ibid.,* p. 97.
[63] *Ibid.,* p. 98.

So he lies, and there lies she,
Who chanted forth a dying groan like a swan's,
And *that* was the lover of *this*.
Not to his bed, but to mine
And my lover's, shall she add
The final relish of enjoyment.[64]

But Orestes, standing above the dead Clytemnestra and the dead Aegisthus in the final scene of *The Libation-Bearers,* is defensive and regretful. Holding his father's blood-stained robe, which he has found, he speaks to the Chorus:

Is she guilty or not guilty? See this robe dyed red
From the work of Aegisthus' sword: there is my evidence.
Yes, it is blood—blood, whose stains have joined with time
To fade and corrode the colours of this patterned stuff.

Now I pronounce the praise I could not utter then;
I offer now my lament, since I may not see his body,
To this treacherous web that caught and killed my father.

Her deed, her punishment—the whole business tortures me!
A victory whose pollution makes my life abhorred.[65]

He tells the Chorus that he will go as a suppliant to Delphi, "Apollo's sacred ground," to ask for refuge. The Chorus sees no reason for such desperate action, praising him for having set Argos free from "the two beasts that plagued us." But Orestes sees the Furies approaching:

Ah, ah!
Look, women, see them, there! Like Gorgons, with grey cloaks,
And snakes coiled swarming round their bodies! Let me go!

The Chorus remonstrates with him:

---

[64] *Agamemnon,* lines 1444-47, translated and quoted by Richmond Y. Hathorn, *Tragedy, Myth, and Mystery* (Bloomington, Indiana, 1962), p. 57. [Translator's italics.] This translation is used because it is much more apt and vivid than Vellacott's.

[65] Aeschylus, *Choephori,* translated by Philip Vellacott in *The Oresteian Trilogy,* p. 141.

> Most loyal of sons, what fancied sights torment you so?
> Stay! You have won your victory; what have you to fear?

But Orestes cries:

> To me these living horrors are not imaginary;
> I know them—avenging hounds incensed by a mother's blood.

When the Chorus still insists that his mind is naturally a bit distraught by the recent killing, he does not seem to hear:

> O Lord Apollo! More and more of them! Look there!
> And see—their dreadful eyes dripping with bloody pus!
>
> . . .
>
> I know you do not see these beings; but I see them.
> I am lashed and driven! I can't bear it! I must escape!

The Chorus pronounces a benediction:

> Good fortune go with you; and may the blessing of God
> Watch over and guide your ways, and bring you peace in the end.[66]

Clytemnestra and Aegisthus have a "blind spot," a vast ignorance of the pattern of universal justice. Their lack of comprehension concerning their personal involvement in this pattern is so fundamental that disaster is inevitable. As Richmond Y. Hathorn has pointed out, in these characters Aeschylus illustrates our human tendency to forget that the observer of the pattern is part of the pattern himself. The greatness of man is his power of transcendence, his amazing ability to make the cosmos, society, and even himself the object of his observation and reflection. But mysteriously and fatefully, the act of contemplation carries with it a temptation to blindness, for when we reflect and contemplate we abstract, and in abstracting we tend to subtract ourselves from the universe, as though we could be mere spectators. Like most of us, Clytemnestra and Aegisthus want justice to pursue and to overtake everyone—except themselves. They regard them-

---

[66] *Ibid.*, pp. 142-43.

selves as instruments of justice, blind to the fact that justice will be fulfilled *on* them as well as *through* them. At this point, the greatness of Orestes becomes clear. His mother thinks that injustice is a problem to be solved, a knot to be cut. To him it is a mystery to be entered into. Apollo has ordered him to become an instrument of justice, but obedience to this command "seems not so much to carry out a just design as to become embroiled in a confusion of right and wrong such that the just and the unjust cannot be disentangled by mortal discernment." [67] He intuits that he is only a part of the universal design of justice and that his human power of transcendence is not capable of penetrating to a perspective from which he can see the total pattern and know that it is orderly rather than chaotic, meaningful rather than senseless. He knows, or rather believes, that whatever measure of wise insight is possible for him can be achieved only through suffering participation in the tangle of guilt and innocence into which his destiny has plunged him. Therefore, he goes to Delphi as a suppliant. The consummation of justice depends on the intermeshing of human activity and divine ultimacy.

The Chorus brings the drama to a close by addressing itself to the audience:

> When shall be solved this long feud's argument?
> When shall the ancestral curse relent,
> And sink to rest, its fury spent? [68]

The third and last drama in the trilogy, *The Eumenides,* answers the question. The scene shifts to Athens, to the temple of Athene on the Acropolis. Advised by Apollo to seek asylum in Athens, Orestes appears before Athene's statue as a suppliant. But the Eumenides have pursued him, and they demand that he be turned over to them:

> For Law lives on; and we, Law's holy few,
> Law's living record of all evil done,
> Resourceful and accomplishing, pursue
> Our hateful task unhonoured, and no prayer
> Makes us relent. All other gods must shun

---

[67] Hathorn, *Tragedy, Myth, and Mystery,* p. 31; see also the author's excellent discussion of the Oresteian trilogy, pp. 38-61.

[68] Aeschylus, *Choephori,* translated by Philip Vellacott, p. 143.

The sunless glimmer of those paths we strew
With rocks, that quick and dead may stumble there.

So, Heaven's firm ordinance has now been told,
The task which Fate immutably assigned
To our devotion. Who will then withhold
Due fear and reverence? Though our dwelling lie
In subterranean caverns of the blind,
Our ancient privilege none dares deny.[69]

At this point Athene comes from her temple, and the conflicting claims of reason (Apollo) and the emotional impulse of retribution (the Furies) are placed before her for judgment. Her response is one of the climactic points in the trilogy:

This is too grave a cause for any man to judge;
Nor, in a case of murder, is it right that I
Should by my judgement let the wrath of Justice loose;
The less so, since you came after full cleansing rites
As a pure suppliant to my temple, and since I
And Athens grant you sanctuary and welcome you.
But your accusers' claims are not to be dismissed;
And, should they fail to win their case, their anger falls
Like death and terror, blight and poison, on my land.
Hence my dilemma—to accept, or banish them;
And either course is peril and perplexity.
Then, since decision falls to me, I will choose out
Jurors of homicide, for a perpetual court,
In whom I vest my judgement. Bring your evidence,
Call witnesses, whose oaths shall strengthen Justice' hand.
I'll pick my wisest citizens, and bring them here
Sworn to give sentence with integrity and truth.[70]

Athene has announced the establishment of the Areopagus, the democratic citizens' court of Athens. Orestes retires into the temple and out of the drama. The second half of the play is devoted to a courtroom scene in which Apollo and the Eumenides present their cases before the Areopagus, presided over by Athene herself. The courtroom process reveals that Orestes' intention was vastly different from his mother's, and also that he has paid

---

[69] Aeschylus, *The Eumenides,* translated by Philip Vellacott, p. 161.
[70] *Ibid.,* pp. 163-64.

for his crime in suffering during the years of exile and of inner torment. The vote of the Athenian court is a tie. Athene casts the deciding vote in favor of Orestes. But the drama has not yet come to a close. Athene now sets out to persuade the Eumenides that they have not been insulted, not really defeated either, since in Orestes' suffering retribution actually has been achieved. She convinces them that their traditional role, closely connected with blood feuds and vendettas, is not broad enough to express the full scope of their dread yet necessary duty. Finally, they agree to become a part of the Athenian state, functioning as the retributive power of the legal sanctions imposed by the Areopagus under the rule of law. Without this retributive power the Areopagus cannot function justly and orderly life in the polis cannot endure. Or, to put it in more general and more positive terms, the reconciliation of wisdom (logic and reasonable persuasion) with the deep emotional desire that evil be punished—including one's own evil—and that the punishment fit the crime makes possible a just life in the polis.

Representing Zeus, the Lord of Heaven, Athene gives orders for a torchlight procession to escort the Eumenides to their new home beneath the Acropolis (a few hundred yards northwest of the theater), and as the procession moves toward the cave all its members sing together:

Pass onward to your home,
Great ones, lovers of honour,
Daughters of ancient Night,
Led by the friends your peace has won;
   And let every tongue be holy!

On to the deep of earth,
To the immemorial cavern,
Honoured with sacrifice,
Worshipped in fear and breathless awe;
   And let every tongue be holy!

Come, dread and friendly Powers
Who love and guard our land;
And while devouring flame
Fills all your path with light,
Gather with gladness to your rest.
   And let every voice crown our song with a shout of joy!

Again let the wine be poured
By the glare of the crackling pine;
Now great, all-seeing Zeus
Guards the city of Pallas;
Thus God and Fate are reconciled.
  Then let every voice crown our song with a shout of joy! [71]

This procession must have moved the Athenian audience to deep religious joy and pride and patriotic feeling. The heroic soul-searching and suffering of consequences portrayed by Orestes must have been experienced as representative suffering, challenging each person to bind his own soul to his own fate, as to the common destiny of the polis.

One aspect of the Oresteian trilogy has not been brought into focus in the preceding description. Aeschylus is presenting in dramatic form the conviction that there is a principle of order in the cosmos by which every man's evil purposes and deeds are balanced by proportionate suffering. How does he symbolize the ultimate that guarantees the proportioning? Very early in the first play, the *Agamemnon,* the Chorus reflects:

Let good prevail!
So be it! Yet, what is good? And who
Is God? How name him, and speak true?
If he accept the name that men
Give him, Zeus I name him then.
I, still perplexed in mind,
For long have searched and weighed
Every hope of comfort or of aid:
Still I can find
No creed to lift this heaviness,
This fear that haunts without excuse—
No name inviting faith, no wistful guess,
Save only—Zeus.

The first of gods is gone,
Old Ouranos, once blown
With violence and pride;
His name shall not be known,
Nor that his dynasty once lived, and died.
His strong successor, Cronos, had his hour,

[71] *Ibid.,* pp. 181-82.

Then went his way, thrice thrown
By a yet stronger power.
Now Zeus is lord; and he
Who loyally acclaims his victory
Shall by heart's instinct find the universal key:

Zeus, whose will has marked for man
The sole way where wisdom lies;
Ordered one eternal plan:
Man must suffer to be wise.
Head-winds heavy with past ill
Stray his course and cloud his heart:
Sorrow takes the blind soul's part—
Man grows wise against his will.
For powers who rule from thrones above
By ruthlessness commend their love.[72]

Thus, we return to the question of appropriate symbolization, but this time it is not an isolated Heraclitus who proclaims, "One thing, which alone is wise, will and will not be called by the name of Zeus." Aeschylus is an acknowledged teacher of the Athenian polis. In a ritual setting he is seeking to initiate his audience into the deepest mysteries of the interaction between eternal ultimacy and human order, as well as to nourish their patriotic loyalty to the distinctive pattern of Athenian civic life. On the surface the speech of the Chorus may seem to be a critical, disintegrative treatment of "Zeus," the traditional popular symbol of ultimacy. Zeus is one of a series, preceded by Uranus (Ouranos) and Cronus; the implication seems to be that he may be superseded by another god. Will not this relativizing of Zeus be disquieting to the audience rather than inspiring?

But what if the Athenians, shaken by the fall of the old aristocratic regime with its ancestral religious faith, and disturbed by the rise of strange new spiritual forces in the wake of the violent efforts and victories that have brought the city to prominence, are *already* aware of the relativity of the gods? What if they yearn for the firm foundation of an eternal ultimate that transcends the Olympian pantheon? Then Aeschylus' point is that however multitudinous and contradictory the various "powers who rule from thrones above" may be, the truly ultimate is

---

[72] Aeschylus, *Agememnon,* translated by Philip Vellacott, pp. 47-48.

one and unvarying. Uranus, Cronus, Zeus—the name does not matter. Given the mythic tradition and customary usage, Zeus is probably the most appropriate personal image. But against the tendency to assume "Zeus" to be an empty symbol, revealing no reality beyond itself, and against the tendency to give in to the idea that "All things flow; nothing remains," Aeschylus is proclaiming deliberately that "All things flow by the will (the just law) of the ultimate, and the ultimate remains eternally."

More than a century later, when the original religious power of tragic drama was no longer vividly experienced, Aristotle theorized about the effects of the tragedies on their Athenian audiences and concluded that they produced an emotional catharsis by evoking feelings of pity and fear. H. D. F. Kitto's interpretation is more convincing:

> In fact, what this religious drama gives us is rather Awe and Understanding. Its true Catharsis arises from this, that when we have seen terrible things happening in the play, we understand, as we cannot always do in life, *why* they have happened; or, if not so much as that, at least we see that they have not happened by chance, without any significance. We are given the feeling that the Universe is coherent, even though we may not understand it completely.[73]

Our own summary is this: in tragic drama the polis is transfigured by the addition of basic convictions about true humanity. True humanity is attunement of the human person with the eternal order—awesome, sublime, severe, but finally just.

Although we have not been able to consider the full scope of tragic drama, certainly we have gained some insight into its possibilities for education through remembrance and renewal in a patriotic ritual setting, through initiation and participation, through emotion and reflective imagination. Unfortunately, this social function of tragedy that affected the populace as a whole soon became problematic and finally impossible. Even in the great personalities presented by Sophocles, the suffering of the hero is far less representative of the common man than the suffering of a Pelasgus or an Orestes; and the dramatist Euripides is preoccupied with the problem of the hero who breaks under

---

[73] H. D. F. Kitto, *Form and Meaning in Drama* (London, 1960), p. 235.

his fate. The capriciousness of *Tyche* (fortune, luck) emerges as a major theme, and the fact that it does points to a serious loss of faith in the ultimately harmonizing order of divine Justice (*dike*). If the order of the polis is to rest on spirit and not on fearful subservience to power, the reasonable influence of persuasion—such as is illustrated in Pelasgus' leadership of his polis in *The Suppliants* and in Athene's resolution of the Oresteian dilemma—must be believed in and exercised. Socrates and Plato take very seriously the Aeschylean symbolism in the *Eumenides;* they search for an educational method that can produce mature and responsible people who will preserve the orderly processes of Athenian civic life through the persuasive excellence of their character. But before we consider their educational concerns, we should point out that a quite different definition of "persuasive excellence" appealed to the Athenians during the fifth century, and we should describe the tremendously influential educational movement that made it possible for the Athenians to achieve the excellence *they* wanted.

The Sophists

The men who developed both the method and the theory of the new education were called Sophists. One way to describe them is to say that they were migratory foreign teachers who possessed some desirable knowledge for which the increasingly affluent Athenians were willing to pay. Aristotle characterizes the situation in a single sentence in his *Politics:*

> For when their wealth gave them a greater inclination to leisure, and they had loftier notions of excellence, being also elated with their success, both before and after the Persian War, with more zeal than discernment they pursued every kind of knowledge . . . .[74]

The new style of civic life, bourgeois rather than aristocratic, called for a new type of education for leadership in a cultivated,

---

[74] Aristotle, *Politics,* lines 28-31, section 1341, translated by Benjamin Jowett in *The Basic Works of Aristotle,* Richard McKeon (ed.) (New York, 1941), p. 1314.

intensely competitive society. Success depended more and more on a man's ability to win friends and influence people; therefore, "persuasive excellence" came to mean the ability to gain the favor of the citizens and to retain this popular support in the face of criticism, gossiping, and intrigue. Voegelin describes the new image of excellence succinctly:

> The mastery of typical situations and arguments in public debate, a stock of thorough knowledge with regard to the public affairs of the polis in domestic and imperial relations, a ready wit, a good memory improved by training, a disciplined intellect ready to grasp the essentials of an issue, the trained ability of marshalling arguments on the spur of the moment, a ready stock of anecdotes, paradigmata and sayings drawn from the poets for illustrating a point, general oratorical perfection, skill in debate leading to more or less graceful discomfiture of an opponent, a good deal of psychological knowledge in handling people, good appearance and bearing, natural and trained charm in conversation—all these were required for success in the competitive game of the polis. Anybody would be welcome who could train the mind in arriving at sound decisions and in imposing them on others in this new form of politics through debate, speech, argument, and persuasion.[75]

Sophistic teachers demonstrated that they could train men for this new form of politics; the demand for their services expanded rapidly, and they flocked to Athens to supply the demand. The course of training varied greatly from teacher to teacher, but it always centered on mastering the skills of public speaking. This including more than one might suppose. The Sophists imparted to the mind of the student an encyclopedic variety of facts, undoubtedly creating the ancient equivalent of what we today call "information input overload." The Sophists also taught formal training of various types—grammar, logic, sometimes arithmetic and geometry. A third focus was more general. The Sophists provided the "whole man" with political and ethical training by making him thoroughly acquainted with the value system of the social order to which he belonged. They appealed to the law of the polis as the ultimately obligatory standard,

---

[75] Voegelin, *op. cit.*, vol. II, p. 270.

and they conceived of the law as the supreme teacher of the citizen.

The conscious raising of the existing law of the polis to a position of ultimacy inevitably led to questions of principle. Laws are made and laws are changed, and in both instances men make the decisions. Thus the rules governing the making and changing of laws rank higher than the laws actually "on the books" at any given time. Therefore, budding political leaders needed to learn principles of justice and of right conduct. This need gave rise to vigorous debates. The excellences recommended in the past were reviewed: heroic courage, savage valor, prudent judgment, wisdom, and so on. The question was raised whether excellence (virtue) was fundamentally one or whether there was an irreducible group of virtues. New medical information brought such virtues as health, beauty, strength, "a sound mind in a sound body" into the picture. Lists of excellences were drawn up, and the rank of the virtues on the lists became a matter of debate. This process may sound "philosophical," but actually Athenian educational and social interests were dominated by the conviction that the end of life was achievement—success in the polis. The intellectual qualities stressed by the Sophists were responsive to these interests and to this conviction. They were not the adventurous, speculative, intellectual qualities of a Parmenides or a Heraclitus. Above all, the Sophists concentrated on their own great discovery, rhetoric, and they developed it both practically and theoretically to a stage that has probably remained unsurpassed to the present day.

The contribution of the Sophists to educational theory in general is best represented by Protagoras. Unfortunately, the almost complete loss of primary sources for the Sophists forces us to rely on Plato, who violently disagreed with Protagoras on the level of basic convictions. On other levels, however, Plato learned a great deal from him and quietly included it in his own teaching. According to Plato, Protagoras pioneered in formulating the theory that a child or student has a "nature" with which the teacher begins and which the teacher aims to modify. He emphasized the importance of early instruction, carefully designed not only to transmit information but also to provide the kind of drill or practice that will make the acquired knowledge "second nature." These ideas seem obvious to us; today these principles, reflected on and formulated consistently for the first time by Protagoras, are taken completely for granted. The curriculum that the Sophists worked out consisted of the so-called Trivium (grammar, rhetoric, and dialectic) and the Quadrivium (arithmetic, geometry, music, and astronomy). This ordering of subject matter was taken over by Plato's Academy, except that in the Academy the formal Quadrivium was given priority over the "communication skills" of the Trivium. In this revised form—Quadrivium plus Trivium—the curriculum became the classical model of liberal education, a model that is still influential today even though the subject matter areas are not the same. As we said before, the Sophists deliberately accepted the polis as the goal and the final standard of all education, the one and only proper educative force. They gave specific, organized content to convictions that supported the claims of Athenian society, to loyalty and commitment.

But great as the contribution of sophistic education was, and brilliantly as Athens played its new role of cultural capital of Hellas, the transition from provincial politics to imperial power and from naïveté to sophistication brought dangers as well as advantages. The Athenian polis made enormous demands on the discipline and self-sacrifice of its citizens, and these demands were sanctioned by the ultimacy of the state, symbolized by its *nomos,* its law. Yet contemporary sophistic analysis of human conduct encouraged a view of life that emphasized the constant conflict between what men like and dislike ("by nature") and what the polis required them to like and dislike ("by law"). The Sophist Antiphon taught that most of the prescriptions of law are hostile to nature because they "keep nature in chains." Through a curious twist of terminology the word "law," which had traditionally been identified with the just cosmic order (the dike of Zeus), came to be identified with the externally imposed control of the polis, experienced as "mere" custom or convention—something a person does not need to obey when nobody is around to witness what he is doing. "Nature" (*physis*) replaced "law" (*nomos*) in discussions about whether there is any order that cannot be transgressed with impunity. These discussions were confused and confusing because both terms were ambiguous. "Law" could stand for the inherited burden of irrational custom; it could stand for an arbitrary rule imposed by one group or another on the entire polis; or it could stand for the rational system of state law which the Athenians proudly hailed as the achievement that distinguished them from barbarians. "Nature" could mean an unwritten, universally valid natural law in contrast to the particularism of local custom; it could mean the natural rights of the individual against the requirements of the polis; or it could mean the natural law of the jungle, the right of the stronger over the weaker. In his dialogue *Gorgias* Plato incarnates this anarchic immoralism in Callicles, who shouts:

> "We mould the best and strongest among us to our will, catching them young like lions, and we enchant and enslave them by telling them that everyone must have equal rights, and that that is the meaning of nobility and justice. But in my opinion if a man of truly strong nature comes, he shakes all that off and bursts through it and escapes, trampling down our letters and spells and incantations and all our unnatural laws, and he our slave rises up to be our master; and then shines forth the justice of nature!" [76]

In the few actual fragments of works by major Sophists available for study, we can identify two basic issues:

1. What is the source and validity of moral and political obligations?
2. Why do men behave as they do and how can they be induced to behave better?

The Sophist Antiphon candidly answered that the natural standard of human conduct is what is useful to the individual, ultimately enjoyment or pleasure. Men can be induced to "behave better" simply by being allowed freedom to indulge in "doing what comes naturally." Probably Antiphon was expressing the secret feelings of the majority of his fellow citizens. Pericles himself, who presided over Athens during the period of her greatest glory, boasted that in Athens the universal respect for law hindered no one from gratifying his private whims without being frowned on by others. Inevitably, the life-orientation of the Athenian polis was subjected to interpretations that tended

---

[76] 183e, translated and quoted by Werner Jaeger, *Paideia,* vol I, p. 325.

to disestablish the traditions and the order of the community through a process of inner disintegration.

When we probe still deeper we discover that a fundamental achievement of the formative period of Hellenic culture was lost by the sophistic culture, namely, a sensitivity to experiences of transcendence like those that had grasped Parmenides and Heraclitus and propelled them into their explorations of the ultimacy of Being beyond man and of mysterious depths of being (selfhood) within him. The Sophists provided no link between the well-observed and classified phenomena of ethics and politics and the invisible divine order that these men believed radiates order into the invisible eternal soul of man. Protagoras insisted that reverence and justice must be living forces in the soul of every person because without them the order of a community cannot be maintained. Yet he is also credited with having coined the famous phrase, "Man is the measure of all things," and he frankly stated that he was an agnostic as far as the reality of an eternal cosmic ordering power was concerned.

That the Sophists were insensitive toward experiences of transcendence is illustrated in one of the few sophistic documents that has been preserved more or less intact. It is an abstract of an essay *On Being* written by Gorgias, one of the four outstanding men who were later remembered as representative sophists (Protagoras, Hippias, and Prodicus were the others).[77] The essay's title indicates that Gorgias was concerned with problems raised by Parmenides. It was organized in three sections and defended the following propositions:

1. Nothing exists;

2. If anything exists, it is incomprehensible;

3. If it is comprehensible, it is incommunicable.

A passage from the first section demonstrates that every predicate of Being deduced by Parmenides leads to logical contradictions. The passage demolishes the symbolic term "everlasting."

---

[77] The following section is directly indebted to Voegelin, *Order and History,* vol. II, pp. 273-75.

> Being cannot be everlasting because in that case it would have no beginning; what has no beginning is boundless; and what is boundless is nowhere. For if it were anywhere it would have to be surrounded by something that is greater than itself; but there is nothing that is greater than the boundless; hence the boundless is nowhere; and what is nowhere does not exist.[78]

Gorgias ignores completely the overwhelming experience of the ultimate oneness of reality that led Parmenides to develop the symbol of Being. He treats the image of everlastingness as though it had a meaning independent of the experience it expresses. Once he has done this, his attack becomes a simple matter of logic: obviously "everlastingness" will lead to contradictions if one assumes that it refers to some object in the world of ordinary experience, to a thing among other things.

Other Sophists applied the same type of argument to other symbols of experiences of transcendence outward toward the universal One and inward toward the "logos that augments itself." Both in the *Republic* (365 d-e) and in the *Laws* (885 b), Plato quoted the following argument concerning the gods:

1. It seems that no gods exist;
2. Even if they do exist, they do not care about men;
3. Even if they do care, they can be propitiated with gifts.

Plato countered each of the three steps: the gods do exist, they care about men, and they cannot be "bought off" by prayer and sacrifice. Plato did not identify the source of the agnostic or atheistic propositions, but undoubtedly they originated among the Sophists. At any rate, Plato deliberately concentrated the core of his philosophizing in an emphatic counterformula to the Protagorean "Man is the measure." Plato's formula was: "The measure of man is the Good (the Eternal)." This formula marks a decisive difference between the worlds of thought of the Sophists and of the philosophers, not because "God" (the Eternal) is brought into the picture, but because the experience of transcendence is reaffirmed. This experience involves a correlation

---

[78] Translated and quoted by Voegelin in *Order and History,* vol. II, p. 274.

between man and an ultimate beyond the polis. It consists not only of an awareness of a dimension of mystery in the cosmic order, but also of an awareness of a dimension of mystery in man himself. In other words, Plato wanted to reestablish creative tension between the claims of the polis and the claims of a true humanity attuned to the ultimate.

Socrates

Two decisive events intervened between the sophistic enterprise during the fifth century and the enterprise begun by Plato during the fourth century. One was the disastrous Peloponnesian War between the Greek city-states, which began in 431 B.C. and ended with the crushing defeat of Athens by Sparta in 404 B.C. The other was the life and death of Socrates. His life spanned both the period of Athens' imperial glory under Pericles and that of the Peloponnesian War. His death came by decree of the Athenian court in 399 B.C., during the political and religious convulsions that followed the loss of the war. In 404 B.C., Plato was about twenty-three years old. The son of a noble family, he was closely related by blood and by family associations to the commission of thirty aristocrats that gained temporary control of Athens immediately after the capitulation to Sparta. Many years later Plato described his experiences between 404 and 399 B.C. as follows:

> I had much the same experience as many other young men. I expected, when I came of age, to go into politics. The political situation gave me an opportunity. The existing constitution, which was subject to widespread criticism, was overthrown . . . and a committee of Thirty given supreme power. As it happened some of them were friends and relations of mine, and they at once invited me to join them, as if it were the natural thing for me to do. My feelings were what were to be expected in a young man: I thought they were going to reform society and rule justly, and so I watched their proceedings with deep interest. I found that they soon made the earlier regime look like a golden age. Among other things they tried to incriminate my old friend Socrates, whom I should not hesitate to call the most upright man then living, by sending

> him, with others, to arrest a fellow-citizen and bring him forcibly to execution; Socrates refused, and risked everything rather than make himself party to their wickedness. When I saw all this, and other things as bad, I was disgusted and drew back from the wickedness of the times.
>
> Not long afterwards the Thirty fell, and the constitution was changed. And again, though less keenly, I felt the desire to enter politics. They were troublous times, and many things were done to which one could object; nor was it surprising that vengeance should sometimes be excessive in a revolution. None the less the returned democrats behaved, on the whole, with moderation. Unfortunately, however, some of those in power brought my friend Socrates to trial on a monstrous charge, the last that could be made against him, the charge of impiety; and he was condemned and executed.
>
> When I considered all this, the more closely I studied the politicians and the laws and customs of the day, and the older I grew, the more difficult it seemed to me to govern rightly. Nothing could be done without trustworthy friends and supporters; and these were not easy to come by in an age which had abandoned its traditional moral code but found it impossibly difficult to create a new one. At the same time law and morality were deteriorating at an alarming rate, with the result that though I had been full of eagerness for a political career, the sight of all this chaos made me giddy, and though I never stopped thinking how things might be improved and the constitution reformed, I postponed action, waiting for a favorable opportunity. Finally I came to the conclusion that all existing states were badly governed, and that their constitutions were incapable of reform without drastic treatment and a great deal of good luck. I was forced, in fact, to the belief that the only hope of finding justice for society or for the individual lay in true philosophy, and that mankind will have no respite from trouble until either real philosophers gain political power or politicians become by some miracle true philosophers.[79]

For Plato, the "real philosopher" was Socrates. But who was Socrates? He never wrote anything, since he insisted that the only important thing was the relation between his spoken words and

---

[79] Seventh Letter, translated by H. D. P. Lee, and quoted in his introduction to his translation of *The Republic* (Baltimore, 1955), pp. 11-14; the concluding sentence is borrowed by Lee, with some alteration, from *The Republic,* whose theme it summarizes.

the living men with whom he was speaking. He considered literary composition dangerous because it created the illusion that truth or wisdom can be fully expressed, stored away in a book, and then taken over by the reader as though it were a piece of information. He believed that a man can demonstrate that he is something more than a poetic, legal, or oratorical craftsman only through dialogue—oral expression subject to immediate critical challenge and response. From the remains of the literature produced by Socrates' friends (Plato's dialogues, Xenophon's *Memoirs of Socrates,* and fragments of dialogues written by Antisthenes and Aeschines), it is clear that the chief aim of his pupils was to keep Socrates alive, not as an intellect but as a person. Both the dialogue and the biographical memoir were new literary forms invented for this purpose. In the light of Erich Auerbach's comparison between Homer's picture of man and the Biblical picture, which we outlined earlier in this chapter, the following observation by Werner Jaeger is especially interesting:

> The literary portrait of Socrates is the only truly lifelike description of a great and original personality created in classical Greece. Those who created it meant neither to explore the recesses of the human soul nor to engage in fine-drawn ethical investigations, but to reproduce the impression of what we call *personality*—although they had neither the concept of personality nor words to express it. Socrates' example had changed the meaning of arete (excellence).[80]

The attempt to give a clear impression of Socrates' intellectual and spiritual power by imitating in literary form his question and answer method of teaching was an unconventional and daring enterprise. But although at times we seem to come close to the "historical Socrates," no definitive picture emerges because his pupils fused their own characters so closely with his. Moreover, the Socratic circle dissolved soon after Socrates drank the hemlock. Its members disagreed so radically and passionately

---

[80] *Paideia,* vol. II, p. 18. The four dialogues of Plato which are most closely related to the project of giving a literary portrait (*Euthyphro, Apology, Crito,* and *Phaedo*) are available in *The Last Days of Socrates,* translated by Hugh Tredennick (New York, 1954). Three of the four (*Euthyphro* omitted) are included in *Great Dialogues of Plato,* translated by W. H. D. Rouse (New York, 1956).

about the meaning of his teaching that they became alienated from one another and formed rival schools. As a result, Socrates remains to this day an enigmatic figure.

Nevertheless, an extraordinarily large number of passages in the writings of his pupils agree that Socrates described the "care of the soul" as the highest interest of man, that he felt his work was basically educational, and that he believed this work to be a religious duty, a service of the Good (his ultimate). There is agreement that he distinguished sharply between the inner core of selfhood (the soul) and the body and that he believed the soul to be the divine in man. There is agreement also that he placed external goods like property and power at the bottom of his hierarchy of values. All these elements were included by Plato in his picture of Socrates in the *Apology,* a dramatic retelling of the trial that ended with the verdict "guilty" and the penalty "death." The charge against Socrates was that he did not recognize the gods recognized by the polis and that in introducing other divinities he was corrupting the youth of Athens. In the course of defending himself before the court, Socrates (via Plato) described his method of philosophizing and his reason for philosophizing in this way:

> "Many thanks indeed for your kindness, gentlemen, but I will obey the god rather than you, and as long as I have breath in me, and remain able to do it, I will never cease being a philosopher, and exhorting you, and showing what is in me to any one of you I may meet, by speaking to him in my usual way: My excellent friend, you are an Athenian, a citizen of this great city, so famous for wisdom and strength, and you take every care to be as well off as possible in money, reputation and place—then are you not ashamed not to take every care and thought for understanding, for truth, and for the soul, so that it may be perfect? And if any of you argues the point and says he does take every care, I will not at once let him go and depart myself; but I will question and cross-examine and test him, and if I think he does not possess virtue but only says so, I will show that he sets very little value on things most precious, and sets more value on meaner things, and I will put him to shame. This I will do for everyone I meet, young or old, native or foreigner, but more for my fellow-citizens as you are nearer to me in race. For this is what God commands me, make no mistake, and I think there is no greater good for you in the city in any way than my service to God. All I do is to go about

> and try to persuade you, both young and old, not to care for your bodies or your monies first, and to care more exceedingly for the soul, to make it as good as possible . . . ."[81]

The speech is too artfully contrived to be merely a revised version of the extemporaneous defense Socrates made originally, but it rings true, especially if we remember that what this man lived for was so overwhelmingly important to him that he was willing to die for it. The greatest strength of his teaching was the change he introduced into the old educational concept of "the heroic example." The heroism with which he pursued his care of the soul during seventy years of life was transfigured into an archetypal pattern through the heroism of his death.

What did Socrates mean by "soul" (psyche) and by "care of the soul"? He seems to have followed the leads supplied by Parmenides, Heraclitus, and Aeschylus to the following conclusion: the soul is the dynamic core of selfhood whose very lifeblood is constant dialogue with itself, with other selves, and with an "ultimate" beyond the self which at the same time is within the self as the source of its true order. In Socrates these three kinds of dialogue became the content of what we have been calling the experience of transcendence. "Care of the soul," therefore, meant the nurture of the excellence proper to selfhood. Socrates brought his convictions regarding this excellence (virtue, *arete*) into focus in four favorite statements: (1) "virtue is knowledge of the good"; (2) "the good is indivisible"; (3) "nobody does wrong voluntarily"; (4) "all true excellence is the companion of thinking." The word Socrates used for "thinking" (*phronesis*) did not mean intuition or comprehension or scientific understanding, but rather a kind of moral pondering in which purposive thoughtfulness leads toward insight into the intrinsic purity and integrity of human selfhood.

The reports we have of the conversations Socrates carried on indicate that he customarily began with questions about the meaning of official ideals of civic virtue—piety, justice, courage, self-control. Through dialogue he tried to awaken those with whom he conversed to the realization that all separate phenomena in the realm of moral standards presuppose one supreme general standard ("the good is indivisible"). He claimed that all

---

[81] Translated by W. H. D. Rouse, in *Great Dialogues of Plato,* pp. 435-36.

wisdom culminates in one knowledge, to which we are brought back by every attempt to define closely any single human good, and that this one knowledge "knows" one reality—the Good Itself, eternal and unchangeable. Jaeger writes of Socrates:

> The knowledge of good which he reaches, starting from all the separate human virtues, is not an intellectual operation, but (as Plato recognized) the now conscious expression of something existing in the spirit of man. It is rooted in the depths of the soul, at a level where to be penetrated by knowledge and to possess the object known are not two different states but essentially one and the same.[82]

What is this "something existing in the spirit of man"? It is the essential structure of human selfhood, an integrated structure which, like the Good itself, is indivisible. Every man experiences a drive toward self-fulfillment, a yearning for individuation. In other words, every man seeks the Good. No man does evil for the sake of evil; he always wants something that promises him good, self-fulfillment. But most men do not "know" the essential structure of their selfhood, and they are beguiled by their ignorance into all sorts of disintegrative attitudes, aims, actions, and relationships. Because he understood happiness as not dependent on any external conditions, Socrates was able to believe that the wise man is both good and happy. Happiness is integrated selfhood, an inner harmony of the self with itself, integrity. Integrity can be achieved through the education of the will by insight. Insight can be trained by purposeful thoughtfulness—plain, hard, honest, humble thinking in the context of the triple dialogue with oneself, with others, and with the mysterious ultimate that lures man toward becoming truly human. On this basis Socrates insisted that virtue can be taught, and he devoted his life—and his death, deliberately accepted—to this task.

Socrates' educational aim was neither the cultivation of certain abilities nor the communication of certain branches of knowledge. He aimed at a fundamental personal "awakening," followed by a lifelong effort to achieve moral and intellectual wholeness. In contrast to the sophists, most of whom were not Athenians and who profited by training their pupils to exploit the state

---

[82] *Paideia,* vol. II, p. 65.

and to carve out profitable careers as soldiers of fortune, Socrates was Athenian through and through, anxious about his city, filled with a sense of responsibility for its future, and critical only because he believed that loyal opposition was needed. Yet he came into tragic conflict with the polis because he appealed to an "ultimate" that was superior to the state. Most citizens invested Athens herself with ultimacy. Therefore, the charge that Socrates did not recognize the gods recognized by the polis had a point, as did the charge that he introduced new divinities. Although Socrates never named any ultimate other than the Good itself, he did make it plain that he must obey "the god" rather than men, which meant that his deepest loyalty was not given to the city-state. Jaeger interprets the situation in this way: the state was no longer strong enough to incorporate the realms of morality and religion as it had done earlier when the state was all. The approach we have been taking leads to a different emphasis: the movement within Hellenic culture from compact to more and more highly differentiated experiences through exploration of the human psyche led to a breakthrough to universality both on the level of ultimacy (the Good) and on the level of order (integrated selfhood). The fundamental motivating image of Socrates was a reformed and revitalized Athens, purified and reestablished on a new basis through the development of balanced, integrated leaders. Athens rejected both the image and Socrates himself.

Plato

Socrates' pupils took various attitudes toward his conflict with the city-state. Xenophon said that the whole affair was just an unfortunate accident due to misunderstanding. Aristippus held that it was an example of the inevitable clash between the spiritually free individual and the tyranny of society. Plato seems to have felt that it was inevitable for both sides to be what they were, and he drew the conclusion that the city-state must be reformed so that real human beings could live in it. He concentrated on educating in his Academy (established in 384 B.C.) leaders—"philosopher-kings"—who would restore the order of Hellenic civilization through love of wisdom. He dreamed of a

Hellenic empire, a federation of city-states ruled from Athens by men infused by the spirit of the Academy. Actually, as we saw earlier, unification came in the form of empire through the power of Macedonia, led by Philip and then by Alexander the Great. But Plato's work was successful beyond any expectations he may have had, for the symbols of a new order of wisdom which he created have entered and influenced the entire subsequent history of the West.

When we turn to Plato's works the amount of material to be covered becomes overwhelming. The English translation of his surviving works is about equal in length to an English translation of the entire Hebrew scriptures. Instead of attempting a survey of Plato's systematic development of the major themes of the entire Hellenic tradition, we shall deal with a single striking feature of his later dialogues, a feature that brings us back again to the first symbolic form we studied. Plato wrote myths. In Chapters Two and Three we noted that within the context of their experience the creators of the Egyptian Memphite Theology and the writers of the Israelite Deuteronomic Torah were aware that they were manipulating the traditions of their people with considerable freedom. In this chapter we have noted that Homer, Hesiod, and Aeschylus freely reorganized and reinterpreted the Hellenic mythical tradition. But, as Voegelin says, "The coincidence that the creator of a myth is at the same time a great philosopher who knows what he is doing, as in the case of Plato, is unique . . . ."[83] Plato inherited the doctrine that the soul (the dynamic center of selfhood) is neither a subject nor an object but a reality that is able to explore its own nature because it is illuminated with consciousness. He also inherited the conviction that the soul participates in the eternal power that orders the cosmos. Finally, he inherited Socrates' search for knowledge of ultimate reality—the Good itself—a search that Socrates was never able to bring to any stopping point where assured results could be formulated.

---

[83] *Order and History,* vol. III, p. 193. Some years ago the present writer did considerable research on Plato's use of myth. In an unpublished manuscript he defended the view that the function of Plato's myths is best understood in the context of convictions. Voegelin's analysis of Plato's philosophy of myth has corrected as well as confirmed the conclusions he reached at that time. See *Order and History,* vol. III, pp. 170-214.

Plato became convinced that nothing at all can be said about the content of the Good itself. The vision of the Good does not supply rules of conduct, or even a hierarchy of excellences (virtues). It is the climactic experience of transcendence. The Good grasps and shapes the inner dynamics of selfhood, yet it remains a hidden factor in the experiential process. Books six and seven of *The Republic* develop this decisive point. In Book six (sections 508-09), Plato illustrates it by analogy with the fact that the sense of sight and the visibility of objects require the light from the sun or else nothing will be seen. Though the sun is not itself sight, it is the cause of sight and is seen by the sight it causes. Plato has Socrates call sight a "child of the Good," and Socrates continues:

> "The Good has begotten it in its own likeness, and it bears the same relation to sight and visibility in the visible world that the Good bears to intelligence and intelligibility in the intelligible world."
>
> "Will you explain that a bit further?" [Glaucon] [84] asked.
>
> "You know that when we turn our eyes to objects whose colours are no longer illuminated by daylight, but only by moonlight or starlight, they see dimly and appear to be almost blind, as if they had no clear vision."
>
> "Yes."
>
> "But when we turn them on things on which the sun is shining, then they see clearly and their power of vision is restored."
>
> "Certainly."
>
> "Apply the analogy to the mind. When the mind's eye rests on objects illuminated by truth and reality, it understands and comprehends them, and functions intelligently; but when it turns to the twilight world of change and decay, it can only form opinions, its vision is confused and its beliefs shifting, and it seems to lack intelligence."
>
> "That is true."
>
> "Then what gives the objects of knowledge their truth and the mind the power of knowing is the Form of the Good. It is the cause of knowledge and truth, and you will be right to think of it as being itself known, and yet as being something other than, and even higher than, knowledge and truth. And just as it was right to think of light and sight as being like

---

[84] C.L.

the sun, but wrong to think of them as being the sun itself, so here again it is right to think of knowledge and truth as being like the Good, but wrong to think of either of them as being the Good, which must be given a still higher place of honour."

"You are making it something remarkably exalted, if it is the source of knowledge and truth, and yet itself higher than they are. For I suppose you can't mean it to be pleasure?" he asked.

"A monstrous suggestion," I replied. "Let us pursue our analogy further."

"Go on."

"The sun, I think you will agree, not only makes the things we see visible, but causes the processes of generation, growth and nourishment, without itself being such a process."

"True."

"The Good therefore may be said to be the source not only of the intelligibility of the objects of knowledge, but also of their existence and reality; yet it is not itself identical with reality, but is beyond reality, and superior to it in dignity and power."

"It really must be devilish superior," remarked Glaucon with a grin.

"Now, don't blame me," I protested; "it was you who made me say what I thought about it." [85]

The transition to myth is prepared for by the sentence: "[The Form of the Good] is the cause of knowledge and truth, and you will be right to think of it as being itself known, and yet as being something other than, and even higher than, knowledge and truth." This ties in directly with what Jaeger says about Socrates' knowledge of the Good in the passage just quoted. Plato seems to have believed that basically this nonintellectual knowledge is awareness, in the unconscious depths of the self, of a point of contact between the self and the primordial forces of the cosmos. His experience of the oneness of all reality is similar to that of Mesopotamia and Egypt, and his answer to the question how what is going on in a depth-dimension of the self that is beyond the subject-object relationship can be expressed is the same answer given by these earliest high civilizations. Although what is going on in the depths of the self cannot ever be expressed

[85] Plato, *The Republic,* translated by H. D. P. Lee (Baltimore, 1955), pp. 272-73.

directly and literally, it can be expressed indirectly, imaginatively, through the symbols of myth.

As noted earlier, the mythical forces in a culture are expressed on the archaic level in rites that are symbolic actions. Myths first appear as tales of anonymous origin that interpret the rites. The traditional body of myths of a people might be called the refraction of its collective unconscious into consciousness. When the individual psyche appears historically, it breaks through the collective character of the traditional myths and uses their symbols to express the inner drama of selfhood. This is the level we illustrated in our analysis of the difference between the tragic drama of Aeschylus and myth in Homer and Hesiod. Plato achieves still greater differentiation. He does not bind himself to the traditional myths at all; he "plays" with symbols, and he creates myths that fit the personal experiences he wants to express. Myth retains the seriousness of its truth, but at the same time it is consciously and deliberately an imaginative play. Voegelin has written so well on the nature and function of myth in Plato's work that we quote him at some length:

> The new dimension of conscious play is the characteristic of Plato's mythical creation. Such play is possible only under certain conditions which are present neither at all times nor in all men; and we have to be clear about these conditions if we wish to understand the function of the myth in Plato's late work. First of all, the nature of the myth must be understood by the creator or poet as the upwelling, from the unconscious, of psychic forces which blossom out into assuaging expression. An awareness of this nature of the myth is probably always present in mythical creation, even on the most archaic level; for without this assumption it would be difficult to account for the range of imaginative play which is considerable even on the ritual level, and it would be quite impossible to account for the bewildering richness of the play on the level of the mythical tale. What is new on the level of Plato is not the element of play itself but rather the inner freedom of the play, engendered by the growth and differentiation of the personal psyche from the sixth century onward. While the inner distance from the myth inevitably destroys the naïveté of the play, and the myth consequently becomes for Plato a work of art, it must not destroy the "truth" of the myth. This is the second condition of the conscious play. Plato knows that one myth can and must supersede the other, but he also knows that no other human

> function, for instance "reason" or "science," can supersede the myth itself. The myth remains the legitimate expression of the fundamental movements of the soul. Only in the shelter of the myth can the sectors of the personality that are closer to the waking consciousness unfold their potentiality; and without the ordering of the whole personality by the truth of the myth the secondary intellectual and moral powers would lose their direction. . . .
>
> As long as the movements of the unconscious are allowed to express themselves in myth in free recognition of their nature, the soul of man preserves its openness towards its cosmic ground. The terror of an infinitely overpowering, as well as the assurance of an infinitely embracing, *beyond* [ultimate] as the matrix of separate, individual existence, endow the soul with its more-than-human dimension; and through the acceptance of the truth of this dimension (that is, through faith) the separateness of human existence can, in its turn, be recognized and tolerated in its finiteness and limitations [italics added].[86]

In *The Republic* Plato projects the soul on the canvas of society. In *Timaeus* he projects it on the still larger canvas of the cosmos. He raises his image of man truly existing in love of the Good to universal proportions by constructing a grandiose myth of creation. The preliminary remarks of Timaeus in sections twenty-seven to thirty are especially significant for the present discussion because they constitute what amounts to a theory of myth. First Timaeus invokes both the gods and human powers. The account of creation must please the gods (deal adequately with ultimate reality), but also it must be communicable (deal adequately with the problem of symbolization). Then he discusses the conditions under which a myth of the cosmos is possible. Is the cosmos eternal and unchangeable, or is it in process of becoming, of change? Since the cosmos can be seen and parts of it can be touched, heard, smelled, the obvious answer would seem to be that the cosmos belongs to the realm of change, process, becoming. But Timaeus goes on to say that the cosmos also participates in the realm of eternal unchangeable being because the creator (the Demiurge) has shaped it as *an image of an*

---

[86] *Order and History*, vol. III, pp. 186-88. See Johan Huizinga, *Homo Ludens: A Study of the Play Element in Culture* (Boston, 1955).

eternal model. Thus the cosmos is neither changeless being nor changeable becoming, but being-in-becoming.

When Timaeus actually begins his story of creation we learn that the eternal model is the Demiurge himself:

> Let me tell you then why the creator made this world of generation. He was good, and the good can never have any jealousy of anything. And being free from jealousy, he desired that all things should be as like himself as they could be.[87]

The eternal being of the Demiurge is orderly; therefore he took over discordantly moving primordial matter and brought it from disorder to order. The eternal being of the Demiurge is intelligent; therefore, since intelligence cannot be present anywhere without dynamic soul (*psyche*), he fashioned intelligence (*nous*) within soul and he gave intelligence in-soul embodiment. The Demiurge is the symbol of *incarnation,* the process of embodiment that bridges the gulf between eternal changeless being and time-and-space changeable becoming, combining both in *the image of the model*—the cosmos, a "living creature" with all things in it "of a kindred nature." In these phrases we encounter again the rock bottom experience of the ultimate oneness of all reality. We should note also that the Demiurge is not to be equated with Yahweh: he is not experienced as utterly transcending his creation although active within it. He is pictured as an artist, working with somewhat resistant materials that he has not made but which he struggles to shape in such a way that they express insofar as possible the goodness and the intelligibility of his model—the essential structure of his own being. The parallel between the Demiurge and human beings struggling to express in their existence the essentially good, orderly, intelligible structure of their selfhood is obvious.

Man is a microcosm. Like the cosmos, he is neither changeless being nor changeable becoming, but being-in-becoming. Incarnation, embodiment, is the secret of his life. Now the question is: what is man's relationship to the eternal model? Does he see it directly with his intellect and then seek to order his life accordingly? Certainly the eternal dimension of reality that

---

[87] Plato, *Timaeus,* in *The Dialogues of Plato,* vol. II, translated by Benjamin Jowett (New York, 1937), pp. 13-14.

manifests itself in the cosmos is the kind of being that intellect can comprehend, but Plato holds that the eternal model cannot be seen directly by man's intellect. The Good is "beyond reality." What can be seen is the cosmos, the *image* of the eternal model. And since the cosmos is an image, a likeness, every human account of "gods and the creation of the universe" will be a myth, a plausible story, rather than knowledge. The correlate, for which we should be prepared by now, is that every comprehensive account of human selfhood is myth rather than knowledge, no matter how much factual information about personality it may contain. Just as the cosmic *image* unites being and becoming, and the *myth* of creation expresses through the sequential process of events in a story the process by which the eternal is embodied, so the image of true humanity unites being and becoming and the myth of the soul expresses its incarnation.

For Plato, then, myth expresses the experience of unity between man's separate conscious existence and the cosmic source of selfhood. Even the theory of myth must itself be a myth because the cosmic depths of the soul that cause reverberations in the field of consciousness are not accessible to the intellect. These reverberations convince Plato that the myth of the cosmos can also be the myth of society; both selfhood and community are embraced in the dynamics of the cosmos. The leaders of the polis should imitate the Demiurge, who creates order out of chaos under conditions that make complete success impossible. Just as every individual is aware of impulses, desires, passions, and anxieties that make achievement of inner harmony difficult, so every statesman is aware of conflicts of interests and aims in society that can never be completely or permanently resolved. This conviction generates the images that Plato expresses in nonmythical philosophical form in *The Republic* as well as those he expresses in his myth of creation. Behind both sets of images lies his myth of the soul.

Plato lived in a period of "enlightenment" much like our own in many respects. Traditional religious symbols were being taken literally and then easily rejected as primitive or irrational. Plato engaged in a project of remythologizing the ancient tradition. He maintained a clear distinction between myth and all knowledge, which today we call objective or scientific. On the level of the myth of the soul, this distinction was parallel to what later came to be called the spheres of faith and of reason. Although he granted primacy to conviction, he insisted that intelligence is of decisive importance in the search for an adequate life-orientation. In a memorable passage from his great creation myth, Plato makes this insistence unmistakable:

> As concerning the most sovereign form of soul in us we must conceive that heaven has given it to each man as a guiding genius—that part which we say dwells in the summit of our body and lifts us from earth towards our celestial affinity, like a plant whose roots are not in earth, but in the heavens. And this is most true, for it is to the heavens, whence the soul first came to birth, that the divine part attaches the head or root of us and keeps the whole body upright. Now if a man is engrossed in appetites and ambitions and spends all his pains upon these, all his thoughts must needs be mortal and, so far as that is possible, he cannot fall short of becoming mortal altogether, since he has nourished the growth of his mortality. But if his heart has been set on the love of learning and true wisdom and he has exercised that part of himself above all, he is surely bound to have thoughts immortal and divine, if he shall lay hold upon truth, nor can he fail to possess immortality in the fullest measure that human nature admits; and because he is always devoutly cherishing the divine part and maintaining the guardian genius that dwells with him in good estate, he must needs be happy above all. Now there is but one way of caring for anything, namely to give it the nourishment and motions proper to it. *The motions akin to the divine part in us are the thoughts and revolutions of the universe;* these, therefore, every man should follow, and correcting those circuits in the head that were deranged at birth, by learning to know the harmonies and revolutions of the world, he should bring the intelligent part, according to its pristine nature, into the likeness of that which intelligence discerns, and thereby win the fulfillment of the best life set by the gods before mankind both for this present time and for the time to come [italics added].[88]

This remarkable passage reaffirms the cosmological convictions that permeated the life orientations of ancient Mesopotamia and Egypt. The parallel can be drawn even more directly. Plato's *Laws* suggest that the most adequate concrete symbols of the divine order are the heavenly bodies, whose ever recurring cyclical

[88] *Timaeus,* 90 A-D, translated by F. M. Cornford and quoted in his *Plato's Cosmology* (London, 1937), pp. 353-54.

courses reveal the eternal, changeless pattern of reality. This seems to bring us right back to the Sumerian breakthrough of 3200 B.C. But now, in addition to the pattern of social organization to which the individual is to conform, the model impinges directly on man as an individual, calling upon him to develop consciously and deliberately the best life, the life that attunes the microcosmic order of personal existence to the macrocosmic order of the cosmos—which, in turn, is an image of the eternal Good. A tremendous process of differentiation has taken place; Plato is not just a supremely gifted Mesopotamian genius. He is a Hellene, a Greek. Yet continuity in the symbolism suggests a fundamental continuity in the experience of ultimacy.

Plato marked an epoch. He was engrossed in the crisis of the polis. A world was dying, but he tried to prepare for its resurrection. He still envisaged society as a compactly integrated unit of political, educational, and religious institutions. In Aristotle we feel a coolness and serenity that stems from the fact that he "gave up." He had no dream of a spiritually reformed, national Hellenic empire. His life was not centered in politics. The plight of Hellas did not excite his deepest concern. Actually, although the order of Hellenic civilization was dissolving, and although various sectors of Hellenic society were being destroyed, other sectors were freed for unprecedented growth. Aristotle was fascinated by the grandeur of the new life of the mind, and through him a second great climax of Greek intellectual achievement was added to the climax represented by Plato. The point, however, is that after Plato philosophy became more and more divorced from the active engagement of men in the ordering of society, more and more concentrated in groups ("schools") that taught individuals how to develop peace of mind in spite of the disorders of society, which they were convinced they could not bring under control. The free and adventurous inquiries of the earlier philosophers were revered, but they were seldom imitated. Instead, their teachings came to be regarded as authoritative disclosures of saving truth, *dogmas* that functioned as anxiety-reducing agents precisely to the degree that they were believed to be fixed and unchangeable. Philosophy suffered a tragic fate, not because it became "religious"—the religious dimension had been present from the beginning—but because the search for a meaningful life orientation for the individual was divorced from the search for a proper ordering of social existence, and because the search for truth was engulfed by the search for security. The very greatness of philosophy—its exploration of the fundamental human experience of transcendence—opened the way for life orientations based on withdrawal from the external world into the inner citadel of selfhood.

Recommended Paperbacks

Dodds, E. R. *The Greeks and the Irrational.* Boston: Beacon Press, 1957.

An illuminating series of lectures that makes use of contemporary anthropological and psychological observations to explore neglected aspects of classical Greek culture.

Frankfort, Henri, *et al. Before Philosophy.* Baltimore: Penguin Books, 1949.

The final essay, "The Emancipation of Thought from Myth," gives Frankfort's comparison of the Hebrew and the Greek traditions. This is important reading because it proceeds on assumptions regarding philosophy which are different from those of the present study.

Guthrie, W. K. C. *The Greeks and Their Gods.* Boston: Beacon Press, 1955.

A valuable inquiry into the tension between conflicting religious traditions and their goals in Greek culture.

Robinson, C. E. *Hellas: A Short History of Ancient Greece.* Boston: Beacon Press, 1955.

One of the better surveys, well-written and useful for gaining a connected sense of historical background.

Snell, Bruno, *The Discovery of the Mind.* New York: Harper & Row, 1960.

Holding that self-conscious knowledge of the human intellect was discovered by the Greeks, Snell traces the course along which this discovery unfolded.

BIBLIOGRAPHY

I

Hardbound Volumes

Audrain, Michael, and Paul Gayet-Tancrede, *The Glory of Egypt,* J. E. Manchip-White, trans. (New York: Vanguard, 1955).

Edmonds, J. M., ed., *Elegy and Iambus* (2 vols.), vol. 1 (Cambridge: Harvard University Press, 1961).

Eliade, Mircea, *Patterns in Comparative Religion* (New York: Sheed & Ward, 1958).

Finegan, Jack, *Light from the Ancient Past* (Princeton: Princeton University Press, 1946).

Frankfort, Henri, *Kingship and the Gods* (Chicago: University of Chicago Press, 1948).

Freeman, Kathleen, *Ancilla to the Pre-Socratic Philosophers* (Cambridge: Harvard University Press, 1962).

Gordon, Cyrus H., *Before the Bible* (New York: Harper & Row, 1962).

Hathorn, Richmond Y., *Tragedy, Myth, and Mystery* (Bloomington: Indiana University Press, 1962).

Jaeger, Werner, *Paideia* (3 vols.), vol. 1 (New York: Oxford University Press, 1945).

———, *Paideia,* vol. 2 (New York: Oxford University Press, 1943).

———, *The Theology of the Early Greek Philosophers* (London: Oxford University Press, 1947).

Kaufmann, Yehezkel, *The Religion of Israel,* Moshe Greenberg, trans. (Chicago: University of Chicago Press, 1960).

McKeon, Richard, ed., *The Basic Works of Aristotle* (New York: Random House, 1941).

Nilsson, Martin P., *A History of Greek Religion,* F. J. Fielden, trans. (London: Oxford University Press, 1949. Rev. ed., 1952).

Noth, Martin, *The History of Israel,* rev. ed. (New York: Harper & Row, 1960).

Oates, Whitney J., and Eugene O'Neill, Jr., eds., *The Complete Greek Drama* (2 vols.), vol. 1 (New York: Random House, 1938).

Otto, Walter F., *The Homeric Gods,* Moses Hadas, trans. (New York: Pantheon Books, 1954).

Plato, *The Dialogues of Plato* (2 vols.), vol. 2, B. Jowett, trans. (New York: Random House, 1937).

Pritchard, James, ed., *Ancient Near Eastern Texts* (Princeton: Princeton University Press, 1950).

Tillich, Paul, *Theology of Culture,* Robert G. Kimball, ed. (New York: Oxford University Press, 1959).

Voegelin, Eric, *Israel and Revelation,* vol. 1 of *Order and History* (Baton Rouge: Louisiana State University Press, 1956).

———, *The World of the Polis,* vol. 2 of *Order and History* (Baton Rouge: Louisiana State University Press, 1957).

———, *Plato and Aristotle,* vol. 3 of *Order and History* (Baton Rouge: Louisiana State University Press, 1957).

Von Rad, Gerhard, *Old Testament Theology* (2 vols.), D. M. G. Stalker, trans. (New York: Harper & Row, 1962).

Wheelwright, Philip, *Heraclitus* (Princeton: Princeton University Press, 1959).

Zuurdeeg, Willem F., *An Analytical Philosophy of Religion* (Nashville, Tenn.: Abingdon Press, 1958).

2

Paperback Volumes

Aeschylus, *The Oresteian Trilogy,* Philip Vellacott, trans. (Baltimore: Penguin Books, 1956).

Albright, William F., *The Biblical Period from Abraham to Ezra: A Historical Survey* (New York: Harper & Row, 1963).

Arnott, Peter D., *An Introduction to the Greek Theatre* (Bloomington: Indiana University Press, 1959).

Auerbach, Erich, *Mimesis* (Garden City, N.Y.: Doubleday, 1957).

Breasted, J. H., *Development of Religion and Thought in Ancient Egypt* (New York: Harper & Row, 1959).

Buber, Martin, *Moses: The Revelation and the Covenant* (New York: Harper & Row, 1958).

Cornford, F. M., *From Religion to Philosophy* (New York: Harper & Row, 1957).

———, *Plato's Cosmology* (Indianapolis: Liberal Arts Press, 1957).

Dodds, E. R., *The Greeks and the Irrational* (Boston: Beacon Press, 1957).

Eliade, Mircea, *Cosmos and History* (New York: Harper & Row, 1959).

Frankfort, Henri, *Ancient Egyptian Religion* (New York: Harper & Row, 1961).

———, *et al., Before Philosophy* (Baltimore: Penguin Books, 1949).

———, *The Birth of Civilization in the Near East* (Garden City, N.Y.: Doubleday, 1956).

Greene, William C., *Moira: Fate, Good, and Evil in Greek Thought* (New York: Harper & Row, 1948).

Guthrie, W. K. C., *The Greeks and Their Gods* (Boston: Beacon Press, 1950).

Homer, *The Iliad,* W. H. D. Rouse, trans. (New York: New American Library, 1950).

———, *The Odyssey,* W. H. D. Rouse, trans. (New York: New American Library, 1949).

Kramer, Samuel Noah, *History Begins at Sumer* (Garden City, N.Y.: Doubleday, 1959).

———, ed., *Mythologies of the Ancient World* (Garden City, N.Y.: Doubleday, 1961).

Lattimore, Richard, ed., *Greek Lyrics* (Chicago: University of Chicago Press, 1960).

Malinowski, Bronislaw, *Magic, Science and Religion* (Garden City, N.Y.: Doubleday, 1955).

Mumford, Lewis, *The Transformations of Man* (New York: Collier, 1962).

Murray, Gilbert, *Five Stages of Greek Religion* (Garden City, N.Y.: Doubleday, 1951).

Otto, Walter F., *The Homeric Gods,* Moses Hadas, trans. (Boston: Beacon Press, 1964).

Plato, *The Republic,* H. D. P. Lee, trans. (Baltimore: Penguin Books, 1955).

———, *Great Dialogues of Plato,* Eric H. Warmington and Philip

G. Rouse, eds., W. H. D. Rouse, trans. (New York: New American Library, 1956).

Robinson, C. E., *Hellas: A Short History of Ancient Greece* (Boston: Beacon Press, 1955).

Rowley, H. H., ed., *The Old Testament and Modern Study* (New York: Oxford University Press, 1951).

Snell, Bruno, *The Discovery of the Mind* (New York: Harper & Row, 1960).

Tillich, Paul, *Biblical Religion and the Search for Ultimate Reality* (Chicago: University of Chicago Press, 1964).

Wilson, John A., *The Culture of Ancient Egypt* (Chicago: University of Chicago Press, 1951).

Wright, G. Ernest, *The Old Testament Against Its Environment* (Chicago: Alec R. Allenson, 1950).

Acknowledgments

(*continued from p. iv*)

DOUBLEDAY & COMPANY, INC. For *The Bible and the Ancient Near East,* G. E. Wright, ed., copyright © 1961 by Doubleday & Company, Inc.; for *Mythologies of the Ancient World,* Samuel Noah Kramer, ed., copyright © 1961 by Doubleday & Company, Inc.

THE FREE PRESS For *Magic, Science and Religion* by Bronislaw Malinowski. Copyright 1948 by The Free Press.

HARPER & ROW, PUBLISHERS, INC. For *Before the Bible* by Cyrus H. Gordon, © 1962 by Harper & Row; for *The History of Israel* by Martin Noth, rev. ed. © 1960 by Harper & Row; for *Old Testament Theology,* volumes I and II, by Gerhard von Rad, D. M. G. Stalker, trans., volume I translation © 1962, volume II translation © 1965, Oliver & Boyd, Ltd.; for *The Transformations of Man* by Lewis Mumford, copyright © 1956 by Lewis Mumford.

HARVARD UNIVERSITY PRESS For *Ancilla to the Pre-Socratic Philosophers* by Kathleen Freeman, copyright 1948 by Harvard University Press; for *Discovery of the Mind* by Bruno Snell, copyright 1953 by Harvard University Press; for *Elegy and Iambus,* J. M. Edmonds, ed. and trans., © 1961 by Harvard University Press and The Loeb Classical Library.

INDIANA UNIVERSITY PRESS For *The Birth of Civilization in the Near East* by Henri Frankfort; for *Tragedy, Myth and Mystery,* R. Y. Hathorn, © 1962.

LOUISIANA STATE UNIVERSITY PRESS For *Order and History,* volumes I, II, and III, by Eric Voegelin. Copyright 1956, 1957 by Louisiana State University Press.

METHEUN & CO., LTD. For *Form and Meaning in Drama* by H. D. F. Kitto.

THE NEW AMERICAN LIBRARY OF WORLD LITERATURE, INC. For *Great Dialogues of Plato,* W. H. D. Rouse, trans. Copyright 1956.

THOMAS NELSON & SONS, LTD. For Homer, *The Iliad,* W. H. D. Rouse, trans.; for Homer, *The Odyssey,* W. H. D. Rouse, trans. Copyright 1937 by W. H. D. Rouse.

OLIVER & BOYD, LTD. For *Old Testament Theology,* volumes I and II, by Gerhard von Rad, D. M. G. Stalker, trans. Translation © Oliver & Boyd, Ltd., 1962, 1965.

OXFORD UNIVERSITY PRESS, INC. For *The Basic Works of Aristotle,* Richard McKeon, ed., B. Jowett, trans., copyright 1941; for *Paideia* by Werner Jaeger, Gilbert Highet, trans., 2nd ed. in English, volume I copyright 1945, volume II copyright 1943, Oxford University Press, Inc.; for *A Study of History,* volume I, by Arnold J. Toynbee, copyright 1935.

PENGUIN BOOKS, LTD. For Aeschylus, *The Oresteian Trilogy,* Philip Vellacott, trans., copyright © Philip Vellacott, 1956; for Plato, *The Republic,* H. D. P. Lee, trans., copyright 1955.

PRENTICE-HALL, INC. For *Eternal Faith, Eternal People* by Leo Trepp, © 1962.

PRINCETON UNIVERSITY PRESS For *The Ancient Near East,* James B. Pritchard, ed., copyright © 1958 by Princeton University Press; for *Ancient Near Eastern Texts,* James B. Pritchard, ed., copyright 1950 by Princeton University Press, rev. ed., 1955; for *Heraclitus* by Philip Wheelwright, copyright © 1959 by Princeton University Press; for *Light from the Ancient Past* by Jack Finegan, copyright 1946 by Princeton University Press; for *Mimesis* by Erich Auerbach, Willard Trask, trans., copyright 1953 by Princeton University Press.

RANDOM HOUSE, INC. For *Complete Greek Tragedies,* volume I (*Aeschylus,* E. D. A. Morshead, trans.), Whitney J. Oates and Eugene O'Neill, Jr., eds. Copyright 1938.

ROUTLEDGE & KEGAN PAUL, LTD. For *The Myth of the Eternal Return* by Mircea Eliade; for *Plato's Cosmology* by F. M. Cornford, copyright 1937.

THE UNIVERSITY OF CALIFORNIA PRESS For *The Greeks and the Irrational* by E. R. Dodds. Copyright 1951 by the Regents of the University of California.

THE UNIVERSITY OF CHICAGO PRESS For *American Life* by W. Lloyd Warner. Copyright 1953 by The University of Chicago; for *Before Philosophy* by Henri Frankfort *et al.,* originally published by The University of Chicago Press as *The Intellectual Adventure of Ancient Man,* copyright 1946 by The University of Chicago; for *The Complete Bible: An American Translation,* J. M. Powis Smith and E. J. Goodspeed, eds., copyright 1931 by The University of Chicago; for *Greek Lyrics,* Richard Lattimore, ed., copyright 1960 by The University of Chicago; for *Kingship and the Gods* by Henri Frankfort, copyright 1948 by The University of Chicago; for *The Religion of Israel* by Yehezkel Kaufmann, © 1960 by The University of Chicago.

VANDENHOECK & RUPRECHT For *The History of Israel* by Martin Noth. Rev. ed. © 1960 by Harper & Row.

VANGUARD PRESS, INC. For *The Glory of Egypt* by Samivel and Michael Audrain, J. E. Manchip-White, trans. Copyright 1955 by Vanguard Press, Inc.